A GUIDE TO THE SOVIET CURRICULUM:
What the Russian Child is Taught in School

A GUIDE TO THE SOVIET CURRICULUM:

What the Russian Child is Taught in School

JAMES MUCKLE

CROOM HELM
London • New York • Sydney

© 1988 James Muckle
Croom Helm Ltd, Provident House, Burrell Row,
Beckenham, Kent, BR3 1AT

Croom Helm Australia, 44-50 Waterloo Road,
North Ryde, 2113, New South Wales

Published in the USA by
Croom Helm
in association with Methuen, Inc.
29 West 35th Street
New York, NY 10001

British Library Cataloguing in Publication Data

Muckle, J Y
    A guide to the Soviet curriculum: what
    the Russian child is taught in school.
    1. Education — Soviet Union —
    Curricula
    I. Title
    375'.00947   LB1564.S6/

    ISBN 0-7099-4667-8

Library of Congress Cataloging-in-Publication Data

Muckle, James Y.
    A guide to the Soviet curriculum.

    Bibliography: p.
    Includes index.
    1. Education — Soviet Union — Curricula. 2. Education —
Soviet Union. I. Title.
LB564.S68M83   1988   375'.00947   87-30314
ISBN 0-7099-4667-8

Printed and bound in Great Britain by
Biddles Ltd, Guildford and King's Lynn

CONTENTS

v

TABLES

THE PURPOSE of this book is to examine the content of the education received by children in the mass comprehensive schools of the Soviet Union, especially in the Russian-speaking areas of that vast country. At the time of writing, the Soviet system of education is undergoing reform, which will continue for several years before its full extent can be estimated. At the same time government in Britain is calling for a national school curriculum. If one purpose of comparative studies is to learn to know one´s own system better, British readers may look on this book as a contribution to the present debate in this country.

It is a straightforward enough task to give an account of the content of the whole curriculum - abbreviated though it must be, since the music syllabus alone runs to more words than the whole of this book. However, baldly to present the content without any indication of what went before, the way that content is taught and assessed, or without even hinting at the political, intellectual or moral context would be meaningless. The "hidden" or implicit curriculum is important too. This book takes all these matters into consideration. It is accepted that many readers will not read the whole book, but will pick out the sections relating to their own particular subject interests. However, whichever parts are skipped, Chapter 3 should not be neglected (for without knowing the moral ethos the rest will be misunderstood), and the reader should understand how achievement is assessed and knowledge presented.

Educators from the English-speaking countries and from Russia have been learning from each other´s schools for a very long time. Peter the Great recruited one Scottish and two English teachers to initiate the Moscow School of Mathematics and Navigation at the turn of the seventeenth and eighteenth centuries. Alexander I, aided by British residents in St Petersburg, encouraged Quakers, one English (William Allen) and one naturalized American (Stephen Grellet), to visit Russia in 1818-19 with a view to the introduction of the Bell and Lancaster system of mutual instruction. Four Russians who trained in London as Lancasterian teachers were befriended by an Anglo-Irish student, James Heard, who learned their language and then spent most of the rest of his life teaching in Russia, where he died, a naturalized and ennobled citizen, in 1875. At the beginning of the twentieth century the most remarkable linguist of them all, Thomas Darlington, one of His Majesty's Inspectors of Schools, visited the country to compile his amazingly comprehensive and perceptive report on education in Russia for the Board of Education.

After the Revolutions of 1917 Soviet Russia looked to America in a brief flirtation with the ideas of John Dewey and with Helen Parkhurst's Dalton Plan, though such methods were dropped at the end of the 1920s. But when the first sputnik went up in 1957 America and the rest of the world looked with a mixture of admiration and uneasiness at Soviet schools, believing, perhaps, that there was a great deal that "Ivan knew which Johnny didn't". Since then there have been frequent visits to the others' countries by Eastern and Western educationists.

The curriculum figured in many of these investigations and visits. Peter adopted the curriculum of the London Mathematical School; Allen and Grellet, despite their limited knowledge of "Russ" quickly spotted what they took to be dangerous and distasteful elements in the curriculum - the passages set for reading and comprehension. They had these replaced by passages from the Bible. It may seem odd that Darlington devoted a very great deal of space to the place of classical languages in secondary schools, but this reflected concern in England at the time about the relevance to modern life of the traditional public and grammar school education. Interest since 1957 has centred more on social, structural and philosophical issues, and the lack of a full study of the whole curriculum of the general-education school is a little difficult to explain. After all, what goes on in the classroom is fundamental to our understanding of the education system - and ultimately the culture - of a society.

It is a pity that, in Britain at least, only a handful of teachers and researchers is presently working on education in the Soviet Union. Education is one of the many aspects of Soviet life and society which we need to understand, since the schooling received by the citizens must be assumed to have some sort of effect on their character, however difficult that may be to estimate. The lack of workers in the field is mainly attributable to the most regrettable neglect of the Russian language in the British education system at present. It is not much better in America. To those who have not had the opportunity of acquaintance with that language and the incomparable literature expressed in it, but who wish to know about the education received by those who speak it as a native language, this study is offered.

ACKNOWLEDGEMENTS

Writing a book like this is a social activity, for without the help of many friends, students, colleagues and kind strangers in Britain and the Soviet Union it could not have been completed. I am grateful for advice and help of various kinds from the following, some of whom have read and commented on sections of the text. At times I despaired as to whether their knowledge of their specialist subject would ever come together with mine of Russian, since translation of many technical passages in the syllabuses gave great difficulty. Thanks to them, most problems have been solved; any remaining insufficiencies are entirely my responsibility. They are: the Library of the Centre for Russian and East European Studies of the University of Birmingham and successive librarians Dr Jenny Brine and Jackie Johnson, Peter Haywood and staff of the Library at the University of Nottingham (who have had to struggle with many difficult inter-library loan requests), Charles Cooke, Dr Alan Bell, Jennifer Suggate, Andrew Pierson, Pam Bishop, Lesley Evans-Worthing, Professor James Riordan, Dr John Screen, Dr Glyn Yeoman, Dr Colin Harrison, Academician Boris Nemensky, Nadezhda Nikolaevna Grishanovich, Natalia Borisovna Romanova, Dr Friedrich Kuebart, Edgar Jenkins, Dr David Shipstone, Dr Frank Molyneux, June Lemon and Siu Fai Tong.

Many thanks go also to heads and teachers of the following schools, who have kindly admitted me to lessons at various times in the last few years and have spared time for discussion: Erevan School no. 19, Minsk Schools 30, 52 and 122 and Kindergartens 280 and 415, Moscow Schools 81, 444 and 905, the one school at Sausti, Tallinn Schools 7, 31 and 24, Tartu School 10, Tbilisi Schools 1, 53 and 161. I am equally grateful to the staffs of more administrative and policy-making institutions than I can possibly mention here: they include the ministries of education of the USSR, and of the Belorussian, Georgian, Armenian and Estonian SSRs, two of the education ministers, several educational research institutes, in-service training centres and local education offices. They have invariably been very kind and obliging, and I hope they will not find anything I have written unduly critical - but if they do, I am sure they will not be hesitant in responding.

J. Y. Muckle
University of Nottingham
School of Education

Chapter 1

THE SOVIET SCHOOL AND THE RUSSIAN TRADITION

THE HISTORY of the school in Russia is relatively short. Three hundred years ago there were very few institutions in the Russian Empire that would be recognised by a modern educator as a school, and certainly nothing resembling a university. For centuries the Russian gentry thought it beneath their dignity to go to school, and those autocrats who were determined to promote development were driven to ingenious forms of extrinsic motivation, such as refusal of permission to marry for those who would not study. The longest established schools and universities on Soviet territory are in non-Russian republics, like Estonia and the Ukraine, and after the revolutions of 1917 Soviet Russia lost some of its most famous establishments when Poland and Finland were separated from the former Empire. Russian scholars in the eighteenth and nineteenth centuries tended to study abroad, creating an intelligentsia which was sophisticated and for the most part westward-looking. The Russian grammar schools, the first of which was founded in 1726, were based on the German *Gymnasium*, as the name, *gimnaziya*, suggests; yet still many of the gentry educated their sons and daughters privately until the end of Imperial rule.

Past and Present

In the two hundred years before the Revolution certain features developed in the Russian school which influenced the system as it is known in the Soviet Union today, and there are, of course, others which were specifically rejected in the new society. There was always some tension between church and secular schools, and between state and private initiatives in the establishment and running of educational establishments. By the nineteenth century government control of curricula and text-books was normal. Schools were never seen purely as places of instruction; in theory at least character training was regarded as essential. Just as in many other countries in Europe, ferocious controversies were carried on in the second half of the nineteenth century as to whether school should be compulsory or not. Access to grammar schools and higher education was regulated by decree, and children from the middle and lower classes were at a disadvantage in the later years of tsarist rule; yet at the same time obedience to such decrees was by no means uniform. Until the beginning of the twentieth century governmental promotion of school education probably outstripped public demand for it, but in the last few years before 1917 the state was being pushed very hard by public opinion and was encouraging private individuals to start and run schools to supplement what the state could provide.

Soviet education has settled many of these issues. Education is compulsory, secular and indeed atheistic, and is provided free of charge and wholly by the state. Only private coaching can be bought informally. Central control of what is taught in school is to all intents and purposes total, though occasional fulminations in the press betray the fact that schools do not always do exactly as they are told. Moral education is still felt to be vital, and the particular morality to be taught is prescribed. Public demand for education is enormous, and the intelligent public is far from uncritical of what the schools provide. Access to educational establishments at least up to age fifteen is restricted only by the pupils' place of abode and the schools they can reach reasonably easily. After that age some more competitive elements enter into the situation, but achievement is the main criterion applied except, perhaps, to those who may have transgressed politically or have influential parents.

Outline of the System and Recent Changes

The features of the structure of the Soviet education system are not particularly unusual and need not detain us long. They are summarised in Figure 1. The Soviet child now begins compulsory education at age six, a year younger than previously. Before that age he is likely to have attended a kindergarten (Russian: *detskiy sad*), in which a certain amount of formal teaching goes on. Provision of pre-school education is not total, nor is demand for it universal, especially among parents from the intelligentsia or those who can cope with children at home. The first year of compulsory education may take place in a kindergarten or in class 1 of the general-education school (Russian: *obshcheobrazavatel'naya shkola*). These schools are co-educational, comprehensive and un-streamed, and the first four years are officially designated "primary". Classes 5 to 9 are termed "incomplete secondary" and at the age of 15 the pupils take a nationally set and recognised examination, conducted by the school. The last two years of compulsory schooling may take place in classes 10 and 11 of the general school, which is the usual route to univer-

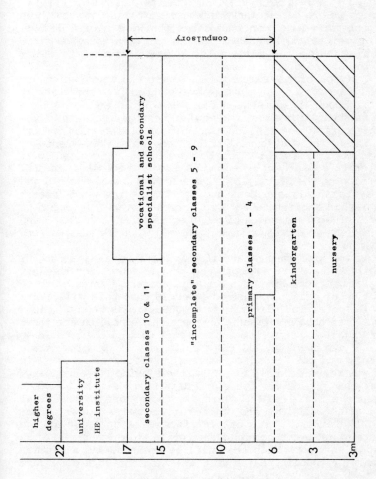

Figure 1   The Soviet Education System (simplified).

sity or higher education, or in a secondary specialist school, often known as a *tekhnikum*, which trains skilled entrants to a range of professions, or in a "secondary professional-technical college" (known in Russian by its abbreviation SPTU), which qualifies rank-and-file workers for the economy.

The most recent reforms were proposed in a document which appeared in the press early in January 1984. After intensive public discussion a revised version of these proposals was issued with the full backing of the Communist Party of the Soviet Union (CPSU) in April of the same year. The document is available in English with the title "Guidelines for the Reform of General and Vocational Schools". Few of the proposals came as a great surprise. Much of the curricular reform, in which we are particularly interested in this book, had been going on for years - in some cases for well over a decade. The intensified public debate, which has been going on since 1984 has provided material of the greatest interest in assessing the state of Soviet education.

Features of the structure of Soviet education which are new as a result of the 1984 measures, then, are the start at six (although in some Union republics children of six have gone to school for some time now) and certain details of the arrangements at age 15. The numbering of classes used in this book is the "new" system, 1 to 11 from age six to seventeen, and replaces the former class 1 at age seven up to class 10 at sixteen to seventeen, even though Soviet schools are still referring to the classes by a chaotic mixture of the old and new systems. It has been decided to use the word "class" rather than English "form" or American "grade" in order to avoid confusion with ages of children in other countries - and also because it corresponds most closely with the Russian word *klass*.

As for what happens at fifteen, until recently about 60% of children have stayed on in the general school for the last two years of schooling, but now this number is intended to be cut by about half. It must be expected that this will cause much dispute, for parents in the USSR are as keen as those anywhere to obtain a prestigious academic education for their offspring. As an inducement to parents to send their children willingly to the SPTU, all these colleges will give both trade training and the secondary leaving certificate - this is in fact why they are known as SPTUs, the S being for Secondary, rather than the former title of PTU pure and simple. A young person who finishes SPTU with all top grades in the final examination will have the opportunity to enter higher education: the others must work for two years at least in the industrial or other economic enterprise to which the SPTU is attached and for which they will be trained. As a further inducement, pupils in the SPTU are paid for work done once they have learned to reach acceptable standards.

Another feature of the system which is new is that all

pupils in every type of school will be taught a trade, and will leave school with a certificate enabling them to be given fully paid and qualified employment immediately. Leavers from general secondary schools enter industry as qualified workers, grade 2, and those from SPTUs grade 5.

That there are economic, political and educational reasons for these changes will be quite obvious from the changes themselves. As for the start at six, the benefits of an earlier start to compulsory education had been recognised for long enough, though the nature of the institutions to which six-year-olds should go has been a matter of controversy There are also social reasons for compulsory education at six: the need for the state to provide a child-minding service for working parents. The stress on labour education and vocational training has roots which go down a long way. On the one hand, traditional Party stalwarts are contemptuous of academics who refuse to get their hands dirty. The attitudes of both teachers and pupils to manual labour were thought to be unsatisfactory and even snobbish. On the other hand, it was becoming obvious that the national work force was not being appropriately trained for the needs of the economy, that many school-leavers were over-qualified and that expectations of the employment they might obtain were over-optimistic. There has been a decline in the population of working age because of the birth-rate in the 1960s. Moreover, it has been argued that the goods the children produce in school can often make a significant contribution to the running costs of the school; some educators take a dim view of this argument.

Responsibility for and Control of Curricula

The point has already been made that central state control of the curriculum and of the syllabus within subject areas is virtually total. Each of the fifteen republics of the Soviet Union has its own Ministry of Education (*Ministerstvo pro-sveshcheniya, Minpros* for short) and there is a Ministry of Education of the USSR, which holds the greatest power of all. Curricula are worked out by the USSR Ministry, or by a body ultimately responsible to it. Thus in September 1984 during a visit to the Ministry in Moscow, it was possible to see the senior official actually scratching his head over the subjects and numbers of lessons to be undergone by every Soviet child for a generation to come as he compiled the charts such as that reproduced as Figure 2. There are Western countries in which a similar sight could be seen, but in England at least the task has traditionally been replicated in every individual school. The Academy of Pedagogical Sciences (APN) is a body of great influence and prestige and of a certain independence, which it is said to pay for by being the most criticised body in Soviet education. The APN controls the bodies which do most of the work on the curriculum: the research institutes (known as NIIs, *nauchno-issledovatel'skie instituty*), some of which are concerned with specific subject areas while others deal with general pedagogy, psychology and the like.   The Ministries of Education of the republics take some responsibility for the curriculum as it affects their own area (see Chapter 13). Curricular reform, in fact, sometimes originates in the republics.

It should perhaps be mentioned here that two other ministries are active in the field of education in the USSR. They are the Ministry of Higher and Secondary Specialist Education, which deals with universities and other higher education establishments and with the advanced vocational colleges from age 15. The Ministry of Culture is responsible for the training of artists, musicians and the like. Where the responsibilities of these ministries overlap, criticism of rivalry and lack of efficient liaison is sometimes heard.

Differentiation

There is little differentiation in the curriculum in the general-education school. Controversy in recent years has surrounded provision for the talented. There are schools "with special profiles" in which a somewhat intensified programme in one subject area is followed. In all schools from class 7 two to four weekly lessons of electives are provided for. Both these issues are briefly discussed in Chapter 13. In the general course of events pupils offer four or five subjects for university entry and it must be assumed that, as examination time approaches, a greater part of their effort is concentrated on these. However, this can hardly be compared with the specialisation involved in an English Advanced Level General Certificate of Education course, for example.

Assessment

Any study of the curriculum in a national education system would be incomplete, probably even useless, without consideration of the way subject content is presented - the preferred teaching methods - and the way achievement is assessed and success indicated. The first of these matters is a constant theme of this book. The second, examinations, requires introductory treatment here.

The standard pattern in Russia has always been for examinations to be oral. Readers of Russian literature will recall famous accounts of exams at school and university, such as those in Tolstoy's *Youth,* and their conduct has scarcely changed. The "papers" are known in Russian as "tickets"; the candidate selects one from a table, where they lie face down, is given time to prepare (and may make written notes), and has to give answers orally - perhaps by reading the notes aloud. This has one or two consequences, not all of which are expected. The spoken word has higher status than in a system where examinations are mostly written. But it is false to imagine that examinations contain much lively debate and argument. Russian examinations have for centuries encouraged pupils to answer by rote. As long ago as the 1840s the writer S. T. Aksakov expressed amazement and delight that pupils of a certain school were allowed to answer in their own words in examinations, instead of reeling off what they had learned by heart. It is often all too obvious 150 years later the drilling of children which goes on in classrooms owes rather too much to a tradition of rote learning which is deeply ingrained in the Russian educational consciousness. Happily, we may be able to qualify this statement as our investigation proceeds.

A very recent (1987) announcement that examinations are to be introduced for classes 3, 4 and 5, and that some of them will be written is, then, a break with tradition. Otherwise, until now, informal assessment of pupils has taken place in all years, and satisfactory marks (that is, not more than two subjects failed) are required in order for promotion to the next class to take place. In the new classes 9 and 11 official examinations take place as follows: in class 9 (age 15) four subjects - written mathematics, oral algebra and geometry, oral Russian and written *izlozhenie* (rewriting a story the pupils have heard read aloud). At school leaving stage six subjects are taken: mathematics, history and social studies, and literature are compulsory (the last in Russian schools only; non-Russian schools must offer Russian language). They may include written composition (Russian language and literature), written and oral mathematics, physics and astronomy, chemistry, and foreign language. Formerly the marks awarded for day-to-day work were averaged and used for entry to higher education, but as this had undesirable consequences. In particular, parents, teachers and pupils developed a complaint known colloquially as "percentomania", and the practice of averaging marks has now been abolished.

Another feature of the examination system which is worthy of note is that the questions to be asked in the state examinations, which take place at age 15 and 17, are for the most part known, because they are published and sold publicly months in advance. Thus, all pupils know that if they pick up ticket no. 4 in the history exam they will have a choice of speaking about Lenin's agrarian reform or the basic rights, freedoms and obligations of a citizen of the USSR. They know that the foreign language ticket no. 7 will require them to speak on a set theme and to re-tell a short text in the foreign language - but they will not see that specific text until the examination begins. They may know they will have to solve a quadratic equation if they pick a certain mathematics ticket, but the actual example will be fresh. In many subjects the exact questions which will be asked are known and the answers will have been rehearsed. The texts and subjects for written exams may be read out on television or radio shortly before the examination starts. The "commission", that is the panel who conduct the exam, is chaired by the head teacher or a deputy and contains the teacher of the subject concerned and another teacher of the same subject or of a related subject. Representatives of the local authority may also be present: this tends to be seen as something of a misfortune. Proposals for fully external examining have not yet come to anything.

Official instructions for the conduct of exams and the promotion and release from school of pupils indicate that only pupils who have received a satisfactory mark for behaviour may be admitted to these official examinations. Pupils who receive unsatisfactory marks in two subjects may be set holiday work and be given a re-examination in the autumn; if they received three or more unsatisfactory marks or failed their re-sits they have to repeat the year. Candidates who fail class 11 exams may take them again the following year. After a second failure, if it is in only one subject, they may re-sit as an external candidate.

Examinations, and in fact all pupils′ work from primary school to university, are marked on the traditional five-point scale of 5 (excellent), 4 (good), 3 (satisfactory), and 2 (unsatisfactory). Criteria are published for marks of 1 and 0, but in practice these lower marks are rarely awarded.

For entry to higher education there is no "clearing house". Examinations are timed so that pupils my have two chances. They offer four or five subjects of which Russian language and literature must be one; the others depend on the nature of the course for which they are applying. If candidates are unsuccessful at getting into either of the institutions they have entered for, but none the less have done reasonably well in the exam, they hawk their results round other establishments in the hope that one will take them.

This examination system, in contrast with the agonizing about standards, differentiation, grade-related criteria and fine distinctions between pupils which goes on in England, is a very blunt instrument indeed. It is not systematically moderated; exams, being oral, are not liable to re-call and re-marking; it is in the hands of regular teachers, who, to judge by the Soviet educational press, are only sometimes "found out" when outside moderators pounce unannounced on a school. Concern surfaces from time to time about inconsistency of standards between schools, especially between rural and urban institutions. It is against this background that discussion of the content of syllabuses should be seen; one does read rash statements about Soviet schools in the Western press of the type "How wonderful that every Soviet child is taught a syllabus which includes... which we only give to the best pupils". Indeed it may be wonderful, but we may legitimately ask how many of the Soviet children actually learn it.

Ethical Content and Cultural Diversity

A feature of Soviet education which needs to be understood from the outset, although we shall of necessity return to it again and again, is the great importance attached to what the Russians call *vospitanie*. This word is translated literally as "upbringing"; it is often used as a synonym for "moral education" and it refers to all those elements in the schooling and socialization of children which could be termed "development of the personality". Soviet educational philosophers are emphatic that one of the most important aims of the system is to produce a new type of person, the "new Soviet man". Again and again it will be discovered that the teaching of academic subjects has this purpose: to develop the desirable characteristics of the new Soviet citizen and to form rounded socialist personalities.

It must also be remembered that the USSR is a multilingual, multi-ethnic, multi-cultural society and that "Russian" and "Soviet" are not synonymous terms. Just as it is sometimes difficult to be strictly accurate and unambiguous in distinguishing between England, the United Kingdom and Great Britain - especially when there is a historical dimension to the dicussion - Russia and the Soviet Union will be seen to have a very great deal in common without being co-terminous. In this book "Russia" and "Russian" will be used in three senses: firstly to refer to the Russian Empire before the October Revolution of 1917, secondly to indicate the Russian Soviet Federated Socialist Republic (RSFSR), the largest of the republics in the Union, and thirdly to identify the language or ethnic origin of citizens. A very great deal of what is said about the Soviet curriculum will be true of both Russian and non-Russian schools, so the difficulty need not retard understanding of the principal issues. Russian is the first native language of more than half the Soviet population. Linguistic and ethnic policies are a subject of controversy, and something will be said about this in Chapter 6.

Discussion of Soviet curricular issues is therefore to be carried on against a background of assumptions, customs, practices, socio-political aims, and traditions which have a character of their own. The book aims to avoid charges from western readers of either dismissing or idealising different aspects of the Soviet curriculum, and may fail to avoid being regarded over there as "bourgeois falsification". So that there can be no doubt about the position from which the book is written, its aim is to describe the Soviet curriculum, to interpret it in the light of its own context and tradition and to discuss it from the other side of the cultural and ideological divide.

Chapter 2

THE CONTENT OF EDUCATION: WHAT AND WHY?

BRITISH governments used to say that they did not seek control of what was taught in schools in the United Kingdom. Recently, however, it has become government policy to establish a national curriculum. Opposition to this has not been total, though in some quarters, there has been strident protest. Russian and Soviet governments, on the other hand, have always had total control of the curriculum, and this control is shared between central and republican administrations. While British head teachers have to decide - with the help of colleagues, school governors or managers (or in Scotland the regional authorities) - whether or not 3B studies German and if so for how many hours a week, their Soviet counterparts are free from such worries. The obvious consequence of this is that senior British teachers are vitally concerned with curricular issues and curriculum philosophy and in communicating their decisions to parents, while Soviet teachers' main task is to put the decisions of others into practice.

Leadership in Curricular Policy

The principal writers and thinkers on the curriculum in the Soviet Union are headed by members of the staff of organizations such as the Research Institute on General Pedagogy of the APN of the USSR, or the same Academy's Institute on Curriculum and Methods of Teaching - national institutions of considerable importance and esteem. The APN and to some extent its elder brother, the Academy of Sciences of the USSR (AN SSSR) enjoy a rare degree of independence. Considerable deference is shown in Soviet society to academics, and there is reluctance even at the highest level to go against the advice of the most senior minds in the profession of education. So it once was, at least; the discussions leading to the 1984 draft Guidelines were initiated by the Central Committee of the Communist Party under Yury Andropov, and chaired successively by Konstantin Chernenko and Mikhail Gorbachev, in each case just before these men succeeded to the most powerful

office in the land. It would seem that educational reform
was felt to be so important that only the most senior figures
in the state were big enough to take it on.

Some slight tension, then, exists between educationists
and government. Something faintly resembling this may be
discerned in the West in the differing curricular demands
placed on the schools by the state and commercial concerns as
opposed to the ideal sought by academic philosophers of education. If one side stresses the requirements of the economy,
the other emphasises the personal development of the pupil.

Integration and Differentiation

Despite the ideological, historical and political differences
which separate Soviet society from our own, many of the same
concerns animate Soviet discussion of the curriculum, though
in the USSR the terms used are not the same. Western philosophers of education look at the material which might conceivably be conveyed to children in school and classify it using
expressions such as "realms of meaning", "modes of thought",
"distinguishing cognitive structures", or "forms of knowledge"; consideration of such categories leads to decisions as
to what knowledge and what learning experiences comprise the
minimum which should not be denied to any child. This discussion has its counterpart in the Soviet Union, where the underlying demand, however, is for the "all-round harmonious development of personality", and communist personality at that.
A particularly, though not exclusively, British phenomenon is
preoccupation with specialization and selection of subjects
and the degree to which it is permissible in school. The
equivalent of this in the USSR is the continuing tension
between general and professional or vocational education, and
the provision of optional courses and schools with specialist
academic programmes.

Knowledge does not exist in isolated compartments; how
should the schools present it? In England, many primary
schools have a curriculum with a good deal of integrated
study; very few secondary schools have more than the token
integration of two or three subjects, and in the late 1980s
interest is discernibly swinging away from integration back to
separate subjects, despite the recent publication of an official report by the Department of Education and Science,
Curriculum 5 - 16, which favours integration. In the USSR
there have been two about-turns since the Revolution: the
enthusiasm in the 1920s for the Dalton plan and the like, and
in the 1930s decisive return to a subject-based programme.

Education in England is often attacked for its "elitism",
and it is certainly true that very many English teachers
believe very firmly that children are different. The very use
of the term "mixed-ability" (for which there is no equivalent
Russian phrase in common use) and the arguments used to advo-

11

cate it underline the existence of this belief. It leads to further controversy: can all children "take" the same programme of general education? Some argue strongly that all normal children should be initiated into high culture while others believe that education for the average and less able child should have different aims. Soviet views are firm that all children should receive the same (but not totally identical) curriculum - for reasons based on psychology and ideology which will be explained later in this chapter.

Soviet Views of Western Curriculum Theorists

How do Soviet curriculum theorists view the work of their "bourgeois" counterparts in the West? To judge by the bibliography of one recent authoritative book on the Soviet curriculum (that by Kraevsky and Lerner), they have not read very much. Nevertheless, B. S. Bloom's taxonomies of educational objectives are discussed at some length with a certain approval. It is J. F. Kerr's contribution to his own book *Changing the Curriculum* (London, 1968) which most clearly reveals Soviet attitudes to western opinion. Kerr's "simple model of curriculum" with its four components - objectives, knowledge, learning experience and evaluation is thought to be worthy of attention. It "highlights many factors which influence decisions on the content of subject programmes". The scheme, however, is "insubstantial, because it characterizes a way of working out a particular methodological system in isolation from the general aims of the school".

V. S. Tsetlin, the contributor of this critique to the book mentioned above, throws doubt by implication on the ability of "bourgeois" philosophers to establish a satisfactory theory of curriculum. He questions the western concept of "curriculum" (using the Latin word) and writes that he is unable to see exactly what the word means to a western educator. It is different, he says, from the Russian *soderzhanie obrazovaniya* [content of education], and he declares that "curriculum theory" for westerners should be seen as a "theory of programmes of instruction". Bloom and Kerr are seen as aiding individual teachers in a given school to construct programmes; they are therefore typically bourgeois pragmatists who have raised the individual child to a preeminent position. They peddle the erroneous notion of ideological neutrality. Bloom at least is a behaviourist (a pejorative judgement in the Soviet Union), and his subjectivism and "pluralism" is a cloak for furthering the interests of capitalism by increasing the likelihood of differentiated standards of achievement while appearing to offer freedom. They are incapable, it is argued, of constructing a satisfactory theory because any theory they produce is based on erroneous notions of children's individual characteristics and readiness for study in a particular school. Such pragmatism demonstrates "the inability of Westerners to create a general theory" of curriculum.

Theory and Practice Since 1917

It follows from all this that any Soviet theory of curriculum must be applicable to the mass of schools and to all children; it must provide a framework for a good education for every child; it should ensure equality of opportunity by guaranteeing comparable standards of achievement in all schools. It must, indeed, be sound and all-embracing. Nothing, said Lenin, is more practical than a good theory. On what theory or theories, then, is the Soviet curriculum based?

Curriculum theory has been worked out by generations of Soviet educators on a foundation of the writings of Marx, Engels and Lenin, but at the same time tradition on the one hand and the desire to experiment on the other have been potent additional influences. The manpower needs of the state and the desire for civil equilibrium have also played their part.

Marx held that children should learn about nature, man and society and the relationships between them. Marxists believe in the unity of theory and practice, and that knowledge is indissolubly bound up with action. It is a feature of Marxist theory of knowledge that "thought develops as it grapples with reality in actual problems". One might expect, therefore, that communist education would show a strong element of problem-solving and emphasise practical activity.

Let us follow these two basic motifs through the early years of Soviet rule in Russia. The task in 1918 - leaving aside practicalities such as protection from foreign invasion, famine and economic chaos - was to make the school in Marx's phrase "an implement for the spiritual liberation of the people", or, in Nadezhda Krupskaya's, "to create a generation capable of putting an end to class domination". The early years of Soviet rule, before Stalin's dead hand fell upon every aspect of society, were a heady time of experiment and adventure, especially in the arts - but it was so in education too. An aim of education expressed at the time was to develop the child's ability as "creator, thinker, discoverer", and to explore relationships between man and nature, the individual and society, economics, politics and culture, past and present. The inventiveness of teachers at the time was illustrated by a great diversity of methods. The ideas of John Dewey and Helen Parkhurst's Dalton Plan were much in favour. The Soviet pedagogue P. P. Blonsky set out "to evolve curricula around problems arriving from the world outside", and in 1924 new syllabuses were introduced for Russian and mathematics, while the whole of the rest of the curriculum was to be integrated under a "complex method". Several methods meriting this name were in use, and a most entertaining novel containing an account of the introduction of the Dalton Plan is

Diary of a Communist Schoolboy, which was published in English under the pseudonym of N. Ognyov in 1926. It was not just that the curriculum became "complex": teacher authority was removed, pupil councils or soviets were running the schools - and in the case of this particular communist schoolboy, very little work was being done. There are parallels in the very much more dramatic events of the Chinese Cultural Revolution of 1966 and the following years.

By the end of the 1920s the complex method, problem solving and the integrated curriculum were felt in many powerful quarters to have failed. They had been in tune with the theory, but presumably the theory was simply not good enough, and another had to be found. It was suddenly discovered that the style of management in schools was not communist, but "liberal-anarchist". There can be no doubt that teachers did not like being ordered around by pupils. Krupskaya, who had supported the experiments, attributed their failure to lack of resources and training, and to the large classes. Worst of all, the teaching was accused of being "unsystematic" and less effective than traditional methods. Complex methods, it was now said, had undesirable social and political consequences and significance.

Consequently a decree in 1931 of the Central Committee of the Communist Party established certain rules for the Soviet school. Education was to be "systematic", the centrality of the teacher was not to be questioned, and the formal lesson was reestablished as the basic way of facilitating learning - with its "clearly defined routine", "order-promoting organization" and the way it inculcated a collective spirit. Six decades later, these principles are still upheld.

For a Soviet educator, then, from 1931 to the present, the only efficient, effective, practical way in which to reveal to pupils the "dialectical unity of the Marxist triad" nature - man - society and to demonstrate that the natural world and the history of human society are one and the same is through a curriculum which firmly maintains the traditional subject divisions. Soviet educators are keenly aware, however, of the need to make connections between traditional subjects. They recognise the existence and the danger of blinkered attitudes among teachers and the distaste some of them have for what they perceive as the "pollution" of their subject. They confess that in a few cases it still proves impossible to persuade teachers of different subjects to co-operate: thus, for example, physics teachers are or were until recently obliged to teach a certain aspect of mathematics because mathematics teachers leave it too late in their courses. Radical measures, say the educationists, should be taken on planning - but have not been taken yet. Nevertheless, all modern syllabuses are required to give prominence to inter-subject links and to suggest ways of establishing them. Such links "create the conditions for a wholeness in the structure of the curriculum". More work, they believe, must be done to create "inter-cycle" links (that is, between arts and natural sciences), since "humanization of the natural sciences was foretold by Marxist-Leninist thought". Despite the political language in which this is expressed, in practical terms the attitude differs little from that of many western curriculum planners.

Moral and Psychological Issues. The Requirements of Society

A central position in educational thought relating to the curriculum is occupied by the notion of the inseparability of instruction *[obuchenie]* and upbringing *[vospitanie]*. A primary aim of Soviet education is the "all-round development of communist personality" - a broad conception, resembling that of the "whole man". The personality conceived of will have knowledge and skills on the one hand and moral qualities on the other; its possessor will also possess adequate professional or work training in order to take part in the labour of socialist society. It is said that the state needs a "well-trained work-force of broad general culture". The implications of this are important: if taken seriously, it means that a boy of fourteen cannot drop all other studies except those which are directly relevant in the narrowest sense to his becoming a garage mechanic, or that a sixteen-year-old may not prepare for higher education by specializing in two or three subjects at the expense of everything else. No-one may devote himself exclusively to academic study and become either a physical wreck or a spoilt egotistical brat - or, if he does, the system has failed in his case. Soviet teachers are not supposed ever to neglect the moral side of education, and their academic teaching should be imbued with communist morality and outlook. This aspect of education is taken very seriously indeed.

Soviet educators have always been reluctant to recognize much difference between the ability of individuals to assimilate a given course of teaching. Materially different aims for strong and weak pupils - or for quick and slow learners or whatever terminology is used - are not set, though it is acknowledged that some children find it very much more difficult to learn than others. If they fall behind, it is the duty of the staff and of their fellows to arrange formal or informal remedial help. Soviet educational psychology is heavily reliant on L. S. Vygotsky, and it claims to have disproved the notions of followers of Jean Piaget about what a child who has reached a certain stage of development can be taught. (The disparity between Piaget's and Vygotsky's views is by no means as great as some Soviet scholars appear to think.) Soviet teaching is intended to "outpace" the child's development, and is supposed to be pitched at such a level that it will bring the child on from the position he has reached to that he can potentially reach, given help from the teacher. The space between what the pupil has achieved and what he can achieve was termed by Vygotsky the "zone of next development"; it is the task of the teacher to fill this zone and that of the methodologist to help the teacher to find the right method in order to fill it. Thus the weak child has greater, not less "potential" than the bright one, because the zone of next development is larger. An English teacher might well say that such a child "has little potential", neatly illustrating that the meanings of that word and the Russian *potentsial* are opposites rather than synonyms. The consequences of this for the curriculum are that a uniform, though not identical, programme of study is planned for all children; classes are unstreamed and teaching methods for the most part uniform. Nevertheless, it is held that it was never intended under orthodox Marxism-Leninism for all courses of study to be absolutely identical, so optional subjects and, to a certain extent, special programmes are allowed. However, no subject vital to the formation of all-round harmonious personality may be optional.

A decisive feature in the construction of Soviet curricula is "the demands of society addressed to the school". The duty of the young citizen to the state is never lost sight of and would never be relegated to a secondary position. This expresses itself in two ways: firstly, in the general requirement to acquire a broad general culture. This is a desirable end in itself; additionally it is now frequently argued that workers in the coming years will be supervising rather than operating machines, and that creative thinking will be necessary in all walks of life. Secondly, the acquisition of work skills has been part of Soviet education since the beginning. Its status and position have recently been strengthened. Educational theorists also stress the need for curriculum content to be up to date and practically related to the economy.

What Should Be Taught: Content and Process

So far, so good - but what subjects are vital to the formation of an all-round developed communist personality? How are subjects selected for inclusion, or how is the choice rationalized and justified? Lenin thought the all-round personality should possess:

    up-to-date scientific (in the Russian sense of "academic") knowledge,

    acquaintanceship with the practice of socialist construction and the ability to apply knowledge,

    a scientific-materialist outlook,

    communist convictions,

    communist morality,

    aesthetic feelings and experience,

    physical fitness.

A. S. Makarenko, S. T. Shatsky and Nadezhda Krupskaya, leading figures in the 1920s and 1930s, saw these "realms of activity" essential for the all-round development of personality: mental activity, physical labour, play, gymnastics, sport, participation in the arts, and organizational-social activity (by which we must probably understand service to the community).

Soviet educators seek to give "a contemporary picture of the world". Of course, they are mindful of the fact that the "picture" in the sense of received knowledge is only one -aspect of education: the content of education implies process as well. Educators recognize knowledge, skills *(umeniya:* knowing how) and habits *(navyki:* near automatic good working practices) as three components of the content of education. These notions are inherent in a categorization of school subjects arrived at by I. K. Zhuravlev and L. Ya. Zorina, which considers traditional subject classification into natural sciences and humanities, and discusses the possible addition to these two "cycles" of extra categories: labour, physical, aesthetic and linguistic. Arguing, however, that every subject has a "leading function", these authors arrive at three categories: (1) subjects containing "scientific" knowledge - physics, chemistry, biology, geography, history, astronomy, (2) means of activity (skills) - foreign languages, technical drawing, physical education, labour and technical disciplines, and (3) subjects imparting a particular way of seeing the world - art and music. Mathematics, literature and the native language are seen as straddling the distinctions. Cutting across these content-oriented categories, Zhuravlev and Zorina envisage a process-oriented classification of "auxiliary knowledge": (1) "inter-science" (logical, methodological, philosophical), (2) historico-scientific, (3) inter-subject and (4) evaluative knowledge.

Curricular Change in the 1980s

The very first paragraph of the 1984 "Guidelines" writes of "stimulating the creative activity of people". (To avoid possible confusion, the rather stilted official translation published in the Soviet Union in 1984 has not usually been amended in these quotations.) This stress on creativity returns again and again. Young people "should have an up-to-date education, be highly developed intellectually and physically, and have a good knowledge of the basic scientific, technical and economic principles of production, and a conscious, creative approach to work". Schools are required to train young people for socially useful work, to mould their characters and better to educate them politically and ideologically. Schools are to employ "more effective forms and methods of instruction" and "to follow consistently the principles [sic] of unity of education and upbringing". They must "eradicate all manifestations of formalism in the content and methods of instruction and upbringing". A further short section indicates that just about everything in schools is to be improved, including curricula, syllabuses and teaching methods, while excessive work loads are to be eliminated. This aim of reducing the overloading of schoolchildren is a constant theme, nicely illustrated by a 1986 cartoon in the satirical paper *Krokodil*. It shows two neighbours leaving their flats on the same landing. One with a rucksack is saying, "I'm going off on a three-day hike". The little boy next door, in school uniform and with a rucksack four times the size is saying, "I'm going to school for three lessons".

Section III of the Guidelines is entitled "Raising the Standards of Education and Upbringing", and here again stress is placed on reducing workloads, bringing syllabus content up to date, improving the teaching of subjects by ensuring maximum clarity in the presentation of content, increasing practical work and activities, relating school work to modern technological and industrial processes, making sure all children have a good command of Russian, whether it is their first language or not, and ensuring good general as well as good vocational education. Teaching methods and materials are discussed: textbooks must be improved, "standard" lessons (traditional formal chalk-and-talk) are to remain the basic educational form, but discussions, lectures, consultations, seminars and the like are to be encouraged in senior classes. Teachers should help "accustom pupils to work with books and other sources of knowledge and help them to think independently".

Little of this is new. In general, it is intensification and reiteration of well-worn principles - improving the standard of teaching of everything, ensuring moral training is given priority, furthering labour and ideological education. Some is plain common sense, like making sure that knowledge and skills taught are up to date. There is evidence of conservatism: obvious faith in the standard lesson and in the total efficacy of clear explanation if it can be achieved. But some of these requirements are progressive: getting away from "formalism", teaching children independent thinking, reducing the factual input, and most of all imparting a creative attitude and approach.

The Programme of Study

The first consideration for improving the standard of education which is expressed in the Guidelines is "to review the list of subjects taught and their scope". The curriculum currently being introduced should be fully operational by 1990/1991 (Figure 2). It differs from its immediate predecessors of 1977/78 and 1981/82. The curriculum displayed in this chart is for the Russian school, and for the most part classes 2 to 11 under the new system are comparable with 1 to 10 of

Periods per week per class

	Primary				Secondary							
	1	2	3	4	5	6	7	8	9	10	11	Total
First language and literature	7	9	11	11	11	9	6	5	5	4	3	81
Mathematics	4	6	6	6	6	6	6	6	6	4/5	4	60.5
Principles of Information Science and Computer Technology	–	–	–	–	–	–	–	–	–	1	2	3
History	–	–	–	–	2	2	2	2	3	4	3	18
Principles of Soviet State and Law	–	–	–	–	–	–	–	–	–	–	1	1
Social Studies	–	–	–	–	–	–	–	–	–	0/2	2/1	2.5
Ethics and Psychology of Family Life	–	–	–	–	–	–	–	–	0/1	1/0	–	1
Acquaintance with the World Around	1	1	–	–	–	–	–	–	–	–	–	2
Nature Study	–	–	1	1	1	–	–	–	–	–	–	3
Geography	–	–	–	–	–	2	3	2	2	2/1	–	10.5
Biology	–	–	–	–	–	2	2	2	2	1	1/2	10.5
Physics	–	–	–	–	–	–	2	2	3	4/3	4	14.5
Astronomy	–	–	–	–	–	–	–	–	–	–	1	1
Chemistry	–	–	–	–	–	–	–	3	3/2	2	2	9.5
Technical Drawing	–	–	–	–	–	–	1	1	–	–	–	2
Foreign Language	–	–	–	–	4	3	2	2	1	1	1	14
Art	2	1	1	1	1	1	1	–	–	–	–	8
Music	2	1	1	1	1	1	1	–	–	–	–	8
Physical Culture	2	2	2	2	2	2	2	2	2	2	2	22
Elementary Military Training (NUP)	–	–	–	–	–	–	–	–	–	2	2	4
Labour and Vocational Training	2	2	2	2	2	2	2	3	3	4	4	28
TOTAL	20	22	24	24	30	30	30	30	31	31	31	303
Options	–	–	–	–	–	–	2	2	2	3	4	13
Socially-useful Productive Labour	–	1	1	1	2	2	2	3	3	4	4	23
Labour Practice (in days)	–	–	–	–	10	10	10	16	16	20	–	–

Figure 2 Model curriculum for the general education school.

the old. The programme of study for the new class 1 can easily be seen from Figure 2.

Russian language and literature have gained two lessons since 1977, but the centre of gravity has moved very slightly towards the younger classes, with, for example, eleven lessons in new class 5 as opposed to 8 in old class 4. Mathematics has lost one lesson since 1981 (or one and a half since 1977). Of course, Russian and mathematics figure strongly in the new class 1, so overall both subjects have gained hours of instruction. The foreign language has fared no worse than it did in 1981, but this was two lessons down on 1977. History and Soviet state and law are unchanged, but an extra half lesson of social studies is introduced. Leaving aside the primary years, of the natural sciences, biology and physics have lost a lesson each since 1981; chemistry has lost half a lesson, and astronomy keeps its one period. Geography loses half a lesson. Technical drawing retains two lessons, but has moved down the school one year (it used to appear in the old classes 7 and 8). Art and music have gained nothing except two lessons each in the new year 1, but music has lost one from the old year 7. Physical education receives, as before, two lessons throughout. Labour training continues to increase its representation; leaving aside the two lessons in the new class 1, it has two more periods than in 1981 and four more than in 1977. Socially useful productive labour accounts for another 23 lessons. Elementary military training is as before. Options enter the programme one year earlier than before, but gain no lessons overall. The new subjects in 1990/91 are information science and computer technology, and ethics and psychology of family life.

Now this does not, perhaps, look like a curricular revolution, but minute alterations to the timetable of every single school in the country affect the professional lives of all teachers and the education of every Russian child. Like the tiny sliver of chocolate which, as industrialists say, accounts for the whole of the profit or loss on the sale of the bar, these adjustments are perceived as having great significance. Alarm has been expressed publicly because Russian literature no longer appears separate from language. In late 1986 it won back one period in class 10. In 1980/81 modern linguists were indignant at the loss of two periods to labour, and have now failed to win them back: such matters can be seen as a threat to the profession. It may seem that anxiety is exaggerated or are due to the same paranoid tendencies which induce members of the British public to write to *The Times* when they imagine that a shift of emphasis in public examination syllabuses at age 16 is threatening the whole fabric of national academic standards. It is worth noting that in the Soviet Union, where science is revered - and that is not too strong a word - physics, chemistry and biology have lost ground in the school curriculum, even if some of the loss is made up by information technology. Likewise, it may seem strange that art and music have maintained and even slightly strengthened their position. It is less obviously surprising that subjects with strong political content have gained a little, and the increase in labour and vocational training must be seen as significant. Much of this, however, is in tune with the theoretical work which we have just been examining. The national curriculum is not constructed on a basis of naive notions about the "usefulness" of one subject or another; leaders of educational thought are convinced of the vital role of both arts and sciences in the development of the Soviet economy.

Summary

The curriculum of the Soviet general education school is designed and controlled by central authority. That authority is represented by the Ministry of Education of the USSR which is informed mainly from the institutes affiliated to the Academy of Pedagogical Sciences. Minpros is not immune from public discussion, which is presently being carried on in a lively manner. National economic needs are crucial, but narrow responses to such needs are rarer than may be imagined. What can be provided depends, of course, on the resources which the state is able to devote to education. The process is carried on, as ever, under the watchful eye and positive leadership of the elite Communist Party of the Soviet Union. It has been noticeable recently that such leadership has been shown at the highest level in the Party. Minpros is ultimately responsible for promulgating the programme of study, the number of lessons per week in each subject, for compiling and publishing syllabuses, and for employing authors of textbooks. It publishes a monthly bulletin of instructions. The curriculum is "subject-based" and is intended to be systematically taught. Up to age 15 it is general. After that age every pupil continues to receive a general education, though as many as 60% to 70% may eventually be training at school for direct entry to a trade, profession or career and the other 30% will be receiving some form of labour or vocational education. Academic specialization is possible only to a limited extent in senior classes. Finally, character training and personality formation are not seen as a desirable side-product of an academic education, but as a fundamental aim of the system.

The vital importance of the moral education given to all Soviet children should not be underestimated. Before examining the content of subject syllabuses, it will be necessary to look at this issue in some detail. Without doing so, it will prove difficult to comprehend some aspects of them. The next chapter, therefore, is concerned with moral and political values and with the development of personality.

Chapter 3

"VOSPITANIE": MORAL, FAMILY AND CIVIC EDUCATION IN AND OUT OF
CLASS

THE WORD *vospitanie*, which is frequently used in educational
discourse, is usually translated "upbringing". The root verb
from which it derives, *pitat'*, means to nourish, sustain or
feed, and its compound *vospitat'* means to cultivate or foster.
One Russian-English dictionary suggests as a possible translation for *vospitanie* "good breeding".

Though it does not have all the overtones of the English
phrase, the concept of *vospitanie* does contain strong elements
of what upper class English might consider good breeding. In
the public debate which followed the promulgation of the draft
Guidelines for reform in 1984 concern was expressed that
schools should pay great attention to upbringing. The public
is conscious of the need to prevent vandalism and rowdiness
and to improve public behaviour by young people in general.
The feeling that youth is going to the dogs has been a feature
of society for millenia. Recently a British Minister of State
spoke of the fear of "creating a yob society" if moral education were ineffective.

Vospitanie means very much more than this. It embraces
moral education in the widest sense: the education of children
in any way other than of instructing them in a particular
subject. It means the inculcation of desirable ethical, social and working attitudes. Children in any country have the
right to expect that their education will equip them to make
ethical decisions. Though it was a Conservative prime minister, Stanley Baldwin, who said that education could never be
morally neutral, there are some teachers in pluralistic western societies who would prefer to remain impartial in ethical
matters. The Soviet view is that this is impossible, and
teachers there receive a grounding in the principles of moral
education which many western teacher-trainees would probably
consider an affront to their freedom of thought.

The all-embracing nature of *vospitanie* is best kept in
mind if we think of it as the development of personality.
This is a very general and holistic definition, which matches
the concept admirably. It does not appear upon the timetable

- every subject in the programme is supposed to bring it about. The way these subjects are taught and the ethos of the school are meant to convey the elements of a "correct" up-bringing. It is not confined to the school: extra-curricular activities, the work of the youth organisations and the Pioneer houses, which provide often admirable recreational and cultural facilities for schoolchildren, television, magazines and books are all expected to convey the same values and to reinforce each other's work.

The would-be moral educator in the Soviet Union might appear from this to have a good start. Nevertheless, educators are not complacent about their success in inculcating values. Theorists of moral education see it as a scientific matter: one recent writer claimed notable successes in the field, but stated that science has yet to answer such questions as "which moral qualities can be formed in pupils at which stage in their development?" The same writer, N. I. Boldyrev, in a series of books for teachers explores a "complex approach" to moral education, "methods of persuasion and application" and the means of assessing the effectiveness of such upbringing, all of which, he believes, require further investigation. The phrase, "complex approach", which is frequently used in contemporary educational discussion, means tackling all aspects of personality - socio-political, moral, aesthetic, etc. - at once, since the personality is a unity, and upbringing is an integral process. Boldyrev sees upbringing as a complex art and a creative process, having its own content, and its own principles.

Soviet Morality

What is the "well bred" young Russian like? Is there a profile for the well brought up child? There would seem to be eleven components: socio-political awareness, morality and ethics, patriotism and internationalism, military-patriotic education, labour education and professional orientation, mental development and the raising of general culture, atheism, knowledge of the law and of the obligations and rights of a citizen, economic, aesthetic and finally physical education. Not for nothing do Soviet educators consider themselves "sculptors of personality".

Let us look at each of these elements in turn. Socio-political awareness means making citizens politically literate and active. Certain subjects on the timetable of schools, such as social studies, history and the basis of Soviet government and law, set out actively to promote political awareness and correct attitudes. All teachers, however, must present the Communist world view.

Patriotism presents some difficulty. Children are taught to love their native land, but the purpose of Soviet patriotism is not purely affection for one's place of residence. It is love for the Soviet Union as the first socialist state ever created and as the homeland of the working class; it can, therefore, and should be, shared by anyone who holds Communist views, whatever their nationality. It is not meant to be empty-headed jingoism or irrational partisanship, such as a supporter might feel for his favourite football team. Soviet patriotism, however, often degenerates into sentimental attachment to birch trees and the "pure Russian sky". The other side of it is proletarian solidarity and internationalism - respect and love for the toiling masses throughout the world. Education for peace is a prominent feature of *vospitanie* and it sometimes conflicts with Military-patriotic education, which sets out to develop in children the desire to defend the socialist motherland. The practical side of this is represented in the curriculum by Elementary Military Training.

Economic and labour education and professional orientation we shall return to in Chapter 4. As well as providing a work-force for the economy and giving children an understanding of the place of their labour within the scheme of the nation's production, the morally improving effects of learning good working practices are of the greatest importance for Soviet educators. Mental development and the raising of general culture really embraces every subject in the curriculum and brings it under the umbrella of *vospitanie.*

Current and past concern with atheism is of considerable interest. The Soviet Constitution guarantees freedom to believe or not to believe, but all religious propaganda is forbidden; only atheistic teaching is allowed. School history textbooks link religion with educational backwardness or even witchcraft. What children think about the atheistic teaching they receive is hard to say, but recent press comment indicates that religious belief survives despite everything.

Knowledge of the law became a living issue a few years ago when it became clear that many juveniles were getting into trouble with the police for offences which they and their parents had seen as purely childish pranks. Often young people proved ignorant too of their rights and obligations.

On aesthetic education we shall have a great deal to say in Chapter 8. Soviet educators are emphatic that an appreciation of beauty both in nature and in the arts is vital to every child.

Physical culture (Chapter 12) is no mere addendum to the list. For the citizen to be physically fit improves production, lessens demands on the public health services and has a beneficial effect on the economy. Soviet educators justify physical education in a similar way to that used by exponents of English boarding-school education: sport and exercise produce determined, disciplined and courageous people who have initiative and who are prepared to work for and defend their native land.

In a syllabus for an experimental course in ethics taught

to eighth-class pupils in Belorussia a few years ago communist morality was described as the "highest achievement of civilized man". The eleven components of this morality were listed above. Let us look at some other expressions of the qualities possessed by that ideal, the all-round harmoniously developed Communist personality. A Party programme for the 22nd Congress in 1961 listed: devotion to the Communist cause, love of the socialist motherland and of other socialist societies, conscientious labour for the good of society, concern for the preservation and growth of public wealth, a high sense of public duty, intolerance of actions harmful to the public interest, a collectivist attitude, mutual respect between individuals, honesty, truthfulness, moral purity, modesty and unpretentiousness in social and private life, mutual respect in the family and concern for the upbringing of children, an uncompromising attitude to injustice, parasitism, dishonesty, careerism and money-grubbing, friendship and brotherhood among all peoples of the USSR, intolerance of national and racial hatred, an uncompromising attitude to the enemies of Communism; peace and the freedom of nations, fraternal solidarity with working people of all countries. The Soviet Constitution of 1978 adds "respect for the environment" to the list, and the phrase "high standards of honour" is used to replace "honesty, truthfulness, etc".

The "Guidelines" of 1984 write, "Of paramount importance... must be the shaping of a politically conscious citizen with strong communist convictions. All the elements of the educational process...should work towards this end." The aid of the whole community - clubs, museums, leisure services, cultural and political organizations, television and radio - is enlisted. Moral and legal education is "of exceptionally great importance and so is the fostering of the spirit of collectivism". Physical fitness, military and patriotic education and communistic education in the youth organizations must be improved. The Guidelines also explore the responsibilities of all agencies outside compulsory education (kindergartens, the family, the work-place, social and voluntary service associations, and extended-day groups - children whose homework and leisure is organized by teachers outside normal school hours) in what is called "social and family education".

The Media and Soviet Morality

An entertaining aspect of Soviet moral education concerns the by-products of this imposing and serious programme, some of which probably derive from distortions of the content of Soviet morality. Others are due to the prejudices of the elderly towards the crazes of youth, and have very little basis in ethical principle of any sort. For instance, the desire of the young to buy imported goods of various sorts is frequently castigated (though why the goods are imported if not for sale is not made clear). Marriage with foreigners is not forbidden by any of the precepts above, but arbiters of social mores speak against it: one popular press columnist praised a young woman for leaving her French husband in order to return to Russia for sentimental reasons - not because it is the "first workers´ state". Patriotism is obviously a greater virtue than marital fidelity (which is apparently less vital if the partner is a foreigner). One should not be too critical of these attitudes - after all, journalists write all the more entertainingly for having prejudices.

Soviet children are constantly reminded in their papers and magazines of the sacrifices made and heroic deeds done by their parents and grandparents during the war of 1941-45. It is easy to understand the motivation of older generations in terms of a passionate desire to avert future wars. There is, however, a fair amount of evidence from the press that children are becoming bored with heroic tales; this has led not so much to an easing-off of propaganda, as to calls for teachers and parents to improve the presentation of their stories. They should speak of the exploits of heroes in the "appropriate tone of voice... not didactically, but with enthusiasm".

The adult press too instils the desirable characteristics of the all-round harmoniously developed communist personality. Particularly prominent in recent months has been a desire to promote the stability of the family. Another constantly recurring motif is criticism of poor standards of public services and of workmanship in the building and manufacturing industries. Corruption, waste and drunkenness, ignorance and suspicion of new technology are all regularly criticised. Not all of these failings would at first glance be accepted as matters for moral education, but in fact they all fall into one or other of the eleven categories which go to make up the harmoniously developed all-round communist personality. Put another way, if *vospitanie* for all citizens in their youth had been faultless, none of these complaints would have arisen.

How Moral Precepts Are Conveyed

This, then, is the content of Soviet personality development and character training, both in theory and as it appears in reality, surrounded by all the quirks and obsessions which accompany the notions. We can now summarise where and how it is taught. Firstly, it goes on inside school lessons in any and every subject: no teacher can escape the obligation to convey political, ideological and ethical teaching. Secondly, there is the work of the class tutor, who has an important role and is expected to train children in all the good qualities of the new Soviet person, both through necessary activities like the organization of classroom duties and in extra matters like setting children specific tasks in preparation for the celebration of Soviet festivals (Lenin´s birthday, the anniversary of the October Revolution, and so on). He or she is to hold talks and debates with the class concerned, and to get them to produce class newspapers and to organize entertainments - among many other possible activities. In all this the teacher should encourage children - we are told in books of instructions and advice for such work - to socialize each other, while keeping a wary eye on the actions both of would-be dominant characters and of passive or idle children. The class tutor should make children aware of the qualities required to carry out joint activities successfully: trust, reliability and initiative. They should give both praise and blame where deserved, and not stint the former.

Thirdly, there is the work of the youth organizations, all - at least in theory - voluntary, and overtly political in ethos and purpose. They are the Octobrists (aged 8 to 10), the Pioneers (the All-Union Pioneer Organization, aged 10 to 15) and the Komsomol, or All-Union Leninist Communist League of Youth (15 upwards). Recently these organizations have been severely criticized for failing to interest young people and attract their active support. None the less, their activities are of great importance for moral and ideological education. In many ways the Pioneers' activities are meant to complement and reflect the work done by the class tutor, and it is expected that the tutors will cooperate with the Pioneer leaders in planning upbringing work. A Pioneer detachment is formed from children in the same school class and has a leader who may be an older child, or a student or suitable adult. In theory, Pioneers are supposed to show initiative and independence in running many of their own affairs; in practice many Soviet teachers find it hard to work *with* children without adopting an authoritarian manner to them and their leader, especially if that leader is a very young person. Every school has one adult paid Pioneer coordinator, who is ultimately responsible for the running of the system. The Pioneers go in for almost every imaginable cultural, sporting and political activity: talks, debates, environmental work, all sorts of crafts and hobbies, making posters and displays, helping Octobrists run their activities, helping other and younger children with school work, organizing socially useful work, arranging games and field sports. The political content is very important: children are taught about the flags, symbols and anthems of their organization, their republic and the Union. Great use is made of ceremony and solemnity, including drumming and bugling, banner-bearing, drill and marching.

A brief account of one such ceremony may convey the flavour. Its purpose was to provide a context for a formal meeting with the older generation, so that they might urge the children to emulate good communists. As the drums rolled, the Pioneer detachment formed up in the hall. The president of the assembly solemnly received reports from each section and formally conveyed them to the senior Pioneer leader. The

children and their guests all sat down. Extracts from Mayakovsky's poem, "Vladimir Il'ich Lenin" were recited. Many of
the older generation, some wearing uniforms or campaign me-
dals, made formal short speeches. Appropriate songs were then
sung. Some of the best Pioneers present were awarded certificates for excellent academic and practical work. During the
singing of another song the children gave flowers to their
visitors and thanked them for their contributions. All present then joined "like one united family" in a Pioneer song.

The fourth area in which *vospitanie* is conducted is the
media. Enough has been said about this, except perhaps to
stress once again that the values conveyed reinforce and do
not conflict with those taught in school. Fifthly there is
the influence of the community, and particularly the home.
The home can be perhaps the strongest, perhaps the weakest
link: the strongest if parents share the values of society,
the weakest if they do not. Schools set great store by their
links with the children's homes, as indeed they do in many
countries, but in the USSR the confidence with which teachers
can call upon most parents for support in ethical and ideological as well as academic issues is considerable. There is
an official monthly magazine for parents with children of
school age, *Family and School*, and much of its space is taken
up with articles and shorter items relating to moral upbringing. Teachers and Pioneer leaders are expected to visit
and get to know the homes from which their children come.
This does not necessarily always happen in practice. But all
is *not* left to the parents' discretion. The "Guidelines"
stress that "the effectiveness of upbringing depends... on the
concerted efforts of the family, the school and work collectives and the coordination of the demands they make on
pupils". The involvement of the community in keeping an eye
on the way parents perform their duty should not be regarded
as a mere formality. The parents' trade union or colleagues
in the workplace are expected to, and often do, concern themselves with matters which would be considered private in other
countries. The "Guidelines" again: "Work collectives are
called upon constantly to watch over the upbringing of children, to help parents in this matter, and to call them strictly
to account for faults and shortcomings in family upbringing."

Vospitanie, the ethical and political upbringing of Soviet children and the development of their personalities,
quite clearly has a very obvious agreed content which is not
neutral, and no attempt is made to disguise it. It is not,
therefore, part of any "hidden" curriculum there might be in
Soviet schools; it is explicit. It permeates the whole of the
rest of the curriculum and, even in "pure" science and mathematics courses, cannot entirely be escaped. For this reason,
the remaining chapters of this book should be read with all of
these issues in mind. Moral education and the propagation of
values is a notoriously difficult area for the practising

teacher in any country. Full success can never be assured, and it would be unfair to stress the shortcomings in Soviet moral education. Nevertheless, Soviet education cannot be understood without full awareness of the nature of the "new Soviet" man or woman, which the system sets out to create.

MORAL, FAMILY AND CIVIC EDUCATION AS CURRICULUM SUBJECTS

There are three short courses in Soviet schools which have a high content of moral education. The first of these is taught in the first two years of primary schooling, and is entitled *Acquaintance with the world around.* Its aims are to give young children some conception of the social and natural environment, enrich their social and moral experience and form habits of decent behaviour. It can be seen partly as the very beginning of scientific, geographical and labour education, but much of its content is moral in character.

More particularly, the purposes of the course are to acquaint children with social life and labour in Soviet society, to instil a respectful and considerate attitude to other people and their work and property, to encourage love of the child's native locality and the country, and to foster a conservationist attitude to the natural environment.

The course comprises four themes. The first is "our house": this includes the family and their jobs and daily work, care for older relations, housework, personal hygiene, caring for oneself and one's clothes, table manners, and looking after house plants and domestic pets. "Our school" deals with the jobs of the personnel, rules of behaviour in and out of class, speech etiquette, interest in school work, and helping classmates. It also seeks to encourage a critical attitude to one's own and others' behaviour. "Our town or village" deals with the main points of interest, historical monuments, industry, geography, cultural and educational institutions, people's work, machines which simplify life, and road safety. "Our native country" makes children look outside the immediate environment, and the course deals briefly with the capital, Lenin, history and the main festivals celebrated in the USSR. Teachers are to stress the "concern of the Party for the people in its care, especially for the happy childhood of the rising generation", and the "scarlet thread" running through all of this is the development of a humane attitude to other people.

Ethics and Psychology of Family Life begins in the second half of class 9 and continues for the first half of class 10. Short though the course is, it merits a fairly full summary here. It begins with four lessons entitled "Personality, society, family", which consists mainly of straight social psychology mixed with some moral instruction on the dynamics of family relationships and their relationship with society. This is followed by eight lessons on inter-personal relationships in youth: two on the psychology of it, two on the moral basis of boy-girl friendships and the nature of young male and female personality, two on friendships in general and two on "love as the highest human emotion" between the sexes and within families. All of this is placed in the context of society and its demands upon smaller groups such as the family. There are then five lessons on marriage and the family: what is readiness for marriage? (2 lessons) - social, physical, economic and psychological readiness and roles within the family. Two more lessons in this section deal with the Soviet family and its functions, and a very sociological approach is adopted; one lesson goes on characteristics of the young family - practical problems of embarking upon a new way of life.

The seventeen lessons in the following year are grouped under two headings: the first is "fundamentals of family relationships" and covers eleven lessons. One of these is on the ideological basis of the family and contains a great deal of what might be termed socio-politics. The next two deal with the moral basis: equality, duty, responsibility, conscientiousness, respect, frankness, etc. Two more are entitled "the collectivism of the Soviet family", a difficult and abstract topic. Consider this paragraph:

> The specifics of intra-family intercourse. Its dependence on multi-faceted family relationships (economic, ideological, emotional and moral, sexual, parental), on naturalness, permanence, mutual interest, and on the purpose of ensuring all sides of the vital activity of the members of the family, etc. The new content of the concept "head of the family". Mutual help by spouses in family matters. The family council.

To make this accessible to children of all abilities would not be easy; nor would the next two lessons on "the psychological climate of the family", which is about compatibility - temperamental, psychological, ideological and so on. One note reads: "exaggeration of the role of sexual compatibility in the creation of a good psychological climate".

Three more single lessons cover the family's working atmosphere, household budgeting, and *estetika byta* (a difficult phrase to translate - literally, "aesthetics of everyday life", a topic which embraces such matters as turning the home into a cosy, inviting and intellectually stimulating environment) and leisure, (culture, the struggle against bourgeois concepts of beauty and comfort, and fashion - the psychological need both to follow it and to adapt it to the individual). One lesson is on the consequences of infringing family relationships: family break-up and divorce.

"Family and children", deals with child-raising: parents' obligations to the children and society (3 lessons), the

upbringing of children within the family (2 lessons), and one
lesson on "the child in the young family" - feeding, daily
routines, the child's emotional and physical treatment.

The sheer mass of the content of this course must surely
mean that it can only be conveyed by a straight didactic lecturing style of teaching. Six-and-a-half pages of indigestib-
le telegram-style Russian is followed by a mere quarter page
containing four subjects for discussions, six for lecturettes,
three for "readers' conferences" - special events with a theme
like "the image of father and mother in literature", four
topics for case-study discussion (or possibly role-playing) -
e.g. "the young family and parents", and a list of six films.
The titles of 26 books are appended, 13 of them Party or other
political documents, and the remainder mainly serious and
academic with the odd popular work thrown in. We must await
evidence of the progress and success of the courses, but it
looks very much as if most teachers will feel that they have
to lecture at the children for most of the time.

There is a fairly obvious omission from this account of
the ethics course. There is little if any sex education in it.
It has already been criticised in the Soviet Union on this
account. This matter of sex education is considered by Soviet
teachers to be "intricate and delicate". They are coy on the
subject, and many of them see it as no business of the school
to become involved. In this whole course of ethics and psychology of family life the word "sexual" is used no more than
four times, always in passing and, as we have seen, in one
case with the specific purpose of deprecating the importance
of sex. The four lessons on human reproduction in the ninth-
year biology class deal with the topic in a purely scientific
way (see Chapter 7).

There have been local experiments in sex education. For
example, in the Stavropol area an experimental course was
designed to strengthen the family and improve preparation for
marriage. Sexual issues are covered among many other matters,
and the local notabilities who planned the experiment were led
by a professor who is a doctor of medicine, and though full
details of the course are not given, it clearly has a strong
health education side - on alcohol and tobacco as well as sex.
Among visitors who come into schools to teach are psychiat-
rists, doctors and a consultant venerologist.

Principles of Soviet government and law is a course in civic
and legal education which is followed by all children in the
ninth year. It contains a great deal of information which
would be useful to any citizen, and much of it is designed to
further patriotic education, the creation of positive attitudes to work and identification with the ideals of communism.
There is, nevertheless, other motivation for its inclusion in
the curriculum. For example, educators write of the "prophyl-
actic" intention of the course - in preventing adolescents

from infringing the law out of sheer ignorance, for one thing, and in averting the possibility of their adopting "views harmful to socialism" for another. The thrust of the course is backed up by popular literature in book and journal form, directed at parents and young people. The introduction to one wide-circulation paperback writes of the need not only to make individuals observe the Soviet law themselves, but to be implacable in their opposition to others who break it. "It is the duty of parents, school, and society to do everything to protect the adolescent from harm."

Proponents of the course, which first appeared in the curriculum in the late 1970s, enunciate the hope that it will change young people's behaviour: They were, however, realistic about the possibility of a few lessons in school achieving this major moral effect. Nevertheless, the optimistic streak in Soviet education inclines teachers to believe that a good methodology may eventually bring adolescents to a fuller realization of their personal responsibilities as citizens.

Section I deals with Soviet government, law and morality (4 lessons): Lenin, the October Revolution and the foundation of the Soviet state, the meaning of "advanced socialism", the leadership of the Communist Party and the concept of a multinational state. Socialist and "exploitative" states are contrasted. Under "Law and morality in socialist society" pupils are taught about the various branches of the law, legal responsibility, and communist morality and its relationship with the law.

Section II is entitled "The Constitution of the USSR. Constitutional law" (16 lessons). The most significant content includes: how the multi-national state is run, the soviets of people's deputies as the political foundation of the state, the Party, trades unions, the Young Communist League and labour collectives; the economy, socialist property, personal property and its protection; the state's concern for people's material and "spiritual" needs; labour as a source of wealth; the indestructible unity of workers, peasants and intellectuals; the leading role of the working class; the role of the state in raising living standards and the distribution of wealth under socialism; and the state's concern for the development of science and culture and for the preservation of the national heritage. Foreign policy figures: the Leninist policy of peace, the USSR as part of a socialist commonwealth, the defence of socialist society, the armed forces, and the privilege and duty of all to serve in them.

The second part of Section II deals with the state and the individual: the notion of citizenship, the passport (the internal identity document which is received by citizens at the age of 16), the attainment of majority. The rights and privileges of citizens are: to work and choose a career (contrasted with restrictions under capitalism), to receive an education, and to enjoy the achievements of culture. Again,

contrast is drawn with what is seen as the lack of real guarantees of education and access to culture in "bourgeois"
society. Political and social freedom in the Soviet Union is
treated alongside study of the supposed absence in capitalist
societies of such freedom. The unity of rights and duties is
stressed; pupils are informed that failure to engage in conscientious labour is incompatible with the principles of socialist society, and they are told of their obligation to
respect the rights and legal interests of others.

A third topic in Section II is the structure of the USSR
and its organs of power and administration. It is emphasized
that the source of the power of the USSR is the brotherly
cooperation of Soviet peoples - unlike the national inequalities which exist in the capitalist world. Local and national
government bodies and the electoral system are described;
attention is paid to the arms, symbols and anthems of the
Union and of the republics.

Section III is entitled "Branches of Soviet law" (11
lessons): labour law (working hours, conditions of employment,
arrangements for seeking work or being discharged, records of
employment, payment, protection of minors, subsidies for those
studying while at work, and the responsibilities of workers;
the concern of the state for people's leisure and the exploitation of workers in capitalist society). Collective farm
law; civil law (property, agreements, injury caused by minors); family law; administrative law (misdemeanours, such as
vandalism, minor financial offences and drunkenness). The
syllabus contains a hefty paragraph on the criminal law and on
serious crime: being involved in a crime, concealing evidence
and making a defence. A section on punishments for adults and
minors deals with mitigating and aggravating factors (drunkenness being prominent among the latter). Offences against the
person, against public order and public safety also figure,
and the final paragraph of this section includes information
about the illegal storing and bearing of arms and the distil-
ling of spirits at home.

Section IV carries the general heading of "Ensuring socialist legality" (2 lessons): the role of the soviets of
people's deputies in ensuring the law is observed, and the
activities of voluntary vigilante groups, both adult and junior; the courts and other organs of justice.

A final lesson sums up the whole course. It is entitled
"To observe Soviet law is the obligation of all citizens of
the Soviet Union". Commentary by Soviet educators indicates
that this lesson is the crux of the programme. It should be
used to revise material from Sections I and II, and to prepare
the ground for extension of the concepts introduced in later
lessons in Soviet history, geography, social studies and optional studies in legal education. Most of all, it is intended to make pupils vividly aware of the importance of the
material covered for every Soviet citizen.

Chapter 4

LABOUR EDUCATION.   THE SCHOOL AND THE WORLD OF WORK

THE DUTY of schools to prepare children for the work of society is widely accepted, but work, particularly industrial labour, has a special place in Communist education and indeed in
the whole Communist cast of thought. Marx and Engels were
scathing about the exploitation of workers; society in their
view should not rob the labourer of the fruits of his toil and
its monetary value. Marx sought to see that the worker was
given back the respect due to him and just recompense for the
products of his labour. This all represents a highly developed work ethic with important consequences for policy.

This ethic is bound up with a number of ideas which have
been current for a very long time. There is respect for the
"dignity of labour" and the skills of the artisan; a belief
that manual workers are entitled to parity of esteem with
brain-workers. There is consciousness of the importance of
industry and the technological knowledge behind it. Awareness
of the vital relationship of work to a person's life and
personality is shared by, for instance, Protestant Christianity as well as Communism; but Soviet educators go so far as to
say, "Labour created man himself". We must not forget the
scorn felt by many self-made people of proletarian origin for
intellectuals who will not dirty their hands: it was this
which forced civil servants and professors to work by the
sweat of their brow during the Chinese Cultural Revolution.
Communists believe in the morally improving power of physical
labour, which, since it is often collectively organised,
creates a feeling of belonging and the motivation to work
responsibly for the good of the group. The working class,
particularly the industrial proletariat, has always had a
special position in revolutionary thought.

The consequence of this for Soviet education is that
labour figures prominently and in ways that do not correspond
exactly with apparently equivalent activities in schools in
non-socialist countries. Firstly there is the concept of
"polytechnical" education. Then there is the obligation to
participate in "socially useful labour". Pupils also carry
out continuous periods of "labour practice", working on farms

or in industrial concerns for ten to sixteen days during holidays. Lastly, there is "labour and vocational training", which forms part of the curriculum for every child throughout the whole period of compulsory education.

Polytechnical Education

"Polytechnical education" in Soviet terminology means acquainting pupils with contemporary production in theory and practice and with the relationship between society and production. (This word "production" is commonly used in Russian to mean "industry" in the broadest sense.) Polytechnical education also means "effective labour training", the formation of working skills, knowledge enough to make a rational choice of career, and a foundation for consequent professional training. Marx, in *Das Kapital*, left readers in no doubt of the importance of *polytechnische Ausbildung* in shaping the worker´s understanding of his ability to control the "means of production". He and Engels believed that it was an indispensable component in the all-round development of personality. They were not alone in that - similar principles were held by Pestalozzi, Fourier and Robert Owen, but Marx and Engels contended that only in socialist society could polytechnical education reach fulfilment, whereas under capitalism narrow professional training was all that could be envisaged.

It is ironic that a system which expresses such firm belief in this principle, and which devotes a great deal of effort to getting the relationship between theory and practice right, should have had problems with establishing rationally organized polytechnical education in schools. In the 1920s the massive problems suffered by the emergent state - especially the need for a trained work force - meant that *poly*technical education, introducing children to a range of skills, was soon replaced by precisely the narrow vocationalism that Marx deplored. Under Stalin polytechnism was abandoned. It was Khrushchev, peasant turned miner as he was, and full of scorn for unpractical and over-fastidious brain-workers, who exerted a determined effort to make it compulsory again. That was in 1958, and his measures led to six or eight years of irritated controversy, based on the objections of the very intellectuals he was seeking to improve as well as on the practical problems of arranging factory work for vast numbers of older school children. During fact-finding expeditions in recent years, questions on the subject have been answered by reference to labour training, which is not the same thing. Most recently some - not all - have said: "We don´t use the word any more." What does polytechnical education mean today?

In fact, the syllabus for labour training in the middle years of education at school answers most of the criteria for polytechnical education. A range of different and useful skills is taught. In the later years, a clear policy of mono-

technism is or will be followed, with the aim of making sure
that every child receives a trade qualification which guarantees employment the day after he leaves school. But that is
not where the matter ends. Polytechnism is a spirit which is
meant to permeate the whole of education. *The Great Soviet
Encyclopaedia* interprets the whole curriculum of schools as an
embodiment of the polytechnical principle: scientific subjects
provide the technological and materialist basis for it, the
humanities enable pupils to see the world of work in perspective, optional courses offer further opportunities for exploration, and labour training gives them actual manual skills.
If this seems a little insubstantial as a philosophical justification, then it must be said that the newest syllabuses for
many subjects pay particular attention to polytechnical knowledge by stressing the practical applications in the economy
of the theoretical information the pupils are given.

Socially useful labour

This is compulsory for all children from the second class.
The phrase covers a variety of activities: helping old people,
routine chores or duties, picking up litter and sweeping out
school rooms, mending and cleaning clothes, collecting scrap
metal, harvesting crops and maintaining school premises and
gardens. It is felt to be important that not only teachers and
youth leaders should assign tasks. If the president of the
collective farm, for instance, does so, pupils feel that their
labour is useful to society and "communist construction".
     A recent official Ministry of Education report held up as
models the work done in two schools in Novgorod and Podolsk.
The very youngest children made stationery for a television
factory; older ones were producing 500 cutting nippers a
month. The girls ran a "children's cafe", made soft furnishings for the school building and contributed to the manu-
facture of garments in a productive clothing concern. Activities were well organized in conjunction with the "base enterprises": factories, farms or businesses which cooperate with
the school. In these cases the base enterprises had actually
placed orders with the school for the goods they wanted the
pupils to produce, so the children knew that they were in fact
a small, but perhaps essential, part of the firms' operations.

Production practice

After learning a trade for one day a week, pupils spend twelve
days in continuous work during one of their holidays. They
would, like real workers, have to meet a production target and
attain normal standards of quality. They might do this in an
actual factory, perhaps substituting for the regular workers
on their annual holiday; otherwise the work might be organized
on a production line exactly similar to that in the factory,

but located in a school training combine (UPK: described below), or in a special factory training shop. Pupils training for agricultural trades work on collective or state farms; others work, say, on building sites or in service industries.

Labour and Vocational Training and Professional Orientation

By making education to age 17 compulsory and by allowing all who wished to continue with general education rather than entering a trade training school, the system gave rise to certain difficulties. Industry was deprived of the labour of certain adolescents who would otherwise have gone into employment at 15. Moreover, children who have been educated academically have higher expectations of the type of employment they hope to find for themselves. Add to all this a sharp decline in the birth rate in Slav and Baltic areas of the country (where the jobs are) and a marked reluctance on the part of the more fertile Asiatic nationalites to leave their sunny republics to make good the shortage of labour in the more bracing climate of Russia, and the supply of trained workers needs to be stimulated.

Children in all primary classes are introduced to many types of hand work for two periods a week. In classes 5 to 7 they receive "a fundamental training in general work skills of a polytechnical character". It is in class 8 that the subject takes on a specific relationship to a trade specialism. Half the lessons are taught in this year and several in the following year to a syllabus entitled "The Basis of Production and the Choice of a Profession" and the remainder is related to a particular grouping of trades, such as metalworking, agriculture, catering or computers. In years 10 and 11 in the general school the pupil will choose an exact specialism from the grouping already studied and receive training as, say, a joiner or lathe operator. On completing their education, pupils receive a certificate entitling them to seek employment immediately in an enterprise at full salary and as fully qualified workers (though, obviously, at a relatively low level). In an ideal world this system would achieve the moral benefits of polytechnical education, answer the demand for careers counselling at school, and provide a steady stream of qualified workers for the economy without industry itself having to be totally responsible for their training after they had left school.

Primary Classes. Children engage in handicrafts, making simple toys, ornaments and useful objects, often with a good deal of teacher assistance. They draw pictures related to this work. They learn general hygiene, washing hands, the use of cutlery, making beds, tidying up, and so on. For the youngest children much of this amounts to elementary health education, but an introduction to productive labour is effected as early as possible.

Years 5 to 7. Aims of instruction are: children are to understand the importance of industry, the organization of the economy, they are to develop creative powers and good working habits, become acquainted with a wide range of trades in order to choose one, and learn to carry out everyday odd jobs involving general trade skills and working with a wide variety of materials, tools, and machinery. Work with animals and plants is included. In the past children sometimes built up these skills while producing a pile of useless rubbish. This will not do now: their work "must be productive".

The syllabus lists eight sections: woodwork, metalwork, electrical work, work with textiles, culinary skills, everyday repairs, agricultural skills - looking after animals and growing plants, and agricultural technology. The syllabus differs according to the nature of local industries. Schools therefore tend to act as recruiting centres for the local factory or collective farm. Not every child can be introduced to each of these eight sections.

"The physiological characteristics of girls and boys must be considered in conducting labour lessons." Girls are not to be given physically onerous tasks. Despite the stereotype of women commanding regiments, driving tractors, hurling discuses and digging holes in the road which some in the West have, the Soviet Union has an old-fashioned attitude to the roles of the sexes. In many schools all the boys do metalwork while all the girls do cookery. Questions about this are brushed aside almost with impatience: "Wild horses wouldn´t get the girls into the metalwork shop". "None of the boys would want to learn cooking."

Whatever sections are chosen, the syllabus is emphatic that the same level of skills development, quality control, organization, observation of safety procedures, "graphic literacy" (when working to plans) and so on should be observed. Collective ("brigade") forms of organization of work are strongly recommended. Waste of materials and effort is to be discouraged, and lessons are to be drawn from this for industrial production. Ecological issues are not to be forgotten.

Three variants of the syllabus are offered for urban schools. The first is for boys and girls, and contains six main headings: pupils spend roughly the same number of lessons in each of the years 5, 6 and 7 on tasks of the same type. They are: working with wood (timber and plywood; hand tools only in year 5, lathe in 6 and 7); work with metal (sheet metal and wire in year 5, high-grade in year 6, and using lathes for more detailed work in year 7); electrical (more theory in this topic, but including practical work in repairing devices, and wiring in year 5, electromagnets and bells in year 6, and various automatic devices in year 7); repairs in everyday life (from wiring a plug in year 5 to refitting windowframes and repairing vacuum cleaners in year 7); textiles (operation of a sewing machine; making clothes - from

hemming a skirt in year 5 to making a dress in year 7);
culinary work (salads, soups and stews in year 5 as well as
the salting of vegetables; by year 7 the preparation of meat
and fish and whole menus).

Variant 2, for boys, contains four of the six topics
given in variant 1, omitting textiles and cookery, and adding
a fifth: agricultural work, though in an urban school some
difficulties may be foreseen: there is a limit to what can be
done in jam-jars and with rabbits. Variant 3, for girls,
contains textiles, culinary work, electrical work, domestic
repairs, and agricultural work.

In rural schools, variant 1 of the syllabus for boys and
girls gives pride of place to agricultural work and technology. The variants for the separate sexes have in common agriculture and electrical work; boys do metalwork, while girls do
textiles and cooking. In all these syllabuses alternative
numbers of periods for the activities are given, depending on
the resources available.

In *classes 8 and 9* there are 272 lessons for labour,
including "socially useful productive labour". This includes
"Fundamentals of Production and the Choice of a Career" (68),
a course seeking to improve "the Leninist principle of the
unity of education and production" and, by introducing pupils
to the "polytechnical bases of production", to help them make
an informed choice of career. The course aims to arouse "socially valuable" motives for choosing a profession, acquainting pupils with what jobs exist in their region and infor-
ming them about the system of vocational training. It is
intended that local industry should be involved to the maximum. The course includes giving pupils some knowledge of
their own psychological inclinations. Group and individual
counselling are practised. This may take place in schools,
UPKs, local firms or "professional orientation centres". After 51 lessons, concentrated in the first half of year 8, the
pupils make a choice of "profile" - a general vocational area
rather than a specific trade - and begin training. The remaining 17 lessons are given in year 9 in parallel with training in the chosen profile and are meant to help the pupil make
a further more specific choice within that career area for
training in the following two years.

The themes covered are given below with numbers of lessons in brackets. Introduction (1), the polytechnical basis
of socialist production (17) - consisting of the structure of
the economy (1), the socialist productive enterprise (2), the
nature of production work (2), visit to an enterprise (2),
fundamentals of technology (5), techniques of production (5).
Choice of a profession (21) - consisting of personnel in the
economy and classification of occupations (3), a person's
interests and inclinations (2), aptitude and professional
suitability (2), health and the choice of a career (1), the
demands placed upon the worker by a job (2), finding a job

(1), excursions to a UPK, an enterprise, a PTU and a training workshop (6), counselling (4), including provisional assignment to a specialism; practical acquaintanceship with a profile or profiles of vocational training (12).

Class 9: polytechnical basis of socialist production (8): economics and organization of labour in a socialist enterprise (3), modern industry and the environment (1), computers in modern industry (2), and trends in scientific and technical progress in production (2). Choice of profession (continued): here the syllabus instructs teachers to compare the situation under capitalism unfavourably with socialism. Notes include references to planning for a lifetime of professional work, obtaining advanced professional training and financial support, and defending one's choice of career (4 lessons).

Professional Orientation

The term is unwieldy, but the concept differs from careers counselling as practised in some other countries. Concern has been expressed at all levels in society about shortcomings in the system of allocation of the work force to careers and training. In the Soviet Union there is a labour shortage. In most societies there is a mismatch between people's desires, hopes and expectations and the requirements of the national economy for workpeople. Inevitably considerations other than those of personal inclination will come into play. Nevertheless, the impression is almost unavoidable that an important purpose of Soviet professional orientation is to make the numbers fit the State's requirements. However, an unhappy worker is not likely to be a good one; persuasion rather than compulsion must be regarded as preferable, and society seeks a skilled and satisfied work force.

Information gathered a few years ago probably still gives a good indication of how the process looks to the individual pupil. He or she first got help from the class tutor, who was expected to provide a profile by the end of incomplete secondary education. Subject teachers advised. The weakest link, according to my informant (from a city education authority), was then the psychological assessment of the pupil's personality from the point of view of professional orientation. The informant mentioned new courses in psychodiagnostics to help careers advisers to assess children accurately. Recently a new post was created in all schools linking labour training with professional orientation. A "commission", consisting of the head teacher, school doctor, class tutor, parents and child met to discuss the matter, and recommendations were made at the end of the (old) eighth year; in case of disagreement, appeal could be made to the regional methodological centre - the next step up from the school.

Labour in the Later Years of Schooling. Let us return to the labour training syllabus for year 8 and look at the process from the point of view of one pupil. He or she has to choose a profile for years 8 and 9. The many dozens of profiles with syllabuses already approved include woodworker, confectioner, secretarial trades, draughtsman, metalworker, catering trades, tailoring and dressmaking, agricultural technology, car mechanics, radio electronics, office skills, lathe operator, weaver, plasterer and computer technologist. Courses in classes 10 and 11 include chemical laboratory assistant, house painter, typist, fashion model, radio fitter, computer operator, agricultural technician (for sheep breeding or electric milking) and joiner (in the building trade). The Minpros *Bulletin of Normative Acts* for November 1986 listed 36 profiles and professions for which syllabuses would be published by the end of 1986/87. Obviously some of these trades have a rather higher status than others, and any given school can offer only a limited choice from such a wide range.

It would be quite impossible to give even the barest summary of anything like this series of syllabuses, and it is assumed that the reader of this chapter seeks mainly an impression of the type of training which a pupil might receive. As an example, let us take a boy (for reasons already discussed, it is most unlikely to be a girl) who decides to select the woodworking profile in year 8, and who goes on to learn building joinery in year 10. He receives theoretical instruction about work in the field (2 lessons), on working practices, health and safety considerations (2), the materials with which he will be working (6), and the technology of working solid timber with hand tools (8). Practical instruction includes excursions to places of work (3), practice in basic woodworking skills (26), and, of course, 34 periods of socially useful work. In the following year he receives more instruction in organization and safety (1), joints (6), glueing (4), the technological processes involved in the production of joinery (17), creative problem-solving in woodwork (4), and economic planning in relation to the woodworking industry (2). Of the practical lessons, ten go on practice in making joints, 28 on making articles which will be useful to the school, and 11 on repairing school equipment, furnishings, etc. As usual, 34 periods of socially useful labour figure in the timetable.

At this stage our budding joiner is faced with a number of choices, or at least a number of possibilities. He may stay on in the general education school, in which case the syllabus he follows will be as described below. As we saw in Chapter 1, if he is not academically particularly able, he will come under pressure to leave and go to an SPTU, where he will continue his general education for three years and most probably work for the same leaving certificate as he would have got in the general school, but at the same time he will receive a more advanced vocational training than that summarised below. A third possibility, unlikely for a joiner, but possible for a number of other higher-status professions such as medical auxiliary, kindergarten or primary teacher, would be to enter a secondary specialist institution. But let us assume that the young woodworker stays on at school.

The titles for the sections in the syllabus which he will be taught in year 10 closely resemble those followed in years 8 and 9 (safety, organization, planning, visits to workplaces, study of materials, etc.), only they are related to building joinery more specifically. However, there are six hours of "tests" and 120 hours of labour practice which is to be carried out in school or in a workshop under the supervision of a master joiner, and which must measure up to professional standards. The eleventh class syllabus includes, under the heading of theory, lathes and electric machines (10), the making of articles (7) and of joinery structures for building (10), new technology in the building industry (3), economics and planning (4). Practical work consists of introduction (2), organization and safety again (4), excursions to building sites (4), production of joinery items (48), repair of the same (32), carrying out work for purposes of the award of qualification (6) and the qualifying examination (6).

Though we have assumed that this trainee joiner stayed on in the general school, it is possible that his labour training does not actually take place in the school building. The difficulty faced by schools in providing adequate workshops and equipment for training in several trades has led to the adoption in many of the cities of a solution first propounded in the German Democratic Republic, that of inter-school centres for vocational training. These are known as UPKs *(ucheb-no-proizvodstvennye kombinaty)*. One visited in 1984 in Erevan, capital of Armenia, saw 2,300 pupils a week from 20 schools; it offered 10 trades, which were: metalworking, woodworking, typing and modern commercial practice, shoemaking, tailoring/dressmaking, electrical maintainence, applied chemistry, carpet making, automobile mechanics, computers. This was at the time the biggest UPK in Armenia, but even ten trades may not seem an enormous choice. It was stated that occasionally pupils from schools outside the normal catchment area of that particular UPK would come to it because it offered a particular trade. Pupils from schools with a special emphasis (on modern languages, mathematics and so on) were not trained at the UPK: "They have their specialism already".

Technical Drawing

One lesson a week in classes 7 and 8 only gives this subject the appearance of an odd corner in the curriculum, a low-status subject which has lost lessons over the years. It is seen as a branch of labour training and the new syllabus sets out to consolidate the links between drawing and production training. The aims previously betrayed some confusion and

uncertainty, and even the subject's main proponents admitted
that they were unclearly expressed. Nevertheless, a respectable argument is put forward for giving every child "graphic
literacy" and "visual-imagic thinking". The literature of the
subject also gives evidence of conflict in teachers' attitudes
and the methods adopted. For example, they have developed
individualised teaching methods, but they are weak on visual
aids and educational technology generally. They express the
desire to develop pupils' creativity, but they wrangle about
the size of the squares on the graph paper, and they criticise
the authorities for allowing teachers to change the recommended order of the obligatory tasks assigned to the pupils.
The 1981 textbook even specifies ten millimetres of graphite
to be exposed by the pencil sharpener and is similarly specific about the dimensions of the lettering on drawings and the
angle at which the letters slant. Such is the essence of
educational controversy in this field.

In the statements of aims from the new syllabus which
appeared in December 1985 there is even some evidence of
hysteria in the argument advanced for learning the subject.
The usual justifications look to be wearing very thin indeed:
technical drawing furthers a dialectical-materialist attitude
in the pupils and it encourages patriotic education. There
are, of course, valid arguments for the inclusion of technical
drawing in the curriculum. In their textbook children are told
of the educational value of learning to interpret graphic
information and instructions not only in technology, but in
geography and pure science as well. The relation of the
subject to art is touched upon. The subject acquaints pupils
with various branches of technology, and it is necessary for
many qualified workers in very many different fields to be
able to interpret drawings. The use of drawing instruments is
a skill relevant to the world of work. The new syllabus also
stresses the importance of design-related thinking and envis-
ages creative outcomes of instruction in the field; it tries
to encourage independent working. Methodological recommendations include the use of as much practical drawing experience
as possible, the choice of relevant objects from other subject
areas for drawing and continuous assessment of pupils' work.

The syllabus covers the following (numbers of lessons in
brackets): Class 7 - rules for drawing (6): what technical
drawing is, where and how it is done in industry (including
the computer-production of drawings), its relationship with
other types of graphic representation; state standards, and
conventional format, scale and lettering.

Projection (10), rectangular and axonometric, central and
parallel; elevations, details. Isometric projection: axes,
distortion, plotting of dimensions. Axonometric projection of
two- and three-dimensional objects. The representation of
circular and elliptical shapes. Technical freehand sketches.
The interpretation and production of drawings (17): analysis

of the geometric form of objects, breaking them down into prisms, cylinders, cones, etc. Recognition in a drawing of planes, edges, apexes, generatrices. Making drawings using all these concepts and conventions. Drawing objects with alterations to their form, the relative position of the parts and their spatial location.

Class 8 - revision of projection (1). Sectional and cutaway drawings (14): the conventions governing representation of these, their role in complex drawings. Assembly drawings (15), including standard drawings of junctions (5) - bolts, pegs, dowels, threaded joints. Work with standards and reference material. Assembly drawings of objects (10), practice in producing and interpreting such drawings. Architectural drawings, their interpretation and execution (2).

The western reader, especially one who teaches in the field, may conclude that the actual content of Soviet labour education closely resembles that in other countries. The "labour" carried out by primary children is similar to the arts and crafts that younger children do in England. The woodwork and metalwork, domestic science and home economics of the British school would be very familiar to the Soviet labour teacher. Some pupils in European countries are given vocational training in an actual trade at school. Technical drawing is widely taught outside the USSR. The "socially useful labour" of the Soviet school is not at all unlike the voluntary social service many English school groups practise. So what is special about the Soviet programme?

The answer is firstly that it is compulsory from beginning to end of the school career, and not an option for those who cannot fill their timetable with other possibly more demanding things. Secondly, the award of a trade qualification which gives the right to paid employment as soon as the young person leaves school is something possessed by relatively few British school leavers - at least, until recently. Finally, the belief in the morally improving effect of the work done, and the range of its social importance, could not be stronger than it is in the Soviet Union. The spirit in which the work is done is also felt to be important. It is not enough, in St Paul's phrase, to "give their body to be burnt": pupils must have communist charity to obtain the true moral benefits from productive labour. No doubt there are many Soviet children who engage in labour merely as a matter of form: something which has to be done in order to qualify. Moreover, recent press reports show beyond any doubt that labour and professional training is not yet remotely adequate in many places - because of poor teaching, poor liaison with industry, unsatisfactory workshops and arrangements. But for Soviet educators, all types of of labour training are of great significance in the moral as well as the vocational education of the citizens of a socialist state.

Chapter 5

MATHEMATICAL EDUCATION AND INFORMATION SCIENCE

MATHEMATICS is studied by all Soviet children for the whole of the period of compulsory education, and at no stage for fewer than four lessons a week.

Aims

The science or indeed art of mathematics may appear to have no political or moral content, but Soviet mathematics educators would not hold that view. The aims they state include many that would be accepted universally: the role of the subject in intellectual development, the need to understand the nature of mathematics, the methods of inquiry specific to the subject, its importance for the understanding of other forms of knowledge, and its vital role in developing the child's ability to think logically. It is not always clear just how teachers conceive of the extra moral function in practice. It would appear to be linked in their mind with two aspects of the *vospitanie* discussed in Chapter 3. The first of these is the emphasis on the practical application of mathematics in life and more particularly in industrial production. The second is the contribution made by the subject to the formation of a "scientific attitude" in pupils: some writers go so far as to say a "communist attitude". This is based on the assumptions that Marxism is scientific socialism, and that study of scientific or mathematical logic will inevitably lead to acceptance of that philosophy. Nevertheless, Soviet advocates of the benefits of mathematics in education speak also of the value of their subject in developing "imagination and creative thinking", and they declare that it is "an indispensable part of the general culture of [any] human being".

Development of Mathematical Education

The Soviet Union has not escaped the radical changes which began in mathematics education some 25 or more years ago. Perhaps the most widely known of many British curriculum development undertakings is the School Mathematics Project, which began in 1961 as a response to international calls for change as well as to dissatisfaction with standards of education in Britain. In the Soviet Union dissatisfaction with the structure of school mathematics courses had been expressed as long ago as 1936 by specialists in the APN. It was not until the mid-1960s that much change took place. The inadequacies were felt at that time to be a certain waste of time in the teaching of arithmetic, which took up about half the lessons devoted to mathematics, the isolation of algebra and geometry from each other and from arithmetic, and poor preparation of pupils in the early years for the concepts involved in tackling algebra and geometry, which therefore gave them great difficulty when they were eventually undertaken. Also, a good start in other science subjects was prevented because the maths syllabus was moving too slowly. This in its turn was having a deleterious effect on standards in higher education. The syllabus was thought scarcely to have advanced much beyond "the level of the seventeenth century".

The 1967 syllabus did something to remedy this. At that time primary education was reduced to three years, with the consequence that children were taught mathematics by specialists rather than by generalist primary teachers from age 10, a year earlier than previously. In classes 1 to 5 elementary algebraic and geometric concepts were introduced alongside an accelerated arithmetic course, which was deemed complete by the end of class 5, leaving the way clear for "systematic" instruction in algebra and geometry in classes 6 to 8. At that period, not all children carried on with full-time education beyond class 8, but the many who did continued with algebra and geometry and underwent an introduction to calculus. The scope of the concepts taught was thereby somewhat broadened.

Teething troubles of this syllabus concerned the effectiveness of textbooks and the accessibility of the material to the mass of the children. This question is a dilemma for any comprehensive system of education. The new syllabus was conceived at a time when Soviet schools were moving towards, but had not yet achieved, a compulsory system for all; it is clear that many children found the course too difficult and too full. As one Soviet scholar wrote, "There is a contradiction between teaching everyone by a single curriculum and the necessity of taking stock within this framework of the different interests and aptitudes of pupils". Discussion between Soviet and British mathematics educators in 1982 elicited the fact that Soviet teachers take account of differing levels of aptitude for mathematics by having "different levels of mastery of a particular skill".

As in many other areas of education, Soviet mathematics educators seek to move forward carefully. They are reluctant to discard well-tried experience. They are wary of "extreme modernism" and are reassured and not surprised when the efforts of the "Euclid must go" school seem to fail. They recognise the need to discard content which has outlived its usefulness, such as the use of the slide rule - which, if it has not gone already, soon will go - and believe in the necessity of renewing the content of the syllabus while preserving a "large stable nucleus". They are aware that the division of mathematics into separate disciplines creates problems of duplication, and they are watching developments in the integration of syllabuses in other countries and in Soviet experimental courses with great interest. The existence of a programme with a large stable nucleus may look rather conservative, but experiment and innovation there have certainly been.

The much discussed syllabus of Academician A. N. Kolmogorov was introduced in the 1970s and was based on sets and structure. Kolmogorov's "graceful attempt to construct a new school geometry" was widely admired, but his moves were found "too formalized" and "far from totally successful". "Structural ideas, such as set, relation and function had to be introduced using non-mathematical examples, which took up a lot of time which could have been used for pure mathematical work. For example, complex numbers had to be excluded. Furthermore, complex symbolism was being used for essentially simple ideas." Academician Kolmogorov's reform of geometry teaching raised two important issues: "First of all, doubt arises as to the possibility of using geometric transformations from the very beginning of the systematic course in geometry because of the complication of presenting the steps of the proof of a concrete transformation to a class 6 [12-year-old] pupil. Secondly, work is not complete on the development of a system of geometric problems which fulfils the natural pedagogic demands of accessibility, gradualness and the use of algorithms."

Attempts to introduce change on these lines have not been abandoned. Educators and academicians go on striving to perfect and adapt their innovations in the syllabus. The experiments of the sixties and seventies were criticized, and "a second wave of mathematical reform has begun". Examination of the most recent available syllabuses (for 1986/87) shows what stage of innovation or retrenchment has been reached.

Pre-school and Primary Mathematics

Those children who attend kindergarten receive a certain formal introduction to mathematical ideas from the age of three. Pre-school teachers are recommended to devote one period of activity to the "development of elementary mathematical notions" once a week for about 15 to 20 minutes.

Articles by Soviet mathematics educationists indicate that in primary mathematics disagreement and controversy surround issues of content and method, but that the profession has been sufficiently open-minded both to experiment imagin- atively and to evaluate the experiments critically. Sixteen or seventeen years ago, when the primary phase of education was shortened to three years from four, significant restruc- turing took place; now that children enter school at six mathematics teachers are not entirely sure what they can expect of six-year-olds. Consequently in this section the primary course will be described as a whole, and remarks will not be specific about what may be expected at the end of each of the four new classes.

The reforms of the early seventies applied the term "mathematics" in place of "arithmetic" to the primary course. The basis of primary teaching has always been the instilling of skills of calculation, but in recent years, the aim has been to convey a much higher degree of theoretical understand- ing than before. Teachers have sought to "facilitate the training of logical thinking". Children's ability to general- ize has been developed, based upon observations made by them- selves and upon class discussions, instead of upon "dogmatic exposition" by the teacher, which is now frowned upon. It is claimed that greater understanding which children now have of the four basic arithmetical skills, has saved up to 30% of the time formerly devoted to rote learning of tables. Further cause for satisfaction – and for discussion – is given by the determination to include elements of algebra and geometry in the primary course, so that it becomes a preparation for work in classes 5 to 11. Doubt, it is true, is expressed as to whether the geometric, and particularly the algebraic, ele- ments really do this, or whether they are not a little forced, such as "the unjustified use of the equation method for sol- ving written problems which are more naturally solvable arith- metically". However, it is claimed that the very simple algebra included in the course has a propaedeutic function (the word is very popular with Soviet educators) – it prepares pupils' minds to receive more detailed instruction on the subject later.

The basic content of the primary mathematics syllabus is the study of natural numbers and the four operations performed upon them. First priority is given to developing skills of calculation; problems based on each operation are designed to reflect real-life situations. Attention is paid to "acquaint- ing children with some of the properties of the arithmetical operations. Their use helps to make the application of me- thods of calculation more conscious, which is important not only for the inculcation of sound calculating skills, but also for the pupils' general development." Along with the concept of number, children are introduced to the concept of magnitude (starting with length).

By the end of the primary course, children are expected to know by heart the addition facts and the multiplication facts for single-digit numbers. They should know the order for carrying out operations in expressions containing three or four operations, and the units of length, mass, area and time, and the relations between them. They should be able to read and write multi-digit numbers under a million, carry out operations within the limit of one million and do so mentally up to 100. Fractions, incidentally, are introduced as shares, but calculations with fractions are not practised at this stage. By age eight they are expected to measure the length of a straight line in decimetres and centimetres and draw lines of a given length; by age nine they should be able to identify, reproduce and designate with letters a point, a line, a segment of a line and a polygon, and by ten to draw a rectangle on graph paper, with a given length of sides, and to find its area. They should be able to solve simple problems involving up to three operations, to solve very simple equations (of the type $2x + 1 = 7$), and find the value of simple expressions for given values of the variable contained in them. They should be able to find the perimeter of a polygon (including a rectangle or square). They should be able to check the correctness of calculations.

While teachers have not yet decided on the exact relationship between understanding, habit formation and rote-learning in the assimilation of arithmetical operations, instructional method is moving away from teacher-talk followed by pupil memorization and reproduction. The old-fashioned teacher doubtless finds it hard to move towards discussion in which pupils play an active part, but they are none the less now expected to link discussion with independent work, and the material-writers are producing work-cards and work-books. Recent articles write of practical work using realia and say it is "occupying an increasingly important position at all stages in the acquisition of mathematical knowledge, ability and skills". Despite the inbuilt resistance the Soviet teacher has for play techniques, games are being used "which provide pupils with tremendous opportunities for the conscious and automatic use of the knowledge they have acquired and for the acquisition of new facts".

Secondary Mathematics

In discussing the most recent syllabuses, published in December 1985 for use from 1986/87 onwards, it is intended to use the theoretical basis which was expounded in the two Anglo-Soviet seminars of 1981 and 1982. The newest syllabus differs in many respects from that published only a few months earlier for use in the 1985/86 school year, and it must be regarded as the set pattern for a few years to come. Interestingly enough the papers delivered by the theorists in 1981-2 appear to be ahead of the syllabus for 1985/86, but not all the prophecies for the future made earlier in the decade have been realized.

Secondary mathematics falls into two divisions. Years 5

to 9 cover basic mathematical information, while the last two years move into the rather more rarified atmosphere of differential and integral calculus and more advanced solid geometry. Geometry and algebra in these important middle years are taught as a "separate but connected" course.

However, when children enter class 5 (the old class 4) teachers note that they are not yet ready for the level of abstraction required for geometry and algebra, and that their capacity to reason logically is as yet insufficient. Years 5 and 6 are therefore treated as a transitional period before the two independent subjects appear in class 7. Children's ability to carry out arithmetical operations with facility and speed are not yet fully developed either, so arithmetic is still the first priority. The greatest weaknesses are said to be in long multiplication and especially division; pupils lack total confidence and "automatism" in carrying out such calculations. They are introduced to negative numbers (class 6) and vulgar and decimal fractions. Decimals are not thought to present any very great conceptual difficulties as the carrying out of arithmetical operations on them resembles work with hundreds, tens and units. Decimals are regarded as having wide practical application and to be vital for other school subjects; vulgar fractions and negative numbers used to be taught mainly as a basis for later algebraic work, but in fact the 1986/87 syllabus now devotes 56 lessons to them. The course for class 5 contains such matters as the calculation of the area of a rectangle, percentages, averages and scale. In class 6 the introduction of negative numbers and the procedures for dealing with them are extended into the solution of equations involving such numbers, the concept of symmetry is introduced. Considerable attention is paid to rational numbers. Proportion is introduced and used in the solution of problems.

In algebra pupils are expected to handle simple equations. The use of letters to represent numbers is extended and developed to their use to represent a variable, introducing the concept of an algebraic expression. Pupils calculate the circumference and area of a circle by the use of formulae.

During these two years children are taught to use drawing instruments in order to "lay the foundation of geometric intuition". Gradually they learn geometric figures, starting with a straight line and a triangle and progressing through squares, rectangles, cubes, circles and spheres; they learn to find the area or volume of many of these. They are introduced to coordinates, right angles and parallel lines. Much of this geometric work is again intended to be propaedeutic.

The broader aims of teaching this content are expressed in terms of "the development of logical thought". Children are brought to the point during these two years where they can "draw inductive conclusions on a basis of particular examples"; they are taught to apply general principles and to take "the simplest steps towards inductive reasoning". They are taught to understand and to use "logical turns of speech" and to be precise and accurate in the use of mathematical language; moreover, they are taught "the ability to use symbolic writing" in the shape of formulae. The content as expressed topic by topic in the very latest syllabus is similar to its predecessor. There is, however, some internal reorganization of the content and strengthening of the algebraic content.

Algebra

The really serious business of algebra and geometry is carried out in classes 7 to 9, and it is claimed that the preparatory work in years 5 and 6 makes possible the inclusion of a number of concepts that were previously restricted to the last two years of school education. With some satisfaction mathematics educators say that this factor has raised both the general educational level of the course and the applied nature of the work done. The algebra course for these three years has four main purposes. Firstly, the pupils are to "generalize and systematize their knowledge of real numbers and develop their skills of calculation". Though this section of the course includes little new conceptual material, great attention is paid and importance attached to increasing both the volume and the complexity of calculations, eventually necessitating the use of tables and later calculators. Theorists speak of "raising the level of the pupils´ calculatory culture". Secondly, children are to "master the skills of manipulation of the basic types of algebraic expression (polynomials, algebraic fractions, powers and roots)." In carrying out the basic operations such as expanding brackets, factorizing, taking the common factor out of brackets, reduction of similar terms, addition, subtraction and multiplication of polynomials, arithmetical operations on algebraic fractions in simple cases, and manipulations of powers and roots, pupils must soundly grasp the principles and procedures and "must not get into difficulties" in solving problems which require any of these algorithms.

The third aim of algebra teaching in years 7 to 9 is to "master the methods of solving algebraic equations and inequalities of the first and second order and equalities and systems reducible to them". Children should learn how to solve basic types of equations, including using graphs; they "must acquire...skills in the reduction of more complex equations and inequalities of basic type". Practical methods for the solution of simultaneous equations are taught.

Fourthly, pupils study simple elementary functions and their properties. They are to "master methods of investigating functions and constructing their graphs...on the basis of relatively little functional material (direct and inverse proportional dependence, linear and quadratic functions and the functions $y = x^n$ and $y = \sqrt[n]{x}$ where n is a natural number)". Teachers attempt to develop, "on the basis of sufficiently simple examples, the ability to express in functional form relationships between magnitudes and to use with ease various methods of representing functions". Mastery of these skills lays the foundation for advanced algebra and basic calculus in years 10 and 11.

Study of the new reformed syllabus for classes 7 to 9 indicates how this content is spread over the three years. Space allows little more than to list the main themes for each class; here they are. Class 7 gives five major topics apart from obligatory revision. They are: equations (34 lessons) – this includes those with one or two variables, the concept of functions and a good deal about simultaneous equations and their geometric interpretation; powers with natural indices (14); monomials and multinomials (28) and the carrying out of some basic operations upon them; formulae for abbreviated multiplication (30): this theme includes the formulae
$$(a + b)(a - b) = a^2 - b^2$$
$$(a + b)^2 = a^2 + 2ab + b^2$$
and their use in multiplying multinomials. Approximate calculations (20): numerical inequalities; absolute and relative error of approximations; carrying out arithmetical operations on approximate values with a calculator.

In class 8 there are four themes: algebraic fractions (30 lessons) – their sum, difference, product and quotient, raising them to a power, identical transformations of rational expressions; square roots (30). The function $y = x^2$ and its curve and others including $y = \sqrt{x}$, finding approximate square roots with a calculator, the concept of irrational numbers; quadratic equations (29) – to enable pupils to solve quadratic equations and the simplest rational equations and to apply this knowledge in the solution of problems; rational equations (14) – checking roots, solution of problems, the curve $y = k/x$. Class 9 covers five topics: inequalities and systems (10) with one variable and their solution numerical functions (20) and properties and curve of $y = kx$, $y = |x|$, $y = kx + b$, $y = x^2$, $y = \sqrt{x}$, $y = k/x$; $y = x^n$ when n is a natural number. Next, quadratic functions (20); $y = ax^2 + bx + c$. Solution of equations and inequalities (30): equivalence, inequalities of the second order with one variable; rational inequalities; the introduction of auxiliary variables in solving inequalities. Elements of trigonometry (30): radian measures, use of a calculator to discover sines, cosines and tangents; basic identities; reduction formulae, trigonometric identities. Progressions (12), arithmetic and geometric; the formula
$$x^n - 1 = (x - 1)(x^{n-1} + x^{n-2} + \ldots + 1);$$
constantly diminishing geometric progression and its sum.

Geometry

Whereas 391 lessons are to be devoted to algebra over these three classes, 221 are allocated to geometry. It is over the teaching of geometry that the greatest disagreement has been registered. The person representing the views which would appear at present to have won out is Academician A. V. Pogorelov, whose experimental textbook *Geometriya* (Moscow, 1981) was in 1982 adopted as standard for Russian schools; a competition for writing the new book to accompany the reformed syllabus has, however, now been announced. Pogorelov's view is that traditional methods of presenting geometry are basically sound, and, though rethinking and updating are necessary, it is possible to use them with "scientific rigour". After a decade or so of enthusiastic experiment with geometry courses based on geometric transformations, which were found difficult by both teachers and learners and which did not seem to lead to any improvement in geometric training, Pogorelov was invited to lead an experiment using a new version of his course, which had long been ignored by innovative educators.

Three aims of geometry teaching are stated by Pogorelov: to prepare pupils for further study of mathematics, to promote active mastery of the subject, and, most importantly, "to teach the pupil to reason logically, argue his statements and prove his point". The vast majority of school leavers, it is argued, will never use Pythagoras's theorem in real life, but all will need to reason, analyze and produce proofs. Because of strong feelings in many Soviet mathematics teachers that children of 12 (in the new class 7) are incapable of grasping the axiomatic structure of geometry, the Pogorelov system does not begin with axioms, but with "the fundamental properties of the simplest geometric figures", and "simple reasoning processes are followed through, in the course of which other properties are deduced from the original ones. Subsequently these fundamental properties will be declared axioms." Realization that geometry is logically constructed is of the greatest importance: "The adoption of the `prove everything´ approach creates in the pupils a powerful psychological sense of purpose which is particularly important in the early stages of learning... It is particularly important... scrupulously to follow logical links."

Themes for the syllabus in class 7 are: introduction to geometry (16 lessons) - the concept of axioms and theorems, the role of practical experience in the emergence of geometry (talk); triangles (12) - evidence for congruence, and properties of isosceles triangles; constructing angles, triangles and perpendiculars, bisecting angles (basic use of instruments) (12); parallel lines (12) and related axioms, the sum of the angles of a triangle; circles and circumference (10) - tangents, inscribed and circumscribed circles. In class 8 the topics are: quadrilaterals (18) - parallelograms, rectangles, rhombuses, squares and their properties; vectors and coordinates (18); theorems relating to measurement (27) - Pythagoras's theorem, distance between two points with given coordinates, cosines, sines and tangents of an angle, scalar product of a vector and its properties; transformations (12), symmetry, equal figures, rotation, translation. *Class 9.* Similar triangles (18); the area of polygons (14) - rectangles, triangles, parallelograms, trapeziums and the relationship of the areas of similar figures; the circumference and area of a circle (6) - radius, the value of pi; the solution of triangles (15) using the sine and cosine theorems and applying algebraic methods to the solution of geometric problems; talks on the logical construction of geometry and the axiomatic method in mathematics; summing up.

Geometry in classes 7 to 9 can be summarised in the words of Professor A. A. Gonchar. He writes that during the course pupils are expected to "acquire systematic knowledge of the basic two-dimensional figures and their important properties". He writes of "active mastery of basic geometric concepts", the ability to reproduce proofs of theorems and solve problems independently. "Considerable importance is attached to geometric intuition" - the development of graphic awareness and the ability to use drawings. Pupils must "acquire an idea of the equality and similarity of figures and of the basic types of geometric transformations and their uses in geometry" (principally congruence of triangles, construction of figures and the solution of related problems). They must also "acquire the skills of geometric construction... necessary for... graph work and also skills of measuring and calculating lengths, angles and areas." Finally, they must "become acquainted with analytic methods (algebraic transformations and equations, elements of trigonometry, analytic geometry and vector algebra) for the solution of geometric problems".

Mathematics After 15

The course pupils follow in whatever institution they complete their secondary education after the age of 15 is seen by mathematics educators as an extension of the essentials acquired in classes 5 to 9. Over the two years in classes 10 and 11, 153 lessons are devoted to algebra and basic calculus and 136 to geometry. Material is chosen, it is asserted, with an eye to practical application. The first topic in class 10 *algebra* is trigonometric functions (12 lessons), including periodic functions. The second is trigonometric equations (20); arcsine, arccosine, arctangent; the application of trigonometric identities for the simplification of equations; approximate solutions. Thirdly, the derivative (18): its geometric and mechanical meaning; derivative of a power function with whole number index, of sine and cosine, the derivative of a sum, of a product, of the quotient of two functions. The fourth topic is the application of derivatives (22): increment and decay of functions, finding extrema, constructing curves; mathematics and the natural sciences (talk). Class 11 has three topics: the integral and its application (17) – the differential; the derivative of the power function $y = x^2$, of a sine and cosine, the discovery of calculus by Leibnitz and Newton, use of the integral in solving simple problems, the differential equation, harmonic oscillations, mathematics and the real world (talk); powers with rational indices (14) – the nth root, the concept of irrational indices; exponential and logarithmic functions (22) – their properties and curves, the quantity e; radioactive decomposition, inverse function, logarithms (of a product, quotient, power), natural logarithms. Fifteen lessons go on final revision and on summing up the whole course.

The *geometry* course for the last two years contains the following topics. Class 10: introduction to three-dimensional geometry (6 lessons); parallel lines and planes (20) – intersecting lines, the relationship of lines to planes, of two planes (parallel or intersecting), parallel projection, depiction of solid figures on a flat surface; perpendicularity of lines and planes (24): theorems relating to this subject, polyhedra: the parallelepiped, regular prisms and pyramids and the area of their surfaces. Class 11: transformation (8) – the concept, point and line symmetry, parallel translation; the concept of equality of three-dimensional figures; regular polyhedra; solid figures (16) – cylinder, cone, and their cross-sections, area of their surfaces, spheres and ellipsoids, intersection of spheres by a plane, tangent planes, the capacity of polyhedra (16); capacity of solid figures (12), area of the surface of a sphere; summing up (16).

Especially from class 7 onwards, this syllabus differs in many ways from its immediate predecessor. To some extent this is a matter of internal organization: some points have been moved about from one topic to another. The promised introduction of information science and computer technology has had some effect: elementary programming disappears from the algebra syllabus of class 9. But most of all a determined effort seems to have been made to tackle the bogey of overloading of the syllabus. Even the casual reader can see that many details have been dropped from the 1985/86 syllabus, and that in several respects the course is somewhat simpler – which must be a great relief to the less mathematically-minded child. None the less, conversations with practising mathematics teachers in 1987 revealed that, pleased as they were with the reduction in content, they were still having to pay great attention to remedial materials for pupils who found the courses excessively challenging.

Assessment

It will be recalled that Soviet mathematics educators are aware, probably more so than teachers of other subjects, of the problems of catering for pupils of all levels of attainment in one class, and that their answer is to expect varying degrees of mastery of the syllabus, all of which is studied by all pupils. It is perhaps significant that papers for the two Anglo-Soviet Seminars in Mathematics Education contain two articles by British participants on assessment, but none by Soviet scholars - who appear also to have remained relatively quiet in the discussion of these papers.

The examinations taken at 15 consist of oral geometry and written algebra. Each of the 23 geometry tickets bears three questions. The first is usually a theorem, definition or formula, and the third is a problem. Thus question one may be Pythagoras's theorem, the theorem of the properties of the diagonals of a rhombus, the deduction of the formula of the area of a parallelogram, etc. In the case of the second of these examples, the pupil will be expected to define a rhombus, state its properties, execute the appropriate drawing and prove the theorem. Examples of question two are: stating the sine, cosine or tangent of an angle, giving the formula for finding the length of a circumference or an arc, the formula for the sum of the angles of a polygon, or finding the angles and third side of a triangle given one angle and two sides. In answer to these questions pupils should show they understand the concept concerned, write the formula down, show they can use it, make any necessary constructions and explain their reasoning. Question three will be taken from the textbook (which contains hundreds of examples), and subjects include similar figures, Cartesian coordinates, geometric constructions, congruent triangles, coordinates of a vector, the sum of the angles of a triangle, or finding the area of a figure.

Algebra written papers are made up of examples taken from a book, to which supplements are occasionally published. Here is a published example of a five-question test for (the "old") class 8 in 1987:-

1. Solve the inequalities
   a) $4x^2 - 4x - 15 < 0$ $[2x^2 + 3x - 9 > 0]$
   b) $x^2 - 9 > 0$ $[5x - x^2 < 0]$

2. Solve the inequalities using the method of intervals:
   a) $(x + 7)(x - 5)(x - 11) > 0$
      $[(x + 3)(x - 1)(x - 10) < 0]$
   b) $\dfrac{x - 4}{x + 6} < 0$ $[\dfrac{x - 5}{x + 14} > 0]$

3. Find all the solutions of the inequalities:
   $0.3x^2 < 1.2$ $[3x > 2x^2]$

4. Find the possible range of the values of x for the following functions:
   $y = \sqrt{x - x^2}$ $[y = \sqrt{4 - x^2}]$

5. For what values of x is the function $y = x^2 + 2x - 15$ [$y = -x^2 + 6x - 8$] increasing and for what values is it decreasing? Find the maximum or minimum value of y.

Soviet Mathematical Education in Context

Western mathematics educators do not all react in the same way to the content and methodology of Soviet syllabuses, but there are certain broad ways in which approaches differ. Over the question of the differing abilities of children to assimilate mathematical concepts and to carry out operations successfully there is probably less disagreement than appears on the surface. In a neat formulation arrived at by participants in the second Anglo-Soviet Seminar, both countries recognise that you can take a horse to the water but cannot make it drink; the Soviets ask, "How much water should we give the horses?" and the British, "How much water have the horses shown themselves capable of drinking?" There is no setting in Soviet mass schools, but teachers may give optional extra work to the more able, and extra-curricular clubs are run to provide mathematical activities outside the standard syllabus. Soviet educators report that often the slower learners respond very positively to "non-standard" material in these clubs.

British educators show some interest in Soviet work on minimum standards of achievement, and also in their experience in the oral assessment of mathematics. Although calculators are used in Soviet schools, teachers in the early 1980s seemed to be much less enthusiastic than the British about the contribution they can make, especially to the teaching of algebra. Nevertheless, the new 1986/87 syllabus makes somewhat more direct reference than before to their use.

On the structure of syllabuses, British practice tends much more strongly towards "multi-topic" or "spiral" organization, while the Soviets find British syllabuses fragmentary. On their content, many British experts would wish such matters as probability and statistics to be included. During the Anglo-Soviet Seminars the Soviets said they intended to introduce both in the next revision of the syllabus; this does not appear to have happened yet. On Pogorelov's geometry syllabus, the British expressed some doubts as to whether it is likely to give a good basis for further education, and feel that more stress on spatial understanding would be essential for potential engineers. The 1986/87 syllabus may go some way to answering this point. Not all British educators would agree with Pogorelov that axioms should be introduced gradually or by stealth, because they feel that a child might receive a wrong impression that "you introduce an axiom when you reach an impasse". In the 1986/87 syllabus, all the references to talks on the logical structure of mathematics, the axiomatic nature of geometry and the like are completely new to the mathematics programme, and this seems to indicate that educators perceive the importance of giving children an overview of the nature of mathematics.

A difference in the work-ethic of the two societies is at the root of one disagreement: Soviets hold that complex calculations inculcate good habits of hard work, while British feel that "mathematics is a subject in which by hard thinking it is possible to avoid hard work" and that calculators should be used to reduce labour and make time for developing mathematical thinking. Finally, rightly or wrongly, not all British mathematics educators are entirely at one with Soviet colleagues about the work applications of school mathematics. A. Fitzgerald is reported at one of the Seminars as saying, "It is not the job of the school to prepare pupils in detail for the mathematics they will ultimately use at work". However, whether or not the Soviet horse drinks the water it is taken to, it must surely be admitted that there is plenty of it, extra pools are provided for those that wish to drink more, it is sweet and clean, and none of the horses are allowed to run away before the water is reached.

PRINCIPLES OF INFORMATION SCIENCE AND COMPUTER TECHNOLOGY

This new course was planned for full-scale introduction in classes 10 and 11 in 1990/91, but it has been widely taught since at least 1985. Its presence in the reformed curriculum illustrates an enormous interest in computers in education. Centres for computers in education are springing up all over the country, and a determined campaign to make teachers and parents aware of computers is being carried on. In the winter of 1985/86 a competition was announced for authors to compile the textbook which will eventually accompany the course. To guide entrants, first a draft and then an agreed syllabus were issued in the journal *Mathematics in School.* This syllabus was the work of research institutes not only of the APN, but of the Academy of Sciences itself. Experimental teaching with the draft textbooks was envisaged for two years before introduction of the perfected publication in 1990.

The criteria for the proposed book include that it must reflect the concern of the compilers of the syllabus that the new subject is of general educational importance (that is, to all children, not as the first step in a professional training for would-be computer specialists). It is to be practical and to involve pupils in active work with computers for at least half of every lesson. Little is said about the methodology, so the authors of the new book will be free to follow whatever line they choose. The themes given in the approved syllabus are, however, obligatory and not to be changed.

It may be necessary to apologise for the translation of the extracts from the syllabus. The English or American equivalents of Russian computer terminology do not always seem to be easy to ascertain. In particular, the Russian word *algoritm* appears to convey "procedure" and even sometimes "program" as well as "algorithm", and in section three of the syllabus it even seems to refer to ways of writing down algorithms on paper, such as by flow-chart. This is only one example of the difficulties faced in preparing this short section; it is hoped nevertheless that the content of the syllabus is reasonably clearly conveyed.

Course Requirements

The requirements or aims of the course are six. Pupils should acquire (1) techniques of reformulating problems in such a way that they can be solved by a computer, (2) techniques of formalized description of problems posed, elementary knowledge of methods of mathematical modelling and the ability to construct simple mathematical models of the problems posed, (3) knowledge of basic algorithms and the ability to apply this knowledge to the construction of procedures for the solution of problems according to their mathematical models, (4) understanding of the construction and working of computers and elementary techniques of writing programs in one high-level language, (5) techniques of the appropriate use of basic modern software tools in order, with their help, to solve practical problems, and also understanding of the basic principles underlying the working of such software, and (6) the ability to interpret intelligently the results of practical problems solved by computer, and to apply these results in practice.

These requirements, it is stated, represent at the least the beginnings of computer literacy, and at best the promise in due course of acquiring "informational culture". The first three topics in the course outlined below represent an elementary level, while the last four impart somewhat deeper knowledge. Which language to teach (topic 5) is not yet decided; however, all children will be taught one.

The authors of the syllabus believe that inter-subject links must be fostered strongly, and that this should be a major feature of the course. They envisage three types of practical activity: demonstrations by the teacher, "frontal" laboratory work in which all the pupils will carry out the same exercise simultaneously and "praxis" - independent hands-on activity. If this appears to be traditional in approach, they warn that in a laboratory in which each child has his own visual display, demonstration may not be like the traditional science lesson but may be barely distinguishable from frontal laboratory work.

The course will contain 102 lessons, but how many lessons should be given to each topic is not stipulated. The topics are: (1) Introduction - what information science is about;

the processing of information in general and automatically by computer technology; examples of what computers do and their role in society today. The teacher should demonstrate inter-action with the computer and games. Under the heading of inter-subject links great stress should be laid on the bene-fits of computers in learning other subjects: their use as dictionaries, as indexes and tables in history and geography, as calculators in physics and mathematics and for carrying out all sorts of processes in other fields. (2) First Acquain-tance with the Computer. This includes its basic construction and running of programs, the local network, familiarity with the keyboard of a micro, and using the computer for calcula-tion, modelling, storing and organizing information. (3) Fundamentals of the Creation of Algorithms. Under this head-ing pupils will be expected to understand what algorithms are and to know their basic properties, how to write them down, the basic types of variables, the rules for carrying out commands and executing algorithms. They should be able to discover typical errors in the writing of algorithms, to write simple algorithms similar to those in the textbook, to execute a dry run while using a table of definitions, and to use a library; to construct a simple recursive procedure according to a given recurrent relationship.

(4) Fundamentals of Computer Technology. On completion of this unit pupils should know about the functional organiza-tion of a computer, the automatic running of programs, the representation of data and commands in the computer, the properties of the binary number system, and the names and characteristics of the commonest types of computer. Pupils should know how to explain, using a wall-chart, the workings of a computer and be able to give examples of computer com-mands. (5) Fundamentals of Programming. The principal con-tent of this unit is the introduction of a language. Pupils should know the rules for writing down a program in computer language and the rules for running the program. They should know how to use basic types of software on the school comput-er, using the menu, "help" and other instructions for use; they should be able to turn a flow chart into a program, to write, debug and run a simple program, and use standard func-tions and sub-routines and organize the presentation of the results of the running of a program on a screen and a printer.

(6) The Solution of Problems on a Computer. This theme falls into two sections entitled "The stages of the solution of problems" and "Applied software and its use in solving problems". The requirements which the pupils should be able to meet after undergoing the lessons include knowledge of the names and content of the basic stages in problem solving on a computer, the names and purposes of the basic types of soft-ware tools. Pupils should know how to construct a simple mathematical model, write and run a programme on this basis and carry out analysis of the results. They should have

experience of text processing and the construction of simple graphics, use data bases and carry out basic operations on data. They should be able to carry out operations on tables shown on the screen and make related calculations, and use software packages to solve problems in a wide range of school subjects.

(7) Computers in Society. This unit contains a short history of the development of computers, their role in industry, automation, their place in administration, planning, science, medicine, education and the home. The importance of computer literacy in the education of members of developed socialist society is to be stressed.

Progress So Far

At the time of writing (1987) the course has not yet entered the mass school curriculum, but it is being tried out in very many schools. How is it going? A report published in September 1986 on its progress in the Voronezh area stated that pupil reaction had been very positive - children were much better prepared for the subject psychologically than had been imagined. Syllabus and experimental textbook were over-full, however, and many teachers could not get through all the materials and were calling for more than one lesson a week. Not every school had suitable equipment, but local industry was helping out. Over 700 experienced mathematics and physics teachers had been trained. Children were said to be better at handling computers practically than at understanding the concepts involved in what they were doing. The general conclusion was that all agencies - in-service trainers, inspectors, schools, research institutes and educationists - should pull together to improve the methodology of the subject and provide more complete teaching materials. These are teething troubles, and it is clear that the present degree of interest and effort being expended will overcome them before long.

Teaching methods have not had time to become established, but one matter does suggest itself very strongly. Reformers are urging teachers to avoid "dogmatic exposition" and overuse of the "word and book" method (Russian for "chalk and talk"), yet some teachers find it very hard to change. In a computer laboratory with pupils all supplied with individual equipment it will be very hard indeed to teach in the old-fashioned way, at least once the pupils are set free to work at their own keyboards. Computer studies is, of course, not alone in this, but it could become an agent of change in Soviet schools through the methods of classroom organization which the teachers will have to employ, and this is indeed what the leaders of the Soviet teaching profession seek.

Chapter 6

THE MOTHER TONGUE: RUSSIAN AS NATIVE LANGUAGE

THE NATIVE language spoken by a person can often be a matter of great emotional significance. It enables the speaker to identify with his nation or with a group within that nation, and it may encourage feelings of kinship with peoples elsewhere in the world. The possession of a particular native language may distinguish the members of a dominant or subservient section of a community and can become a means to exclude others from the group. Willingness or refusal to learn the language spoken by a community into which a person has fortuitously moved may be the decisive element in the acceptance or rejection of the migrant by that community. When a dominant power forces subject peoples to neglect their native tongue or belittles the expressive, cultural or poetic powers of that language, resentment is aroused. The possession of one particular language may become a matter of intolerance, arrogance or even fanaticism. In some parts of the world it is necessary to have a command of more than one language in order to live and carry on business. These issues are reflected to one degree or another in Great Britain, the United States, Switzerland, Belgium, India and many African nations, but the position of Russian in the Soviet Union is not exactly comparable with any of these.

Russian and Linguistic Diversity in the USSR

As the 1990s approach, it is very probable that ethnic Russians will lose their overall majority among citizens of the Soviet Union. In the 1979 census they comprised 52.4%, and in view of demographic trends - the relatively low birth-rate in the Slavonic and Baltic areas of the Union and the much higher figures in Central Asia - they are likely be less than 50% before long. However, over sixteen million non-ethnic Russians (over 6% of the total population) claim Russian as their native tongue. The other citizens of the country speak many different languages. The exact number is difficult to establish, but it is reckoned by one recent scholarly survey to be

130. These include the two closest relations of Great Russian
- Ukrainian and Belorussian, a whole range of different Balto-
Slavonic and other Indo-European tongues, Finno-Ugric languages (Finnish and Estonian) and Turkic ones (Uzbek and
Kazakh). Some of these languages are spoken by many millions
(Ukrainian has 42 million native speakers) and others by a few
score. Some of the minor languages have never been written
down, while others, such as Armenian, have an important written culture. The Soviet Union, therefore, could scarcely be
more multi-ethnic, multi-cultural and multi-lingual. Most of
the speakers of languages other than Russian are not recent
immigrants, but have occupied the territories where they live
for centuries.

The state needs a language for the government and administration of the whole Union and for general communication
within it, whatever recognition is accorded to national languages in the regions. Before the Revolution, Lenin is believed to have suggested that a foreign language might be
adopted as a neutral means of communication; he was certainly
against compulsion to learn Russian ("We do not want to drive
people into paradise with a stick"). Russian is now dominant,
however, and its status is much greater than purely that of a
handy means of communication. Spurious reasons for this are
sometimes given. For example, Russian is said to have been
"freely chosen" as the language of friendly communication
between peoples. This is absurd - it is the language of
cooperation because there is no realistic alternative. Again,
it is implied that there is something special about Russian
because it enshrines Communism and is the language of those
who brought about the first Communist revolution in the world.
This is the doubtful rationale or rationalization provided for
a current vigorous drive to improve the teaching of Russian
both as a native and a second language in the USSR. A further
slight irritant to good relations is the proverbial unwilling-
ness of the Russians to learn the local language if they
migrate to a non-Russian area (only 3.5% of Russians claim
fluency in another Soviet language); there is also evidence
that some non-Russians refuse on census forms to admit to
fluent command of Russian even when they have it.

Educational Consequences of Soviet Linguistic Diversity

The Soviet Constitution and laws establish in principle a free
choice of the language of education, Russian or another Soviet
language. In ideal conditions all children would receive
education through the medium of their native tongue. In fact,
schooling is carried on, according to recent figures of likely
accuracy, in 45 of the nation's 130 languages. The exact
meaning of this is variable: education is available to age 17
in the principal languages of the Union republics - and even
in higher education, where unrest has resulted from attempts

at forced Russification. Depending on the size of the population speaking a given language, schooling in a local language
may be offered at primary level only, or up to the end of
incomplete secondary education. Elsewhere Russian is used
throughout, and teachers use the vernacular informally until
children's performance in Russian is adequate. Non-native
Russian speakers may choose to be educated through the medium
of Russian, and Russian is the only language available in this
way in every part of the Union. In all non-Russian schools
Russian is taught as second language.

The Russian Language

Russian is not widely understood in many countries outside the
Soviet Union, and in some places where it is studied compulsorily it is not spoken gladly. As a literary language it did
not settle down and achieve a stable form until the early
nineteenth century. Even then not every Russian intellectual
accepted it as a respectable and cultured medium of discourse.
The recognition of Russian as a world language, studied outside the Soviet sphere of interest, has only recently been
achieved; but it still tends to be a minority interest. This
is the background against which educators see the teaching of
their native Russian as likely to arouse patriotic feelings in
children. Every Russian child will know Turgenev's famous
poem in prose "Russkiy yazyk" (1882): the poet expresses the
feeling that, despite the troubles of his native Russia, he
remains convinced when he contemplates the "great, powerful,
true and free" language that it must have been given to a
great people. Mikhail Lomonosov's eighteenth-century reflection on the Russian language - that it possesses "the splen-
dour of Spanish, the vivacity of French, the strength of
German, the tenderness of Italian and the richness, brevity
and vivid imagery of Greek and Latin" - is also very familiar.
     A further most interesting point is that the Russians
value the spoken form of the literary language highly, which
explains the stress on "expressive reading" as an activity in
Russian classrooms. It is further illustrated by the popul-
arity of public poetry recitals and radio programmes and by
the very wide variety of spoken word gramophone recordings
available for sale in the Soviet Union. Many of these are
intended for children, and not merely as a means to save
parents the trouble of reading bed-time stories.
     Many details of the syllabus for Russian will not be
fully comprehensible without some knowledge of the nature of
the language itself and the way in which it is written. Russian belongs to the Indo-European family of languages and is
the most widely spoken member of the Slavonic group within
that family. It has a very large vocabulary indeed. It is
highly inflected, having three genders (which give small Russian children a great deal of difficulty), six cases of nouns,

pronouns and adjectives with appropriate endings (and many irregularities and oddities), but only three tenses of the verb; nuances of meaning here are conveyed by the use of two verbal aspects. Verb forms are by no means totally straightforward. Words are longer than in English, but meaning is conveyed in fewer words, so that a translation of 100 words of Russian is likely to contain 145 of English. This is partly because of a total lack of articles and the present tense of the verb "to be", and partly because of a tendency to abbreviate utterances and to take as understood items which would be expressed in other languages. Pronunciation, even for Russian children, presents some problems, such as the distinction between palatalized and non-palatalized consonants, and the highly mobile word stress. The language is written in a Cyrillic alphabet of 32 letters, and whereas spelling does not present the mass of illogicalities of English orthography, Russian is by no means "phonetic". Particular difficulties for children include the spelling of unstressed vowels and of final unvoiced consonants: a child who had not been taught would not know how to spell the last two letters of the word *gorod* [town]. It could, by sound alone, be *od, ad, ot* or *at*. There are, of course, Russian dialects, but they do not differ enormously or create serious problems of comprehension, surprising though this may be in a language which is spoken over such a wide area.

None of this answers the question as to whether and to what extent Russian children need the help of teachers to master their difficulties or whether they would overcome them just as well without professional help. Children scarcely need to be taught basic case-endings by teachers, since they learn them "naturally" anyway, as is well established by research and observation. An argument put forward for the formal approach to language study which is carried out in schools is that it is imperative to teach clear pronunciation and accurate writing as a meas to unambiguous communication in a standard language. The feeling excists too that the language represents a cultural possession which is to be valued and conserved, and that children must be taught to speak it properly. However, Soviet educators are aware that theoretical teaching does not necessarily have the desired effect of improving children´s performance in written communication.

The Aims of Native Language Teaching

The principal aims begin with that of giving children "a profound knowledge of the language". This includes consciousness of it as "an historically developed social phenomenon", feeling for its beauty and the desire to strive for mastery of its richness. The second and third main aims are to give pupils the ability to express thoughts coherently in speaking and writing, and to instil literate habits of writing the

language down.   Closely related to these aims is the wish to
arouse a conscious awareness of the use of words and a careful
(in the sense of "concerned", "sensitive", "thoughtful")   attitude to them.   There is a strong feeling that a literate
person not only uses language well, but understands and is
aware of it *as* a means of communication.   The study of Russian
is claimed to arouse patriotic feelings and to establish a
dialectical-materialist attitude.   This includes making pupils
gradually realise that "language reflects a reality which is
quite independent of our consciousness", showing them that
mastering it "deepens their grasp of the real world which is
perceived by us" and revealing to them the "social essence of
language in the spirit of Marxist-Leninist theoretical lin-
guistics".   The purposes of Russian teaching, then, are to
give factual knowledge, to impart practical skills and a
scholarly attitude, to develop powers of thinking, to arouse
aesthetic awareness of the beauty of the language and to
dispose pupils towards a particular philosophical standpoint
in regard to the language.

Syllabuses

The Primary Classes.   In the words of a recent statement, the
objectives of the primary course in Russian are "to teach the
children to read, speak and write in an intelligent manner; to
enrich their language; to impart elementary information on
language and literature, to develop children's attention to
and interest in language and reading; to develop and enrich
children's conceptions of the world around them; to facilitate
the acquisition by the children of a command of the oral and
written forms of the language within the limits determined by
their age".   The tasks most in teachers' minds are instruction
in reading, writing and the "development of language", and
this last phrase denotes a concept which is not separated
from, but is regarded as an integral part of instruction in
reading, writing, grammar and orthography.

The whole word "look-and-say" method has or had its
adherents in the USSR, and controversy about the teaching of
reading is alive there.   Nevertheless, literacy is now taught
everywhere by a method known as the "sound analytic-synthetic
method" *(zvukovoy analitiko-sinteticheskiy metod)*.   It represents a development of work done last century by K. D. Ushinsky, a venerated figure in Russian educational history.   In
its modern manifestation there is a "pre-alphabetical" period
of a few days or weeks in which children engage in conversation, story telling and recitation with the teacher.   Their
vocabulary is enlarged, attention is directed to the structure
of simple sentences, words and syllables, and, most importantly, they are taught to distinguish the phonemes from which
words are made up, and the order in which they come in a given
word: д, о, м, *дом* [house].   This naturally leads, as the

shape of the letters is taught, to the building up of words from cut-out cards with one letter on each. At the same time, great importance is attached to the recognition and reading of syllables, since it is argued that children who read letter by letter miss out non-final vowels when they come to write. When compulsory schooling began at seven, teachers were expected to have completed the introduction of the alphabet by 15 December (term begins on 1 September), and by the end of the old class 1 pupils were meant to be able to read aloud at a rate of 30 to 40 words per minute.

Because of the nature of language teaching it is not easy to set out the content of the primary syllabus in a way the reader will necessarily find helpful. Russian educators conceptualize the primary syllabus as containing the following interdependent elements: writing, reading, phonetics, grammar, word-formation and orthography, and the development of language. The content of primary education is perhaps best understood if arranged under these broad headings, and if occasional comment is made about the methods used.

The teaching of *gramota*, literacy, has been briefly referred to above. Methodological handbooks make reference to the desirability of dividing up classes by attainment, in order to achieve more effective instruction; a simple division into two groups or a more intricate one into five are suggested as a means to putting the "differentiated approach" into practice. This method of class organization is rarely found otherwise in Soviet education. Before literacy is achieved, pupils are taught to recite poetry "expressively and using correct intonation", to recount their experiences to the whole class, to re-tell a story which has been told them or answer questions about the content of what they have heard. In the teaching of writing, emphasis is placed on the correct handling and care of paper and implements, posture and, when it comes to the actual written text, calligraphy: the shape, size and slope (65 degrees) of the letters. There is a standard form prescribed for the letters and figures, and writing exercise books often, though not always these days, have sloping lines to indicate the 65-degree slant.

Reading in class includes passages from the reader about the life of the family and young people, festivals such as International Women's Day (8 March), Lenin's birthday (22 April), May Day and revolutionary anniversaries, the Soviet Army, nature and work at different times of the year, moral tales ("What do `good´ and `bad´ mean?"), "What life was like before the Great October Revolution", scenes from the life of Lenin, the Revolution itself, fables and folk tales. Poetry is learned by heart at all stages. Out-of-school reading is required too, and a weekly, or later fortnightly, lesson is devoted to preparation and follow-up; it begins with very simple tasks - riddles, puzzles, verses, and proverbs, and leads on to standard children's books. One function of this is to make "propaganda for books" in the children's homes.

The pre-alphabetical period of reading instruction at the very start of primary schooling is the introduction to phonetics, which is linked closely with graphics. In other words, pupils' attention is drawn to the phonetic construction of words, to the correct articulation of sounds in language and to the contrast between the actual pronunciation of a word and its representation in written form. Correct standard pronunciation and stress are taught.

The teaching of grammar includes punctuation and word-formation. Children learn to distinguish the parts of speech, to recognise the different cases, different types of sentence (narrative, interrogative and exclamatory), to understand the persons and tenses of a verb, to point out the subject and predicate of a sentence and to tell the root of a word from its prefix, suffix and grammatical ending (essential for word building). They learn the correct use of capital letters, full stops, question marks and exclamation marks.

The development of language, both spoken and written, is a continuous process throughout primary and incomplete secondary education, and it is carried on in conjunction with all the parts of the syllabus. Broadly speaking, Soviet educators see it as having three purposes: to teach the "literary linguistic norm" (whether in its artistic, scientific or colloquial register) and distinguish it from dialect, slang and "simple talk" *[prostorechie]*, secondly to teach reading and writing and the differences between spoken and written language, and thirdly to achieve for every pupil a minimum level of "culture of language". The meaning of this phrase implies the ability to use language sensitively, persuasively, considerately, skilfully and even artistically. Soviet teachers develop language on a basis of the idea that language and the development of thinking are interdependent; thus, the extension of the range of concepts possessed by children is carried out as their vocabulary is systematically enlarged, work is done on (often metaphorical) turns of phrase and proverbs. Attention is paid to the logical organization of thought in children's analysis of texts they have studied and their answers to questions. Phrases and sentence structure are studied. "Continuous language", oral and written, consists of answers to questions, single sentences about pictures, dividing a text into sections and providing a title, short summaries of texts, accounts of the children's games, hobbies and work. By the end of primary education, the children will be telling the story of a film or a series of pictures, writing accounts of incidents from their own life, or re-telling a story from the point of view of one participant other than the original narrator. In all composition exercises the compilation of a plan is very important - whether done by the class with the teacher's help or eventually by the individual pupil.

Brief accounts of two or three Russian language lessons

in primary classes may help to show how such material is presented. In a class for six-year-olds the children were asked to perform the following tasks: to identify individual letters and read syllables consisting of a consonant followed by a vowel from a chart displayed by the teacher and to make up three and four-letter words from letter cards. They worked out the number of syllables in a given word, answered riddles and made suggestions of suitable words to describe a model house. They made up their own sentences based on a coloured picture, recalled proverbs and sayings when prompted, and recited a poem with actions. Among the tasks the teacher performed were stimulating child response by asking questions, insisting that they always replied using complete sentences, correcting their pronunciation and articulation, checking their spelling and attending to their physical posture.

In a second-year (age 8) class, children carried out quite a wide variety of tasks. For example, the lesson began with their being asked to invent sentences based on a diagram on the board of this type: WHO? / WHAT IS [S]HE LIKE? / WHAT IS [S]HE DOING? / WHEN OR WHERE? Grammatical-morphological activities, written and oral, included distinguishing between animate and inanimate nouns (which has morphological consequences in Russian) and between masculine and feminine gender, parsing, supplying the correct grammatical ending to nouns and spelling words which contained one particular problem (whether to represent a certain sound by letter o or a). A minute or two was spent on word-building: pupils were invited to suggest words containing the roots *kholod* [cold], *skaz* [tell] and *niz* [low]. A gramophone record of music was played and children were asked to suggest adjectives which appropriately described the mood of the piece; this presented an opportunity for aesthetic response which the children entered into with some enthusiasm. While most children were completing the grammatical exercises, those who had finished were invited to write poems, and some did. Also the homework set was a piece of creative writing: "a poem or a story about springtime", which had been the theme of the music.

Russian in Secondary Education

The systematic course begins in year 5 and is regarded as complete by the end of year 9. It is clearly divided into sections, although a good deal of overlapping is discernible: syntax and punctuation, phonetics and graphics, lexis (vocabulary), word-formation and orthography, morphology and orthography, and the development of continuous language.

The syllabuses have closely resembled their present form since the late 1970s (and are not too different from those of the late 1960s). Discussions held with leading figures in native language teaching of the Institute for Research into Content and Methods of Instruction of the APN SSSR in 1980 elicited the following particular concerns at that time, which are reflected in the syllabuses presently in force.

The Research Institute has teams of experts working on each section of the course. The work leads to the compilation of improved textbooks, teaching aids and supplementary materials (including at that time a new defining dictionary for schoolchildren). There was a strong feeling that the time was ripe for change in the teaching of language development. The former attitude had been to emphasise the structure of language, but now pure language was preferred, and the aim was to arrange the teaching of the native tongue around "language activities". Functional stylistics (the question of register) was to be studied in situational context. There was also a move away from artistic literature as models for children´s writing towards other types of text which children might be expected to understand more easily. Language was seen as both an activity and an end, as illustrated by the three aspects felt to be of particular importance: the mastery of certain linguistic norms of pronunciation, lexis and grammar, the enrichment of children´s vocabulary and the range of grammatical structures they can use, and communicative skills - the ability to compose texts in different functional styles (the "use of Russian", as it might be termed). When tackled about method, the reaction was to say that the Institute was not greatly worried about finding new methods. The main issue was to make the old ones work more effectively. The main interest was in methods which developed cognition. On creative work, the attitude was very much that the place for this was out of class in clubs and optional courses. It was rarely practised in lessons, where writing was usually closely based on models.

The sources for the information on syllabus content given here are the 1983 syllabus booklet along with several much more recent "instructions" and "methodological letters", pointing out amendments to this syllabus. Numbers of lessons stated in brackets for each topic do not necessarily mean that complete lessons are devoted to these topics.

Class 5. An introductory lesson is entitled "Russian as a means of communication". Revision of the primary school course runs to 21 lessons, and advice to teachers implies transfer problems when it stresses the importance of secondary Russian teachers being well acquainted with the content of the primary course. Syntax and punctuation (34 lessons) includes word combinations, types of utterance and sentence and the appropriate final punctuation, sentence structure (main and secondary elements, simple and extended sentences), the use of a comma between clauses and before conjunctions, speech marks; the use of correct intonation when reading the different types of sentence aloud.

Phonetics and graphics (15) embrace vowels and consonants, word stress and its effect on the disparity between spelling and pronunciation, hard and soft consonants, the alphabet and the use of an orthographic dictionary. Lexis (9) deals with the meaning, literal and figurative, of words, homonyms, synonyms and antonyms, how to refer to a defining dictionary and the correct use of words in context. Word formation and orthography (20) involves the analysis of words into root, prefix, suffix and inflexion, and the consequences of all this for spelling. Morphology and orthography includes nouns (22) - certain matters peculiar to Russian, such as the animate/inanimate distinction, gender agreement with verbs in the past tense, more difficult case inflexions that young children might not be expected to know, also the use of synonyms to avoid repetition in good style; adjectives (11) involves similar points; the verb (31) - aspect, person and gender agreement, correct stress in pronunciation and the sequence of tenses in past tense narrative; consolidation (12).

The development of continuous language (34) includes the concept of a text, its organization and planning; style (colloquial, scientific and artistic, narrative, descriptive and reflective); summary of a narrative text; writing descriptions of objects and animals; "reflective" answers to questions related to the pupils' own experience or on a work read by them; written accounts of incidents from the children's lives or based on pictures.

The syllabus, like all such documents, contains a section for each class of "Basic abilities and skills" which pupils are to attain. For class 5 much of this is made up of a list of the specific types of word which children are to be able to spell and the punctuation marks they are to use correctly. It also states that pupils must be able to distinguish the theme and basic idea of a text and compile the plan of a narrative text; they should be able to analyse a narrative text with elements of description in it. When composing essays they should be able to "use lexical synonyms for the more exact expression of thought, the expressiveness of utterance and the avoidance of unjustified repetition". Recent methodological instructions ask teachers to concentrate on a host of issues, raising the question as to whether "concentration" really is the appropriate word: punctuation, use of dictionaries, correct oral articulation, extension of vocabulary through word-formation, spelling of case-endings and the characteristics of individual parts of speech, to mention only a few.

Class 6 begins with a lesson on "the Russian language - one of the world's developed languages". There are twelve lessons of revision, nine on lexis (general, professional, dialect, borrowed and obsolete vocabulary, neologisms and the concept of "phraseologisms"). The content of the section on word-formation and orthography (27) has, it is said, been cut down; it extends previous work. Under morphology and orthography, work on the noun (21), adjective (22), numeral (14) pronoun (23) and verb (30 lessons) is completed; after all of these lessons and 12 of consolidation, pupils are expected to have acquired a whole series of abilities and skills which are almost entirely expressed in terms of correct spelling and punctuation (except for the identification of parts of speech and the analysis of the structure of words). The development of continuous language (33) contains revision of the previous year's work, more stress on the planning of essays, writing more descriptive essays than previously, and more work on resume of narrative texts. It includes some imaginative writing: "essays or reflections of imaginary content". Requirements for the abilities and skills include the collection and organization of essay material and the polishing both of the content and the linguistic formulation of the pupil's own texts. Recent methodological instructions to teachers mention particularly that they should stress correct spelling, teach "literary" norms of language and extirpate dialect characterisics, make a point of linking teaching with life by including professional work vocabulary, speak to pupils about the development of Russian and the enrichment of its vocabulary since the Revolution, and see to it that pupils get used to handling reference works.

Class 7. The theme of the introductory lesson is "Russian as a developing phenomenon". The principal themes of the course are revision (7 lessons); participles (31) - these are difficult for Russian children, since there are four different types, they are not used much in spoken language and there are certain spelling problems. The gerunds (7), though not used in speech at all, create fewer problems. Adverbs (22) are puzzling to a native speaker, as there are difficulties of various types regarding their spelling, stress, the use of hyphens, the number of words or whether they are to be written as one. Auxiliary parts of speech are treated in five divisions: introduction (1), prepositions (7), conjunctions (7), particles (18), interjections (1). This whole topic is seen as being closely linked with syntax and morphology, since many auxiliary parts of speech in Russian can belong to one or the other category. Consolidation lessons (9). Development of continuous language (25) introduces the concept of "publicistic language", which is seen as a style designed to persuade an audience, affect its emotions and change its behaviour. Composition work is much as before, but adds description of people's appearance and of "labour processes"; some essays are now to involve discussion.

Classes 8 and 9 have fewer lessons allowed (102 and 68 respectively) and it is regarded as difficult to squeeze in all the material. The course involves much systematizing of previously studied topics, and teachers are advised not to waste time going over known matter as if it were new, but to organize

teaching so that revision is a constant process. The introductory lesson to class 8 is entitled "Russian as the language
voluntarily adopted by Soviet people as their nationwide means
of communication". Teachers are recommended in revision (6)
to concentrate on punctuation and orthography (missing out
lexis and phraseology if time is short). The principal preoccupation in this class is syntax (and punctuation), and much
very systematic study of sentence structure goes on. The
topics are: phrases and clauses (5) - to introduce analysis of
language units grammatically; simple clauses wih two main
parts (12), simple sentences with one main clause (9), incomplete clauses (2), sentences with homogeneous clauses (12),
sentences with forms of address, introductory words and interjections (9), sentences with isolated clauses (18), direct and
indirect speech (6) and revision (5). The development of
continuous language (17) includes more work on descriptive
writing, particularly of historical, architectural or artistic
monuments and places of interest, discussions of moral and
ethical matters and of subjects arising from literary works,
including character-descriptions of literary personages.

From published advice to teachers it is clear that the
principal obsession of the course planners is to improve
pupils´ punctuation (which depends more in Russian than in
English on appreciation of syntactical structures) and the
intelligent reading aloud of sentences of the types studied.

Class 9. The introductory lesson is entitled "The international significance of Russian". After two lessons of revision the theme of the complex sentence occupies 34 lessons:
main and subordinate clauses, sentences with several subordinate clauses, the use of subordinating and co-ordinating conjunctions, various marks of punctuation and the ability to use
this theoretical information in practice. Then follows a
short section of general information on language (2), embrac-
ing its social role, the historical and recent development of
Russian, and the Russian literary language and its styles. 12
lessons are devoted to "systematizing and generalizing all
that has been learnt on lexis, phonetics, grammar and spelling". The development of continuous language (17), apart
from revising and extending previous work, contains compositions in publicistic style on socio-political, moral-ethical
and historico-literary topics, an oral report on a socio-
political theme based on two or three sources, and summaries
and abstracts of articles on such subjects. With the end of
class 9 formal study of the native language is concluded, and
if it continues, it does so within literature lessons.

Additional Remarks on the Development of Continuous Language

Russian educators use two forms of composition, *izlozhenie* and
sochinenie, and each exists in spoken and written form. [A

difficulty arises in making sense of translations of Soviet writings on the subject, since the word *rech'* can mean either "language" in general or specifically "speech", a fact which translators are not always too careful about. In the phrase "development of continuous language", this is the word used.] The word *izlozhenie* means "analysis" and is the re-telling of a text in the pupil's words. In its most rigid form it is the more or less word-for-word reproduction of a text, but the term also includes precis, selective analysis (picking out one line of argument only from a text), and an exercise involving an additional task, such as telling the story from the point of view of a character other than the original narrator. *Sochinenie*, literally: "composition", is more free and creative and is likely to require the child to show some imagination and independence. In both types of writing pupils are trained in narrative, descriptive, reflective and publicistic styles, and are expected to use them appropriately.

Soviet educators express some unease about the place in education of the spoken language. It has tended to be neglected, it is said, but recent methodology books devote great attention to it. The problem is not helped by the fact that talk in the classroom has traditionally been over-formal, with insistence on full-sentence utterances at all times, lack of pupil-pupil communication and almost total teacher dominance. Leading educators now seek discourse of a more communicative nature as a pre-requisite for improvement in language work.

The Soviet teacher does not accept undisciplined outpourings from pupils, and all essay work is prepared, executed and polished (or "perfected", as the terminology has it). Polishing is not possible in spoken composition, and, as any teacher knows, it is hard to get young pupils to edit their own prose except for correcting obvious orthographical errors. However, preparation receives great attention: children are taught to draft plans (in the earliest stages the teacher provides the plan), which the teacher then discusses; they collect material, which is again discussed, and they write an abstract before they are allowed to draft the full text.

Sochinenie begins in the lower classes with such simple topics as "My hobby" or "The street where I live". A leading Georgian exponent of primary education, Shalva Amonashvili gives his six-year-olds as their first topic "What makes me sad and what glad", and he graphically describes the contempt and disbelief of professional colleagues at the idea that children of six could conceivably handle such a theme; he deplores the tendency of such teachers to underestimate what children of any age are capable of. Much work is based on models, so if pupils are writing personal descriptions they will be given examples from good literature to study and emulate. Essay titles set for the public examination at age 15 amount to 200, and here are ten typical examples: "Why I love the region where I live", "My favourite literary character", "Heroes are born in labour", "My favourite writer, composer, painter or architect", "They fought for the fatherland", "An interesting excursion", "A good name depends on good deeds", "The person most dear to me", "An unforgettable meeting" and "Reading is the best education".

The Syllabus in Action

The content of this programme of study looks daunting, technical and perhaps unutterably boring from the summaries given here, but in fact Russian language lessons are among the more stimulating and enjoyable that one sees in Soviet schools. This is due to the skill of teachers in varying their approach, and to the fact that, in younger classes especially, activities are changed frequently. For example, in a lesson to the (old) fourth year, the first year of secondary education, the two themes of the lesson were anounced as "the verb as a part of speech" and "the Russian language as a phenomenon expressing national character".

The lesson began with discussion of quotations from Lenin and Ushinsky, to the effect respectively that people should love their language as they love their country and that the character of people and their natural surroundings is reflected in the language they speak. The children were asked to elucidate the meaning of the quotations and to define individual words. The style of the Ushinsky quotation was described by the children as "artistic" and his emotional stance as "love for his country". At different times in the lesson children were asked to identify parts of speech, especially verbs, and to make up sentences including examples of them. They were asked to spot the subject, predicate and object of sentences, and to identify the morphological features of a word (the conjugation of a verb). They were given two exercises to complete in writing: one on morphology (in which they had to supply missing verb-endings in a poem by Bunin which had been written on the board with the endings omitted), and one on punctuation. The pupils were later invited to respond to the poem both intellectually and emotionally. A reproduction of a painting by Levitan ("Fresh Wind on the Volga") was then used to stimulate the children to find words and later sentences to describe it. The most sophisticated response from the class was: "The wind plays on the river as on the strings of an instrument". The teacher spoke for a little while on Levitan's place in Russian art.

The lesson described here was typical of others in the native language which I have attended. Language and content were linked, the lesson was competently planned and variety of activity provided, and the arts were used to stimulate productive language by children. Music is frequently used too. Children are often reminded of the cultural heritage that is theirs.

Assessment

Tasks set in examinations include the following. In the primary classes, dictation, copy-writing, grammar, *izlozhenie* and reading aloud are required. At the end of primary schooling, dictations of about 80 words are set, and a child who makes three mistakes fails. The grammar tests include underlining the letters in a given phrase which would require checking for correct spelling, analysing a word into root, suffix, etc., identifying nouns in a sentence with their declension and case, conjugating verbs, making up an interrogative sentence with pronouns in it, finding synonyms for certain words, parsing the words in a sentence. *Izlozhenie* passages are about 100 words long, and a plan consisting of three sentences is given to help the pupil. Passages for reading aloud are about 120 words long. The purpose of this part of the test is to assess the teacher as much as the pupils, since a form is to be filled in indicating how many of the pupils have reached certain standards, estimated by the way they read (syllable by syllable is not acceptable at the end of year 4), how many mistakes they make and of what type, correct placing of the stress, reading grammatical endings correctly and understanding what they have read.

At the end of incomplete secondary education all pupils are subjected to formal examination. The conduct of this examination is described in Chapter 1. The published question "tickets" number 30, and here are one or two typical examples. The teachers are expected to provide texts and examples as mentioned on the tickets.

A

(1) Speak about vowels and their correct spelling in the root of a word. Insert missing letters into a word indicated by the teacher [i.e., the examiner] and explain their spelling. Carry out a phonetic analysis of specific words.

(2) Extract from a sentence indicated by the teacher some word combinations [phrases] and analyse them. Speak about the construction of phrases. Compose some phrases using the prepositions "thanks to", "in accordance with" and "contrary to" [these are single-word prepositions in Russian].

B

(1) Speak about the way common nouns decline and about the spelling of the sounds -o and -e in the singular. Find some indeclinable nouns in the sentences indicated by the examiner; state their gender. Insert missing letters in certain words and explain their correct spelling.

(2) Speak about direct speech and the punctuation signs used in sentences including speech. Insert and explain punctuation into a sentence indicated by the examiner.

C

(1) Define a numeral, speak about the declension of numerals and the use of the soft sign [a tricky letter of ·the alphabet] in them. Find numerals in the text supplied, insert missing letters and explain the correct spelling. Carry out morphological analysis of certain numerals.

(2) Describe the use of the dash in conjunctionless complex sentences. Find examples of such sentences in the texts supplied, insert punctuation and explain.

Performance in the oral part of the examination is assessed according to carefully defined criteria. Examiners are instructed not to interrupt candidates while they are speaking, but published critique of the conduct of examinations indicates that this rule is often disregarded. To get a mark of 5, the pupil must answer fully, correctly, literately, logically and with understanding; for a mark of 4 one or two errors and one or two logical faults are allowed. For a satisfactory mark of 3, the pupil must still show basic understanding, but makes more serious errors in the explanations and fails to give good examples to illustrate answers. The unsatisfactory mark of 2 is given if the pupil shows ignorance of the major part of the topic under discussion, and distorts the sense of replies by their incorrect formulation. Total ignorance or lack of understanding gains a mark of 1.

Dictations in class 9 are about 150-170 words long and perfect work or one mistake only gains 5 marks. Four mistakes - 4 marks, eight - 3. More than this gains a failing grade. A more complex exercise is sometimes set, comprising a dictation with certain other supplementary orthographical, lexical or grammatical exercises; in this case two marks are given.

Sochinenie and *izlozhenie* are assessed regularly. In class 9 texts of 350-450 words are used for detailed *izlozhenie*. The "norms of assessment" suggest three to four pages as the appropriate length for a free composition in year 9, but allow considerable discretion (the number of words on a page is not stated). Both types of composition are assessed for content and language on the one hand and their literacy on the other. For a mark of 5, they must be factually accurate, relevant to the subject, logically planned, show richness and variety in vocabulary and style, and must have achieved "stylistic unity and expressiveness"; two or three minor errors in content or language may be disregarded. Only one mistake in either orthography, grammar or punctuation is allowed for a 5. For 4: exactly the same criteria apply, but not quite the same standard of excellence is attained; if there are no basic errors the mark will be given. A total of no more than six grammar, orthographical or punctuation errors is allowed for 4. For 3, substantial irrelevancy, occasional factual errors, occasional infringement of the logical scheme, a poor vocabulary and monotonous language, and weakness in the overall style will be present; up to twelve mistakes in the presentation will be tolerated. Irrelevant, inaccurate, illogical and linguistically feeble essays are given 2 or 1.

Problems and Prospects.

Comparison of the latest syllabus with its immediate predecessor does not reveal a radical reform in content or methods of instruction. The evidence presented in this chapter is scarcely characteristic of radical reform, and teachers might be excused for even failing to notice that any changes had taken place. Some slight amendment is made to the number of lessons allocated to the various sections of the syllabus: what does it matter if the verb now gets 30 lessons in class 6 instead of 29? And what about the introductory lesson to each year? - It's only one lesson; does it matter? So they can miss out some minor component of the previous syllabus - so what? And they have to "pay particular attention" to so much now that there seems little point in it: if everything is emphasised, what meaning is left to the word "emphasis"? Such was the attitude of many teachers to the amendments to the syllabus.

Not all of them, however, got away with it. A report from the Ministry of Education in late 1985 wrote of the introduction of the new syllabus in schools in seven or more regions, including the cities of Moscow and Orenburg. It praises warmly and blames sharply: some teachers seem to be unaware of the changes in the syllabus and are wasting time on topics which have now been excluded. They are ignoring the new introductory lessons, despite their obvious moral benefit. They are failing to use audio-visual aids, and are not teaching the children to use reference material: in 29 lessons seen in Orenburg the inspectors saw a film-strip being used once only and a dictionary twice. Teachers are failing to teach children to plan their essays and are very slow to mark written work, often handing it back long after the children have lost interest in it. On the other hand, many teachers are praised for their acceptance of the new syllabus, but most of all for attempting to use a new approach: in the region of Kostroma 82% of lessons had made use of some form of educational technology. Analysis of written compositions showed an improvement in work on language development; the essays were varied in content, showed a personal attitude to the subject, for the most part were at least well enough planned to have a beginning and an end, and showed evidence of better command of language. Certain spelling and punctuation rules are more widely observed than before, but several aspects of the theoretical work on grammar are not yet well enough mastered by a significant number of pupils.

So much for the new syllabus in practice; how is it seen by the theorists? An essay by Belen'kiy and Snezhnevskaya returns several times to the basic problem: how to relate technical information about the structure of language to the ability to use language. Syllabuses, it is stated, have tended to list factual material in such a way as to suggest that it must be learned by rote - which is just what is not required. Hands are wrung because it is so difficult to teach children the participles, adverbs and particles in class 7, because syntax teaching is not a success, and because so many entrants to higher education make more errors in punctuation than in spelling. What is not questioned is the notion that there is a fairly direct connection between grammar and the effective use of one's native language. The assumption is made that there is such a link and that it is the task of the linguist-educator to discover and exploit it.

Chapter 7

SCIENCE EDUCATION

THE SCIENTIFIC education of Soviet schoolchildren begins seriously in class 6 (age 11) with two lessons of biology per week; physics starts in the following year and chemistry the year after that. Physics receives the lion's share of the lessons, as will be seen from Figure 2. Science is concentrated in the last years of compulsory education: in the final year pupils receive an average of 14.5 lessons a week on mathematics and scientific subjects, including one lesson of astronomy. For the purposes of this book geography is treated in a later chapter, though the syllabus contains a good deal of relevance to the natural sciences.

Primary Science

Observation of the natural world is present in pre-school education, where it amounts to recording the passage of the seasons and some work in the kindergarten vegetable plot; it is closely connected with the development of language and with the beginnings of labour training. In primary education, nature study used to be taught from class 2, but under the new dispensation the first two years have a course entitled "Acquaintance with the world around" (see Chapter 3), followed by three years of nature study. The "world around" syllabus has at least as much to do with moral and labour education and with social training as with nature, but about one third of it is concerned with the natural environment: gardens, parks, the countryside, the changing seasons and caring for pets and indoor plants. As part of these lessons children are taken out of school and taught to observe simple natural phenomena and to some extent to record their observations.

Primary school *nature study* from year 3 relies heavily on the theme of the changing seasons. The weekly lesson is concerned with observing weather, plants, the behaviour of wild creatures, and the consequences of all these for human health and agriculture. There are lessons which deal with the thermometer, the parts of a plant, coniferous and deciduous trees, ice and snow and the germination of seeds. In class 4 "nature in our region" leads on to "our country on the globe and on the map" and "the variety of natural surroundings in our country". The last part of the year is given up to the human body and its health and fitness: the skeleton, muscles, heart, diet, teeth, the nervous system and the senses, and "the concern of the Party and the Soviet government for the health of its people". A few lessons go on the use and conservation of nature by man.

Nature Study in Class 5

In the first year of secondary education the propaedeutic purpose of the course in preparing the ground for future work in geography, chemistry, physics, astronomy and biology is emphasized in the new syllabus of 1986. It is claimed that the revision of this syllabus has allowed the exclusion of extraneous content and the inclusion of new elements which strengthen its polytechnical and ecological character and its power to influence children's attitudes. The aims include developing in pupils an holistic picture of the natural world, as well as the usual, almost ritual, claim to lay the foundations of a dialectical-materialist attitude which is made on behalf of every subject in the curriculum. General educational aims are mentioned too: the development of observation, reasoning and language. Children are to be given the ability to distinguish between the vital and the incidental features of a natural object, to compare, deduce, generalize and describe natural phenomena. The are also to be taught to orient themselves in the open and to carry out observations.

Content. Introduction (1 lesson); the earth and other celestial bodies (6 lessons): sun, moon, stars, constellations. Air (6): its composition, properties, how man uses it, its temperature in different conditions, wind and weather. Water (6): change of state, as a solvent, the sea, the effect of water on the formation of features of the landscape, water conservation, protection from pollution. Rocks (5): some elementary geology - the formation of rocks, minerals, weathering, metallic and non-metallic useful minerals, conservation. The soil (3): how it is formed, its significance for life on earth, its conservation. Living organisms and their environment (5): the variety of these on earth, their relationship with the environment, the use made of them by man, the effect of human activity upon the living world. One lesson is devoted to an excursion to study this out of doors.

At the end of this course, the children are expected to know the difference between animate and inanimate nature and to be able to point out the links between them. Apart from mastering the content of the syllabus, they should be able to measure temperature with a thermometer and wind strength with a weathervane, to represent weather using conventional symbols on a weather-calendar and to interpret such signs, to orient themselves by local features, and to indicate upon a globe the position of continents, oceans, poles, hemispheres and the equator. Comparison of the content and requirements made upon the children with those in a previous (1983) syllabus does indeed confirm a slight strengthening of the ecological emphasis and the relating of the subject matter to human activity and technology, but in fact the content has been subjected only to minor reorganization. If anything, the statement of "requirements" as to what pupils should be able to do by the end of the course has been tightened up, and now says a little less about their ability to make deductions or observations and more about factual mastery of the content.

BIOLOGY. *Structure and Aims*

The subject is broken down into component parts: botany is taught in classes 6 and 7, zoology in 7 and 8, and human biology in class 9. In classes 10 and 11 a course of general biology is followed. This basic structure has not changed for generations. Actual details of the material covered will be given later, but the information will appear in clearer perspective if something is known about the aims of biology teaching and the importance attached to it in the field of character-development.

The aims of school biology are expressed in various ways. Firstly there are objectives concerned with the nature of the subject and its content: children must receive a rounded picture of the scientific basis of animate nature. They are to learn especially about evolution and the work of Charles Darwin, and the scientific principles which operate in nature. Pupils should learn skills of scientific observation and discover how scientists reason, themselves developing logical thinking and an understanding of cause and effect. Secondly, and closely related with this, pupils should form "a scientific picture of the world", and, more than that, develop a dialectical-materialistic outlook and understanding from their biological study. Now, we have already said that this phrase is used almost invariably in statements of the aims of the teaching of a subject - it is even claimed for technical drawing. But in the case of biology it may be possible to show that, from the Soviet point of view at least, the claim is more than a mere formality. Thirdly, children should come to understand the biological basis for the development of agriculture and for certain industrial processes.

This character-forming and ideological role of school biology is not underestimated. In a recent essay A. N. Myagkova argues that biology "convinces the pupils" of the material basis of the functioning of human and animal bodies and of all their activities, including intellectual ones. Biology teaching establishes scientific materialism in children's minds, and understanding of Darwin´s work gives a concept of evolution in historical development which contributes to a correct interpretation of social issues. The logical exposition of biological principles gives children a scientific outlook and "exposes the anti-scientific character of religious belief". It is stressed that biology teaching cannot be neutral; it must engage in systematic atheistic education and confrontation with "modern religious dogma". (This is a rare admission that present-day Christianity is not the dogged biblical fundamentalism that was once dominant.)

The achievements of Soviet biologists are used to further patriotic education, internationalism is fostered by studies of world figures in biological sciences: Darwin, Linnaeus, Lamarck, Pasteur and Mendel. Biology is important both for ecological and aesthetic education: the natural world should be used to arouse in children a feeling for beauty. Human biology shows children the basis for hygienic, labour and sex education and explains the need for physical fitness and sport. The relation of biology to agriculture and industry contributes to labour and poytechnical education and assists with career orientation. Therefore, the ideal biology pupil will receive a scientific, dialectical-materialist, atheistic outlook from his studies; he will be both a patriot and an internationalist, he will have been introduced to certain scientific ways of thinking, he will be alive to the working of his body, he will respect the environment, and he will have a sense of beauty. Here are eight or nine of the characteristics of the "new Soviet man" which the whole education system seeks to develop.

Criticism and Reform

The Soviet school biology syllabus before 1985 was subject to criticism both from inside and outside the profession. Zverev and Kashin describe it as the most traditional in its structure, scarcely having changed since 1931 and being based for the most part on the series of separate subject courses which date back to pre-revolutionary Russian education. Biology had largely resisted the modern tendency to integrate material. It was even hinted that overseas countries were doing better, that theorists in the field had not been working long enough ("less than a decade") on a new theoretical basis for a non-fragmented syllabus, which should establish some principles in pupils´ minds and give them an holistic view of what biology is. Myagkova´s spirited claims for the importance of biology in attitude and character building, which is summarised above, may be something of a smoke-screen.

Earlier syllabuses were said to be overloaded with secondary material which was too complicated (a common enough complaint about Soviet syllabuses in very many subjects). Some narrowly specialised content of interest to future serious students only has now, it is claimed, been deleted. The age of the pupils, the time available, and the work being done in other subjects were none of them sufficiently considered in the formulation of the syllabus. Knowledge retained from former syllabuses was out of date and ecological aspects were not strongly enough represented. All these faults are held to have been corrected, at least in part, by the latest syllabus published in December 1985.

Syllabus Content, Classes 6 - 11

The 68 lessons in class 6 are devoted to botany. The topics are little changed from the 1983 syllabus, and they are:- plants (3 lessons of general information), the cellular structure of growing organisms (4 lessons), the root (6), the shoot (19) including bud, leaf and stem, reproduction in plants (2), flower and fruit (7), the seed (5) and plants and their environment (8). Five excursions are planned to observe plants growing wild, in hothouses, outdoors in winter and spring, and for study of the interdependence of plants in nature. The syllabus's statement of the requirements upon the pupils include that they should know the principal parts and structure of flowering plants, the meaning of photosynthesis, transpiration, respiration, movement of materials, the role of plants in nature and their importance to man, reproduction by seed or vegetative organs; they should know about the adaptation of plants to the environment and their relationship with other living things. Children should be able to recognize the organs of a plant, to carry out simple experiments related to functions of plants (transpiration, nutrition, etc.), carry out simple plant care (gardening tasks), observe and record seasonal changes, prepare slides for and use a microscope, and take cuttings; they should observe good behaviour in the countryside, and be able to work with graphic and printed material on botany. (Pretty well all statements of requirements for a wide variety of subjects now include this element of textbook, reference-book and resource-based working.)

Botany continues in class 7. The topics are revision (2); angiospermae (10); agricultural plants (6), classification of plants (10: algae, bryophyta, gymnospermae, angiospermae); the development of the plant world (5, including historical development and stress on evolution, the dominance now and wide variety of the angiospermae), and a final section on bacteria, fungi and lichens (8).

The teaching of zoology begins two-thirds of the way through year 7. Two general lessons on animal life are followed by instruction about the simplest single-cell animals (4), coelenterata (4), flatworms, roundworms and annelids (6), and molluscs (3). There are several interspersed lessons of review and revision, and excursions to observe animals in the wild. Summer tasks set for the children to do during the holiday involve them in making a collection of cultivated and wild plants and carrying out various observations. The stated "requirements" of the seventh year biology lessons include mastery of the content, knowing the differences between the types of animals and plants covered, recognition of the signs of evolutionary development and the role of animals and plants in nature and the economy. The children should be able to recognise agricultural plants and to identify them by particular features, to carry out work on the school plot and to recognise different animals in the wild and in pictures.

Class 8 continues with zoology: arthropods (13 lessons): crustaceans, arachnids, insects; chordates (44) - lanceolates (1), fish (7), amphibians (4), reptiles (4), birds (12), mammals (13). Next comes the evolution of the animal world (5) - proof of the historical development of species, the work of Darwin, relationship of man to the animal kingdom, "the lack of substance in the view that the animal world is immutable"; natural associations (4): habitat, the effect of the environment on plants and animals, the need for the preservation of the balance of nature, and the concern of the Soviet government for conservation. Three excursions are allowed for: into the country, to a zoo and a museum. At the completion of this the children are expected to know among other things about the skeleton, organs, respiration, nervous system and blood circulation of animals, the stages and proofs of evolution, the importance of the balance of nature in itself and to human life and activity. No new skills other than those implicit in the syllabus or already mentioned are required of the children, except the ability to collate and present information from their work and observations.

The class 9 course on the human body and its health is intended as a logical continuation of the zoology already studied, as well as an important part of health education. It "serves the aims of developing anatomic-physiological understanding, understanding of the organismal form of life, and also ecological and evolutionary concepts". It extends pupils' understanding of phylogenetic links already received and further demonstrates the relationship of man to the other animals. The main ways in which man is distinguished from them are examined: work, speech and consciousness of his social nature. The syllabus falls into 10 main themes which cover a general introduction (6), bones and locomotion (7), circulation of the blood (8), respiration (5), digestion (5), metabolism and excretion (5), the skin (3), the nervous system and sensory organs (15: including higher nervous activity and sleep) glands for external secretion (3), and reproduction and development (4). This last topic includes the reproductive organs, pregnancy, childbirth, suckling, the growth and development of babies, "youths' and girls' hygiene", and the characteristics of adolescence. This is the nearest that Soviet children get to sex education in the mass school, and if four lessons does not seem very much, then the newest syllabus is a good deal more helpful and explicit than the eqivalent passages in textbooks printed as recently as 1983. (The subject is dealt with in Chapter 3 under the heading of "Ethics and Psychology of Family Life".) The stated requirements for the ninth-year course indicate that the authorities attach particular importance to the implications of the matter studied for health education: choice of lifestyle, diet, alcohol, sport and physical activity and personal hygiene.

Classes 10 and 11 move on to a course in general biology. At this senior stage the aim is to systematize and deepen the pupils′ knowledge and understanding of evolution and the "levels of organization of biological systems". However, the topics covered in this general course are in year 10 evolutionary theory (8 lessons - biology before and after Darwin), the development of the organic world (5 - an historical account of evolutionary development through the ages), the descent of man (4 - Darwin on man′s emergence from the animals, Engels on the role of labour in changing prehistoric apes into men). Social and biological factors are both stressed here and the opportunity is taken for an attack on racism and "social Darwinism" in a topic entitled "human races, their origin and unity". Next come principles of ecology (8) - ecosystems, food chains, the ecological pyramid, and self-regulation; the year ends with two lessons of revision.

Class 11 continues general biology: the biosphere and man (5), principles of cytology (18) - cellular theory, organic substances, the chemistry of cells, metabolism and the transformation of energy as the basis of the activity of the cell, the significance of ATP in cell metabolism, photosynthesis, the gene and its role in biosynthesis, the DNA code and viruses and their activity. Reproduction and the individual development of organisms (6) - division of cells, meiosis and fertilization, the replication of molecules of DNA, chromosomes and their haploid and diploid composition, constant number and form; sexual and asexual reproduction, and development of the embryo. Elementary genetics (12) embraces the basic principles of heredity, variability in organisms, the work of Mendel, chromosome theory of heredity, and mutational variation. Selection in plants, animals and microorganisms (5); revision and overview (4). The "requirements" include that the pupils should know how to propagate plants by various means, to describe certain varieties and species, to indicate examples of adaptation and mutation, to carry out simple cytological and genetic experiments, to work out a scheme for a cycle of matter, indicate the components of a cell and an ecosystem, compare animal and plant cells, and describe types of cell division and cross-breeding.

Biology: the Discussion Continues

A British exponent of biological education, surveying this syllabus, commented that it was "heavy, very traditional, and rather teacher-directed". She remarked upon the "enormous emphasis on factual content", but noted that some indication was given of the need to develop in the child skills of observation, interpretation and problem solving. The division into botany and zoology and the great stress on the theory of evolution (which reflects Soviet emphasis on classification, systematization and an historical and logical approach) are not found in current British practice.

Soviet educators, as indicated earlier, are not entirely satisfied with their biology syllabus. They are concerned that ecological concepts should not come too late in years 6 to 9: "insufficient knowledge of superorganic systems" does not allow pupils to become acquainted with the scientific basis of conservation in nature or lay a firm foundation for an understanding of agricultural production. The most serious weakness appears to lie in the manner in which the theory of evolution is presented to the pupils. To survey it at the start of the course, when pupils know nothing of cytology or genetics, is felt to be unsatisfactory; the view is that it should, perhaps, appear twice, firstly in its "classical" form, and later in its modern development, as a broader conception: a synthetic theory of evolution. This appears to be the current solution, since the topic arises in both year 8 and year 10 and is treated with different levels of sophistication. Nevertheless, for a course of instruction which places such emphasis on the importance of children's understanding of evolutionary theory, this apparent failure over many years to get the presentation of it right does seem to be a serious shortcoming. Myagkova's essay concludes by indicating the direction future change is likely to take: a considerable improvement in the theoretical planning of work in classes 6 to 9, a "fuller realization of the ideas of evolution and the levels of organization of animate nature, and the use of these ideas as integrative theses". these words must have been written at a time when the newest syllabus (published December 1985) was well in hand. It is true that this syllabus shows evidence of some internal reorganization, but there is little radical reform as yet. It remains to be seen if Soviet biologists will be satisfied with progress achieved.

PHYSICS

The syllabus content in this subject has changed much more obviously than the biology course in recent years.   Comparison
of the 1983 approved programme with that for 1980 shows that
considerable reorganization of material took place even in
that short time; the greater part of the syllabus from the
late 1950s is now unrecognizable. Writings of physics educators show that a great deal of assessment of performance of
pupils has gone on, that considerable thought has been given
to methodology and motivation of pupils as well as to theoretical issues concerned with the presentation of concepts in
physics to children of school age.   The very latest syllabus,
published in late 1985, is again different from that of 1983,
though the alterations are in matters of detail rather than
major restructuring.

Aims

The moral and ideological aims of physics teaching resemble
those of the other science subjects.   Five primary objectives
were stated in the 1983 syllabus.   They were: (1) to communicate the basis of physical science - experimental facts, concepts, laws, theories and their practical consequences, (2) to
acquaint pupils with the methods of enquiry used by physic-
ists, (3) to give pupils the ability to carry out experiments
and process the results, (4) to enable pupils independently to
acquire knowledge and explain physical phenomena and (5) to
develop love for and interest in physics and to foster the
cognitive and creative capabilities of pupils.   The most significant features here are the use of the word "independently"
and the onus upon teachers to impart love of the subject.   The
1985 syllabus preserves these objectives in essence, though
more is said about acquainting children with physics-based
technology, making them aware of the unity and universality of
physical laws and helping them choose a career. "Love for"
physics has been deleted from the statement of aims, but
"motivation to learn" is mentioned.

Lesson Content

Increased emphasis on independent ability to discover facts
and interpret them is doubtless linked with the increased
share of the time devoted to demonstration by the teacher and
to experimental work by the pupils themselves. Hints in the
methodological literature suggest that the new increased reliance on experiment is due to observation of practice in
other countries, both socialist and capitalist. Time for
experimental work is said to amount to 16% of the total physics allocation now, and it is intended eventually to raise it
to 20%. As for motivation, theorists believe this will rise

if the latest syllabus can really engage the cognitive activity of pupils and ensure their success in learning the subject. A recent nationwide enquiry to determine how successful pupils were in mastering the concepts of physics showed the best results for the (old) classes 6 and 7, and problems mainly in class 9. Success rates in tests administered by the APN´s Research Institute on Content and Methods of Instruction Laboratory in Physics are claimed to be well over 80% and often over 90%. Such problems as remain relate to specific issues (e.g. the solving of problems on the kinetic theory of gases, the first law of thermodynamics and the explanation of Boyle´s law. Nevertheless, it is admitted that higher education establishments receive specialist students lacking in motivation. This cannot entirely be due to "poor careers guidance" as one writer suggests, though better counselling might, obviously, be all to the good.

Structure of the School Course and Underlying Principles

The physics syllabus is divided into two stages. The first week in classes 7 and 8 is a first introduction to physical phenomena and their explanation in scientific terms. The second in the last three years of schooling, studies fundamental theories in modern physics. The material in classes 9 to 11 is based on four major areas: mechanics - broadly speaking, those aspects concerned with motion; molecular physics and the fundamentals of molecular-kinetic theory; electrodynamics and the elements of the special theory of relativity (the work of Michelsen); and quantum theory. V. G. Razumovsky, an academician and a leading figure in physics education, writes in an essay summing up the syllabus:

> Each theory contains theoretical generalizations on various levels: facts, basic physical concepts, idealized models of physical manifestations, principles and laws, theoretical deductions, the most important physical experiments and practical applications of the theories in industry, agriculture and everyday life. These forms of theoretical generalization are linked cyclically in conformity with the basic tenets of Marxist-Leninist gnoseology: from actual observation (facts) to abstract reasoning (concepts, abstract models, principles, laws, theoretical deductions), and from this to practice (experiments and practical applications of the theory).

A particular preoccupation of educators is "the generalization of educational material", the conveying of overall principles of the subject, rather than fragmented facts. On the "humanization" of science teaching, pupils are taught about the work of many scientists, including Lomonosov, Ohm, Ampere, Joffe,

Galileo, Newton, Tsiolkovsky, Korolev, Zhukovsky, Faraday, Maxwell, Lentz, Lebedev, Stoletov, Planck, Einstein, Rutherford, Bohr, Popov and Korchatov. Questions of the application of physics to industry are thought out in some detail, and it is believed that systematic relation of theory to applications in modern industry and technology increases motivation, reinforces learning and "raises the ideological content of the subject". On practical work, it is worth mentioning that laboratory facilities in Soviet schools, though undoubtedly adequate, are not particul~rl el bo at , a d S vi t visitors to English schools often express admiration for what they call the "subject rooms for science". As with much in Soviet education, lavish facilities are not seen as necessary to ensure good teaching and learning.

Syllabus Content

The course in class 7 covers the following topics. A short, general, introduction (2 lessons) to physical phenomena includes a talk on what the subject embraces. (An account of the nature of the subject and why it is studied is rarely, if ever, missing from Soviet syllabuses.) Topics which follow are: the structure of matter (6) - molecules, their movement, attraction and repulsion; the interaction of bodies (20) - motion (uniform and non-uniform), inertia, mass, density, gravity, weight, friction; pressure in solids, liquids and gases (26) - Pascal's law, atmospheric pressure, Archimedes' principle and its application to water transport; work, power and energy (12) - levers, moment of force, efficiency, potential and kinetic energy. Two lessons are set aside for outside visits.

Themes in class 8 are thermal phenomena (24) - intrinsic energy and ways of transforming it, work and heat transfer; changes in the aggregate state of matter, specific heat, melting, the temperature of ignition of fuel, melting, evaporation, boiling and condensation, thermal engines (internal combustion and steam turbines). The study of electrical phenomena (24) includes the two types of electrical charge, electrical fields and the structure of atoms; electric current strength, voltage and resistance, circuits, current in metals; resistivity; energy and power of a current (including heat generated by a current, incandescent lamps, calculation of energy used by domestic appliances, short circuits and fuses). Electromagnetic phenomena (8) deals with the magnetic field of a current, electromagnets, relays, electrical measuring instruments, DC motors. The final theme in year 8 is light phenomena (10): rectilinear propagation of light, eclipses, reflection and refraction, lenses, the eye, spectacles, cameras and projectors. Excursions (2).

Class 9 (three lessons per week) is devoted to mechanics. Themes are: fundamentals of kinematics (20) - relativity of movement, trajectory, path length, translational motion, velocity, acceleration, circular motion; fundamentals of dynamics (35): Newton's laws, the inertial system, mass, force; gravitational, elastic and frictional forces; laws of conservation (22): momentum, mechanical work, energy (practical application of this includes some account of Soviet advances in rocketry); oscillations and waves (12) - amplitude, period, frequency, the simple pendulum and the formula for its period of oscillation, transference of energy in oscillatory motion, oscillations, resonance; "laboratory practice" (10) of eleven series of experiments; excursions (2).

Class 10, spends 44 lessons on molecular physics and 62 on electrodynamics. The first of these themes is divided into two, firstly principles of molecular-kinetic theory (34) - Brownian motion, mass and dimensions of molecules, the basic equation of molecular-kinetic theory for an ideal gas, Mendeleev and Clapeyron's equation, saturated and unsaturated vapours, air humidity, surface tension in liquids, capillary action; properties of solid materials. Principles of thermodynamics (10) deals with the first law and its application, the irreversibility of thermal processes, the principle underlying thermal engines and their use in the economy. Electrodynamics is divided into four; firstly, the electric field (20): the law of conservation of electric charge, Coulomb's law, Joffe and Millikan's experiment; potential difference, voltage, electrical capacity, the capacitor, insulators in an electrical field, the dielectric constant. Secondly, direct-current laws (11): electromotive force, Ohm's law for a closed circuit, joining conductors in series and in parallel. The third section in the study of electrodynamics is magnetic field (12): magnetic induction, current, Ampere's force, the work of Lorentz, how electrical measuring instruments work; ferromagnets, the magnetic recording of information. Finally, electric current in various media (18): conductivity in metals, semi-conductors - intrinsic and extrinsic conductivity, practical applications of semi-conductors, electronic emission, current in electrolytes, the concept of plasma. Excursions (2), laboratory practice (10), consolidation (1).

Class 11 continues with electrodynamics (63): electromagnetic induction (9) - Faraday's law and Lentz's law, the electromagnetic microphone, self-induction, inductance; electromagnetic oscillations (18) of various types (free, harmonic and attenuated), oscillatory circuits, forced electrical oscillations, the AC generator; reactance, capacitative and inductive resistance, the transformer; transmission of energy and its application in industry and agriculture; Lenin's ideas for the electrification of the country, prospects for the development of the Soviet electrical energy industry. Finally, pupils study electromagnetic waves (36): their properties, their speed of propagation, intensity; the invention of radio by A. S. Popov, principles of radio transmission, radiolocation, television, the development of media of communication in the USSR; the speed of light, Huygens's principle, reflection and refraction, coherence, interference of light and its application in technology, diffraction, dispersion and polarization of light; electromagnetic radiation of various wavelengths - radio waves, intra-red, ultra-violet, visible and X-ray radiation; applications of these.

The course finishes with 37 lessons on quantum physics: light quanta and light action (12) - photoelectric effect and laws governing it, the photon, Compton effect, light pressure, Lebedev's experiments, the chemical effect of light and its application; the atom and its nucleus (25) - Rutherford's experiment, the nuclear model of the atom, Bohr's postulate, wave-particle duality, emission and absorption of light by the atom, continuous and line spectra, the laser; the structure of the nucleus, the binding energy of atomic nuclei, energy output of nuclear reactions, radioactivity, detection, measurement, biological effects of and protection from radiation; splitting an atom of uranium, chain reactions, prospects for the nuclear power industry; particles and anti-particles and their properties.

After all this, follow "generalizing studies" (4: including talks entitled "the modern scientific picture of the world" and "physics and the technological revolution") and further revision of the whole course (15).

Assessment

Since all pupils are likely to face formal assessment in a physics examination at the end of the school course, the "norms of assessment" are of importance to them. They do not differ in principle from the standards expected in other scientific subjects, so the norms given here can be taken by the reader as typical for biology and chemistry too. Pupils are assessed under two headings, "oral answer and test" and "laboratory work". For the former, a mark of 5 is awarded if the pupil displays correct understanding of the physical essence of the phenomena, principles, laws and theories and can give a clear and accurate exposition of them, if drawings, maps and graphs are correctly and appropriately executed, if the answer is planned independently and good illustrations chosen, and if the pupil shows understanding of links with other parts of the course. To be marked at 4, the same qualities must be present, but the pupil may show lesser ability to plan, make links, choose examples or apply knowledge in new situations. Three is awarded if the answers are still basically sound, but certain gaps are apparent; the pupil must be able to solve problems using ready-made formulae, but may have difficulty in adapting a formula to solve less obvious problems. Failing grades are given if the pupil "does not possess the skills and knowledge which correspond with the requirements of the course".

The "tickets" published in early 1987 for the final e aminations at age 17 number twenty-five. There are three q'estions on each, the third of which is always a problem (which the teacher will have to set and which is not known in advance by the examinees) or a practical laboratory exercise - usually carrying out a measurement of some sort (density, resistance, coefficient of s''rf⁼ce ten ion). Here are three examples of examination tickets in physics.

A

1. Newton's first law. Inertial systems of obtaining a reading.
2. Chain reaction of the uranium nucleus. Thermonuclear reaction.
3. Problem on the application of Ohm's law for a complete circuit with conductors linked in parallel and in series.

B

1. Electrical current in a vacuum. Thermoelectric emission and its use.
2. Laws governing the reflection and refraction of light. Total internal reflection.
3. Laboratory work: obtaining the modules of elasticity of rubber.

C

1. Radar and its use.
2. Mechanical work and power. The efficiency of simple mechanisms (exemplified by an inclined plane).
3. A problem on determining trajectory and translational motion.

In practical work, for 5 the pupil must carry out experiments and take readings completely, in logical order, setting up apparatus him- or herself, ensuring that correct readings will ensue, observing safety procedures, presenting all notes, drawings, graphs, figures, and calculations neatly and accurately and carrying out error analysis without mistakes. Pupils will receive 4 if they meet these same requirements, but have made some mistakes or omissions; 3 if the result is near enough to allow reasonably correct deductions to be made but a number of mistakes were made in the course of the experiment. Failing grades are given if the results do not allow correct deductions to be made. As with all assessment criteria described in this book, it is obvious that a good deal of scope is left for the discretion of the teacher or the examining commission.

Good Practice in the Physics Lesson

The qualities expected of an excellent teacher of physics are indicated by a recent press article devoted to the work of E.

I. Afrina. She teaches children to read passages aloud with appropriate expression, showing them how to seek relevant information for the answers to questions. She stresses independent activity and gives little direct information. For experimental work her class is divided into ability groups, and graded experiments are given according to the prowess of the group. Homework consists of experimental work which requires no more equipment than any home possesses; it has an investigative flavour through which children learn the essence of scientific inquiry. She does not neglect the historical and human side of science; pupils read about the lives of scientists in antiquity and in the recent past, learning to summarise what they read and to express the ideas in modern terms. She works closely with the mathematics and sociology teachers, holding discussions of such questions as: "Give examples of the interrelationship of the laws of the dialectic from physical phenomena" or "Substantiate or refute the notion that there can be no conflict of opposites in inanimate nature, and that they occur only in animate nature and human society".

In senior classes Afrina uses "conferences and seminars" in which problems are discussed such as "Is the special theory of relativity appropriately named? Does the title reflect the essence of the theory?... How does Newton´s conception of space and time differ from Einstein´s?..." She encourages private study by making the physics laboratory available for the viewing of films and by providing supplementary material for each topic in the course.

The message is clear: a good teacher is a scholar, she is a thorough planner, she develops pupils´ cognitive abilities rather than drilling them by rote, she is inventive, relies on practical activities, uses audio-visual aids, instils a dialectical-materialist world-view, encourages inter-subject links, she provides extra materials and adapts lessons to the ability of the pupils. The lady in question is obviously outstanding; nevertheless, the portrait shows what the best physics teachers are meant to be like.

Other sources confirm the importance attached to independent work. Under the new syllabus, pupils in the two senior classes do as many as 300 problems independently; under the old dispensation it was at most half of this. Priorities now include teaching children about the "electronicization" of society. Polytechnical links are achieved in two ways: by establishing inter-subject links with labour training (thus pupils training for certain professional profiles are made aware of the physical basis for the techniques they use), and by organizing visits to factories.

ASTRONOMY

The one weekly lesson in class 11 is intended as a finishing touch to the education in physics and mathematics of school leavers. Five aims are stated. The first is to pass on a contemporary view of the universe, the second is to explain the practical uses of astronomy, the third to facilitate the development of dialectical-materialist attitudes and describe the evolution both of concepts of the structure of the universe and of the conflict of science with religion. The fourth aim is to present the significance of astronomy for the acceleration of technological and scientific progress, and the fifth is to develop Soviet patriotism and proletarian internationalism by studying Soviet success in astronautics and the development of international cooperation in the field. The anti-religious aim receives particular emphasis in the most recent variant of the syllabus.

Rationale of the Course Content

It is frequently noted in connection with science education that children should be told that there is no limit to the knowledge which human beings can gain about the natural world. In the introduction to the latest astronomy syllabus human ability to transform the environment too is described as "boundless". The new syllabus contains more about astrophysics than the old: it "reflects the current situation in the science". A new feature of the latest syllabus and accompanying advice to teachers is a particular stress on photodocumentation, educational films and visual aids generally. On teaching method, apart from "frontal" instruction, visits to a planetarium for lectures are highly recommended, and observation with telescopes and the naked eye are provided for. Educators are acutely conscious that, in a subject like astronomy which deals with processes which go on for almost inconceivable periods of time, what a child can do on a few occasions with a school telescope is limited; nevertheless, these observations are not optional and their value to the pupil is neither under- nor over-estimated.

The syllabus published early in 1986 contains seven themes. After an introduction setting the subject in perspective (its relationship with other sciences and with the economy, its dialectical-materialist significance) and outlining general notions of the structure of the universe, the themes are: I - practical principles of astronomy (5 lessons). This covers: apparent movement of celestial bodies as the consequence of their actual movement in space, the Earth and its rotation round the Sun, celestial coordinates, the stellar map, magnitude of a star, the elevation of a body at culmination, the ecliptic, phases of the Moon, lunar and solar eclipses. II -

Movement of celestial bodies (5): Copernicus and the heliocentric system as a revolution in science and philosophy; the scale and structure of the solar system; measuring distances to celestial bodies; Kepler's laws. III - The methodology of astrophysical research (3): the measurement of electro-magnetic radiation as the basis of modern all-wave astronomy; telescopes and radio-telescopes; observation from outer space - the discovery of the physical characteristics and velocities of celestial bodies by their spectra.

IV - The physical nature of bodies in the solar system (5): the common ancestry of the solar system, the relationship between the Earth and the Moon, planets, satellites and rings, smaller bodies, meteorites; modern explanations of the origin of the solar system; achievements of the USSR in the peaceful conquest of space; applications of cosmic discoveries in the economy. V - Stars and the Sun (7): stars as the fundamental bodies in the universe, measuring distances, annual parallax, binary stars; the temperature, brilliance, radius, and mass of stars, their interdependence; the laws of Wien, Stefan and Boltzmann; sources of stellar energy; variable and unstable stars; the evolution and final state of stars; white dwarfs, neutron stars, black holes; the Sun as our nearest star: spots, flares, protuberances, the role of the Sun's magnetic fields, radio emission and corpuscular radiation of the Sun.

VI - The structure and evolution of the universe (7), seen as a manifestation of the physical laws of a material order. This topic embraces the constitution of the galaxy, its rotation, the activity of the nucleus of the galaxy, the large-scale structure of the universe, and the philosophical implications of all this. VII - a lecture on "contemporary achievements and the role of astronomy today".

Observations prescribed (for the naked eye) are to find and identify the planets, some of the brighter stars and more prominent constellations with the help of astronomical maps, to estimate the geographical latitude of the place of observation by the Pole Star, to observe the phases of the Moon, the revolution of the earth as reflected in the position of the stars and the variety in brightness and colour of the stars. With a telescope pupils are to observe the surface of the Moon, the rotation of the Sun, sunspots and flares, the phases of Venus, the rings of Saturn, Mars, Jupiter and its satellites, binary stars, the Milky Way, star clusters, nebulae and galaxies.

Teaching Aids. Six films are available to accompany the course: on the solar system, the Moon, the Sun, the structure of the universe, "astronomy and world-view", and the origins and development of celestial bodies. There are also six shorter film clips. Fourteen items of essential equipment are listed. These include charts, maps and tables, models of celestial bodies, globes, an orrery and the like, and the list also includes binoculars, refracting telescopes tellurions and spectroscopes.

Assessment. The instructions for testing pupils state that the main method is to be oral answers and practical work with a moving star chart. Formal written tests may not be given more often than once in six months, though written work may be used for day-to-day informal tests; these, however, should not involve extended answers and should contain straightforward calculations only.

CHEMISTRY

The last of the major science subjects to be introduced is chemistry, which is taught from classes 8 to 11. Soviet educationists believe that a scientific picture of the modern world, both in theory and in its application in daily life, is impossible without a knowledge of chemistry.

Aims

The usual moral and ideological aims are stated for the subject and tedium will be avoided here by not repeating them again. The academic purposes of teaching chemistry are given as: communicating the basis of the science; acquainting pupils with the practical applications of chemistry in industry, its role in the economy and the nature of the chemical worker´s job; fostering a conservationist attitude to natural resources and socialist property; developing the ability to analyse, explain and compare chemical phenomena, to understand cause and effect, to make generalizations, expound material studied logically and to acquire and apply knowledge independently; enabling pupils to carry out chemical procedures and experiments, to make observations and present accurate results, to organize work independently and use reference literature.

Rationale of the Course Structure and Content

In a recent publication for UNESCO Soviet science educators discussed the content of the school chemistry course (but, despite the recent date of the publication, not the most recent version of the syllabus). They stated that there are two basic systems of knowledge involved in the discipline of chemistry, namely substances and processes: on which of these should the main emphasis be in school teaching? Their answer is that it is self-evident that study of substances should have priority, for without a knowledge of substances, processes appear meaningless. Secondly, teaching of substances is easier to structure pedagogically. Thirdly, the study of substances is a sound way of presenting the necessary knowledge concerning processes anyway; fourthly, the traditional study of inorganic and organic chemistry is an excellent means of acquainting pupils with the applications, particularly industrial applications, of chemistry. (The term "physical chemistry" is not used in the Soviet syllabus.) It must be left to experts on chemistry teaching to decide for themselves whether the authors of the UNESCO document have been overtaken by the newest syllabus, which does in fact claim to pay a good deal of attention to processes.

Despite the emergence of several new branches of the subject - biochemistry, radiochemistry, geochemistry, etc. - educators maintain that, for the school child, study of substances and processes forms a basis for fundamental comprehension of all those other chemistries, and that this avoids danger of fragmentation and superficiality. In support of this attitude they quote the theoretical work of Dmitriy Mendeleev (1834-1907), whose name appears frequently in studies of chemical education and the school syllabus.

Structure of the Course

A fairly strict distinction is made between inorganic and organic chemistry within the school syllabus, but there has been a change recently in the way instruction in these two branches is spread over the four years available for study. Previously the period allocation was 2 + 2 + 3 + 3; inorganic chemistry was taught for three years, organic for one. Now that the allocation is 3 + 2.5 + 2 + 2, the first two years go on inorganic, the next year and a third on organic and the final two thirds on revision, consolidation and enrichment.

The linchpin of the course is molecular theory and the periodic system of Mendeleev. Next in importance comes electrolytic dissociation and the basic features of chemical reactions. Organic chemistry is based upon the theory of chemical structure, and extended by the electronic treatment of various forms of chemical bonding; attention is paid to the spatial structure of molecules. Finally, theory is related to practice in a study of the role of chemistry in achieving industrial and economic objectives.

This structure goes back to the early 1930s, but in view of some fairly significant revisions of the syllabus over the years chemical educators claim to be reasonably satisfied with the course. The latest re-jigging is fairly significant at least in the last two years of schooling, and it remains to be seen how pleased they will be with the new arrangements.

New Features of the Latest Syllabus

Proponents of the latest syllabus claim that material is now more accessible to the mass of pupils in the early stages. There has been controversy between those who sought to introduce more theory earlier in the course and others who take more cognisance of the pupils' stage of development. Even though more weekly periods than before are allocated in the first two years, the temptation to follow the tendency towards early introduction of theory has been avoided. The theoretical-ideological content of the last two years has been strengthened; then, it is said, pupils´ knowledge of other subjects can be built upon.

Features conserved from earlier syllabuses include the concentration upon substances familiar to pupils and likely to be used by them in their daily life and eventual workplaces, and its practical orientation: more experiments are recommended in the latest syllabus. As for *razgruzka*, the reduction in syllabus overloading, some over-complicated material has been cut. For example, five items (not whole topics, but matters formerly covered within main sections of the course) go from class 8, sixteen from class 9 - despite the increase in lessons in these years. Further topics are now merely to be touched upon rather than taught thoroughly. Important concepts are now more skilfully dispersed about the course so that children have a better chance of picking them up gradually. To ensure that pupils appreciate the importance of periodic laws, the structure of the atom and chemical bonding, the topics are met three times in the course.

Syllabus Content

The topics covered are listed below with numbers of lessons noted in brackets. The syllabus gives rather more detail than it has been possible to present here; chemistry teachers reading this should be able to fill obvious gaps. Exhaustive lists of experiments and demonstrations are also printed in the syllabus, but have been omitted here, though some indication of their scope will be given later. Class 8 - Topic 1: elementary chemical concepts (24): matter, molecules, reactions and the conditions in which they occur; atoms, molecular and non-molecular substances; elements and their symbols; relative atomic mass; the mole as a unit of quantity; Avogadro number; molar mass; the law of constant composition; formulae; valency. Atomic theory and the part played by Lomonosov and Dalton in its formulation. Law of the conservation of matter; chemical equations; types of reaction. Topic 2: Oxygen, oxides and combustion (10): symbol, valency, relative atomic mass of oxygen, its presence in nature, physical and chemical properties, interaction with phosphorus, carbon, sulphur and iron; oxides. Calculations using chemical formulae. The oxygen cycle; combustion; exo- and endothermic reactions; conservation and transfer of energy in reactions. Fuel types in the nation´s economy and their rational use; prevention of atmospheric pollution and Soviet law on conservation.

Topic 3: hydrogen, acids, salts (11). Obtaining hydrogen in the laboratory, physical and chemical properties; reversible and irreversible reactions; use of hydrogen as an ecologically pure fuel and raw material for chemical industry. The molar volume and relative density of gases. Acids, their general characteristics, interactions with metals and oxides; concept of displacement series; exchange reactions. Salts - composition, names and formulae composed on a basis of their valency. Topic 4: water, solutions, bases (14). The importance of water and solutions in life, prevention of pollution; purification; molar concentration of solutions. Composition of water, chemical properties, reaction with sodium, calcium, iron and some oxides. Bases; the hydroxide group, alkalies and insoluble bases, reactions with acids; neutralization; effect of alkalies on non-metallic oxides; decomposition of insoluble bases subject to heat. Topic 5: revision (6).

Topic 6 is Mendeleev's periodic law and system of chemical elements; the structure of the atom (15): the classification of elements, metals, non-metals; oxides and hydroxides showing amphoteric properties; concept of groups of like elements. Atomic number; periodic dependence on the charge of the nucleus; protons and neutrons; isotopes. Distribution of electrons in atoms of elements of the first four periods; groups and sub-groups; characteristics of elements of the main sub-groups on the basis of their position in the periodic system and the structure of the atom. Significance of the periodic law for understanding of the universe and the development of technology; Mendeleev - patriot, citizen, scholar. Topic 7: chemical bond; the structure of matter (8): covalent bond, polar and non-polar; electronegativity; ionic bond; degree of oxidation. Ionic, atomic and molecular crystal lattice. Topic 8: halogens (10): position in periodic system; atomic structure; structure of simple substances. Chlorine: properties, reactions with metals, hydrogen, water; redox reactions; obtaining hydrogen chloride, its properties; Avogadro's law; hydrochloric acid and its use. Comparison of the ability of the halogens (fluorine, chlorine, bromine, iodine) to form oxides, identification of chlorides, bromides, iodides. The use of halogens.

Class 9 begins with revision (2). Topic 1: electrolytic dissociation (13): of substances with ionic and polar covalent bond; of acids, alkalies and salts; degree of dissociation, strong and weak electrolytes; ionic substitution. Properties of acids, bases, amphoteric hydroxides, and salts in the light of electrolytic dissociation and redox processes; concept of the hydrolysis of salts. Topic 2: oxygen subgroup (7): position of these elements in the periodic system, structure of their atoms, concept of allotropy. Sulphur: its properties, reactions, presence in nature; sulphuric acid and its use in industry, sulphate ion reactions. Topic 3: basic regularities of chemical reactions; production of sulphuric acid (6): the speed of chemical reaction, its dependence on natural conditions, area of contact, concentration of substances involved, temperature and presence of a catalyst. Chemical equilibrium.

The reactions concerned in the production of sulphuric acid; automatization of the process, jobs of workers involved, concerns relating to efficiency and conservation. Topic 4: nitrogen subgroup (19): nitrogen - properties, reactions. Ammonia; formation of ammonium ion; ammonium salts; reactions; their use in industry and relevant workers´ jobs. Nitric acid, reaction of dilute and concentrated acid with copper; nitrogen cycle in nature; use of nitric acid and salts in industry; chemical reactions involved in production of nitric acid. Phosphorus. Fertilizers, simple and complex; their rational use and conservation; ecological issues; development of mineral fertilizer production in USSR, the role of chemistry in agricultural production.

Topic 5: carbon subgroup (7). Carbon; allotropy of carbon; adsorption; properties. Carbon monoxide and dioxide: properties and reactions; carbonic acid; carbonates; the cycle of carbon in nature. Silicon; silicon(IV) oxide; silicic acid; silicon compounds in nature; glass, cement, concrete and ferro-concrete. Topic 6: general characteristics of metals (7): their properties, electrochemical series of metals; electrolysis and its application in obtaining metals, hydrogen, chlorine and alkalies. Alloys. Chemical and electrochemical corrosion; protection of metals. Topic 7: metals of the main subgroups I-III in the periodic system (8): their general characteristics. Magnesium and calcium and their compounds; their uses; transformation of calcium carbonate in nature. Hardness of water and its removal. Aluminium; its amphoteric oxide; use of the metal and its alloys.

Topic 8: iron (4): its oxides, hydroxides and salts(II and III). Naturally occurring compounds of iron; the uses of alloys and compounds. Topic 9: metallurgy (4): metals in modern technology; how they are obtained industrially; production of cast-iron in blast-furnaces; production of steel, aluminium; ecological issues in metal production; development of Soviet metallurgical industries and their importance for the development of other branches of industry. The final topic is consolidation of the inorganic course (6).

Class 10 begins with three more lessons of revision of the inorganic course. Topic 1: theory of the chemical structure of organic compounds; the electronic nature of chemical bonds (5). Basic propositions of Butlerov´s theory of chemical structure; the interaction of atoms and molecules; dependence of a substance´s properties upon the structure of the molecules; isomerism; the significance of the theory of chemical structure and its development. The state of electrons in atoms of short periods, s- and p-electrons; forms of electronic clouds; formation and separation of covalent bonds (ionic and radical); energy and direction of a bond. Topic 2: saturated hydrocarbons (7): methane, its structural formula, tetrahedral structure of its molecule, the character of its bonds, sp^3-hybridization. Homologous series of methane, physical properties of homologues. Spatial structure and chemical properties of saturated hydrocarbons; systematic nomenclature; combustion, chlorination, thermal decomposition, isomerism; obtaining synthesis gas and hydrogen from methane. Cycloparaffins.

Topic 3: unsaturated hydrocarbons (9): ethylene, its formula, double bond, sigma and pi bonds, sp^2-hybridization, homologous series. Isomerism of the carbon skeleton. Geometric isomerism; chemical properties of ethylenic hydrocarbons: combustion, combination with hydrogen, halogens, hydrohalogens, water; oxidation, polymerization; Markovnikov´s rule. Production of hydrocarbons by dehydration. Uses of ethylenic hydrocarbons. Dienes; structure and properties of hydrocarbons with conjugate double bonds; natural rubber. Acetylene: triple bond, sp-hybridization; homologous series, properties, applications; obtaining it by carbide method and from methane. Topic 4: aromatic hydrocarbons (5) - benzene (structure, properties, etc. as for other substances above), various reactions. Obtaining benzene; the concept of toxic chemicals, their use in agriculture and ecological consequences. Homologues of benzene; the mutual effect of atoms - toluene. The relationship of saturated, unsaturated and aromatic hydrocarbons. Topic 5: natural sources of hydrocarbons and their refinement (4) - petroleum gases, their uses. Oil, structure and properties; fractional distillation; cracking; aromatization of petroleum products; ecological issues. Coking of coal. Uses in the economy of hydrocarbon material. Problem of obtaining liquid fuel from coal. Contribution of chemistry to the success of the energy programme of the USSR.

Topic 6: alcohols and phenols (7) - structure of saturated monohydric alcohols; the functional group and its electronic structure; hydrogen bond and its effects on alcohols; isomerism of the carbon skeleton. Nomenclature of alcohols. Properties; combustion, interactions with alkali metals and halogen hydrides; dehydration. Uses of methyl and ethyl alcohols; their toxicity and harmful affect on human organism. Industrial synthesis of ethanol and methanol. The link between hydrocarbons and alcohols. Polyhydric alcohols. Phenols; structure, etc. (as before); uses; protection of environment from industrial effluents. Topic 7: Aldehydes and carbonic acids (9) - homologous series of aldehydes, properties (etc.) Carbonyl group. Use of formaldehyde and acetaldehyde; obtaining them by oxidation of alcohols; obtaining acetaldehyde by hydration of acetylene and the catalytic oxidation of ethylene. Homologous series of saturated monobasic acids; carboxylic group - properties, reactions, etc. Formic, acetic, palmitic and stearic acid; soaps as salts of higher carboxylic acids; production of acids and use in the economy. Acrylic and oleic acids as examples of unsaturated acids. The link between hydrocarbons, alcohols, aldehydes and acids.

Topic 8: Esters and fats (5) - structure, hydrolysis and

Plate 1. Six-year-olds learning to read in a kindergarten. The lesson is referred to on p. 177.

Plate 2. Seven-year-olds viewed from the teacher's desk. The display boards at the back are headed ''Our homeland'' and ''Learn to learn''.

Plate 3. Senior pupils in an advanced mathematics class. They are working independently while one of their number is tested at the board. The quotation is from Leonardo da Vinci: "No human discovery can be called true until it has gone through mathematical proof".

Plates 4, 5. Labour training: boys at their benches in the workshop while girls are in the domestic science room next door.

Plate 6. Vocational training. Senior boys and girls learn to make slippers in a UPK, using an assembly line taken from a nearby factory.

Plate 7. One aspect of "Vospitanie": children demonstrate for nature conservation. "Don't harm the birds!" says one banner.

uses of esters, esterification and its reversibility. Fats in nature, their properties; processing of food fats in the organism; hydrolysis of fats in technology; problem of the substitution of natural by synthetic fats. Detergents, their significance and ecological problems. Topic 9: carbohydrates (10) - glucose as a hexose; properties; structure as an aldehyde alcohol; reactions, reduction, fermentation; uses. Ribose and deoxy-ribose as pentoses. Sucrose: properties, where found; formation of saccharides; hydrolysis. Starch: properties, etc., conversion in digestive system. Cellulose: structure, etc.; artificial fibres, e.g. acetate fibre.

Class 11 continues organic chemistry for 23 lessons. Topic 10: amines and amino acids, heterocyclic compounds containing amines (6) - amines: structure, etc.; amines as organic bases; aniline, its production from nitro-benzene and uses. Amino acids: structure, properties, etc., combination with carboxylic group; isomerism; alpha-amino-acids; synthesis and structure of peptides. The concept of heterocyclic compounds containing amines; pyridine and pyrrole; purine and pyrimidine bases as nucleic acids. Topic 11: proteins and nucleic acids (4) - proteins of substances of high molecular weight; primary, secondary and tertiary structure of proteins; properties: hydrolysis, denaturation, colour reactions; conversion in digestive system; success in synthesis of proteins; role of microbiology in Soviet economy. Nucleic acids; structure of nucleotides; principle of complementarity in constructing the double spiral of DNA; role of nucleic acids in the vital activity of organisms.

Topic 12: synthetic high molecular substances and polymer materials based on them (8) - monomer, polymer, structural link, degree of polymerization, mean molecular mass; methods of synthesising such substances: polymerization, polycondensation. Linear, branching and spatial structure of polymers; non-crystalline and crystalline construction. Thermoplastic and thermosetting polymers: polyethylene, polypropylene, polyvinyl chloride, polystyrene, polymethylmethacrylate, phenolformaldehyde resins, their structure, properties and use; saturated plastics. Problems of synthesizing rubber; types, properties and use of the wide variety of synthetic rubbers available; stereospecific rubbers. Synthetic textiles; polyester and polyamide textiles. Prospects for the development of polymeric materials. Topic 13: consolidation of the organic course (5).

The remaining 43 lessons are devoted to consolidation and extension of the whole chemistry syllabus. An overview is given of the chemical laws and theories studied, information about substances, processes and production methods is generalized at a level corresponding to that reached in theoretical work by the end of the chemistry course. Knowledge about chemical industry is "systematized". The culmination of the course consists in the presentation of the place of chemistry among the natural sciences, its importance for building up a scientific picture of the world, its significance for the development of the national economy and the solution of problems in production and energy programmes.

Assessment

"Requirements" for pupils are formulated and assessment is carried out under four headings: the assimilation of theoretical material, chemical language, performing experiments and solving problems. "Recommendations for testing and assessment" are related to these four requirements, and the application of the five-point scale resembles very closely the system described in relation to physics; it will therefore not be repeated here. However, a number of criteria are stated in order that teachers should be able to assess pupils' performance, especially in oral answers to examination questions. These are depth (corresponding with the theoretical generalizations studied), conscious understanding (ability to apply the information received) and completeness (in regard to syllabus content).

Recommended Teaching Methods

Again, many of the new approaches mentioned in relation to the other sciences are recommended to chemistry teachers, and they will not be reiterated here. A particular point is made of the advantages of an historical approach: an account of the "struggle of ideas". As noted in connection with some other science subjects, it is suggested that stress be placed on the achievements of scientists - which some studies in the West too have found may improve pupils' attitudes to the subject. Chemistry educators believe that children should be encouraged to understand the value of knowledge and how it has been fought for. Chemistry teaching methods should be active and pupils involved in independent work. Excursions are included in this category of "independent" work, and a feature peculiar to the chemistry syllabus is that suggestions are made as to how children can take an active role and show initiative when visiting professionals at their place of work. Much of this will not surprise British teachers accustomed to project work, but it is fairly new in Soviet education.

The syllabus for each topic lists demonstrations, experiments and "practical activities". For example, under the very first topic in class 8, there are 7 demonstration experiments, 7 laboratory experiments and a number of practical activities related mainly to the correct use of apparatus, safety rules and the like. By the eleventh class the number of teacher demonstrations far outweighs the laboratory experiments and practical activities, which in some topics seem to disappear altogether.

Chapter 8

ARTS EDUCATION

APPRECIATION OF beauty, particularly in the arts, figures
prominently among the characteristics of a communist personality. It is, moreover, seen as a desirable feature of an
efficient worker in any field. The 1984 "Guidelines" speak of
Party policy "to stimulate the creative activity of people"
and state, "Our young people... should have... a conscientious, creative approach to work". It is the duty of arts
education to give them this "creativity" and creative approach. The "Guidelines" devote a substantial paragraph to
aesthetic and artistic education:

> It is very important considerably to improve the artis-
> tic and aesthetic education of pupils. It is essential
> to develop a sense of the beautiful, to form good aes-
> thetic taste and the ability to understand and app-
> reciate works of art, historical and architectural monu-
> ments, and the natural beauty and wealth of one's own
> country. Better use must be made of every school sub-
> ject for this purpose... More teachers must be
> trained... The professional creative unions and all
> cultural institutions must help in this work... Every-
> where the work of amateur theatrical circles must be
> improved or started and constant attention paid to their
> repertoires. It is imperative to erect a reliable bar-
> rier to ideologically worthless, cheap and banal works
> that might reach young people.

In all subjects, then, the development of creative powers is
to be encouraged. In arts education, good taste must be
taught as a defence against artistic pollution, including
corruption from abroad. Pupils should learn to appreciate the
cultural heritage and the natural beauty of their country.
Agencies outside the schools are to be enrolled in the cause
of aesthetic education, most of whom in other countries would
see it as no part of their job to take orders from any educational authority. And moreover the moral and ideological

implications of aesthetic education are integral to the whole spirit of such work.

There is, however, a pitfall which it may prove difficult to avoid. While formalism in instruction is to be eliminated, resource-based learning and independent thinking encouraged and dogmatism avoided, *correct* political, moral and ideological attitudes must nevertheless be fostered. It will not be easy for teachers to solve this problem, but the perhaps optimistic Soviet view would be that, if indeed there is a conflict, it has a methodological root; by getting at that any apparent contradictions can be resolved.

Justification for Arts Education

In Chapter 2 we saw that the arts were at least holding their own in the Soviet curriculum, despite fears about an apparent loss of literature teaching. Even if some parents doubt it, in the official view the arts are not a "frill", but a fundamental part of the education of all children. They have a political and moral function which is held to be of the greatest importance, but it would be quite wrong to give the impression that the inclusion of the arts in the curriculum is purely political or pragmatic. Educational theorists clearly desire that children should be brought face to face with artistic experience in schools. The political arguments often serve this end. A recent important book on aesthetic education concluded that teachers will have failed if their pupils do not show motivation to pursue the arts for themselves after they have left school.

Soviet arts educators are firmly convinced that it is a prime duty of teachers to pass on to children the cultural heritage as currently valued by the adult world. The notion that children should not be introduced to the works of Mozart, Shakespeare or Leonardo on the grounds that the great artists of the past are irrelevant to them or "form no part of their culture" has not been heard in the Soviet Union for at least sixty years. The value of "realised form" in the arts, such as theatre plays, is not doubted. Musical, dramatic and literary performances, and exhibitions of children's painting are all commonly practised in schools. On the other hand, really adventurous projects, such as recent developments in creative music education in Britain, are lacking in the Soviet Union. A discussion of the differing concepts of "creativity" will be found in the section below on music.

What may be termed psychological justifications are used for arts education. Educationists write of children's and adolescents' "spiritual" needs and the sense of fulfilment they obtain when they come into contact with the arts. The word "spiritual" *(dukhovnyy)* here has no religious connotation, needless to say, but refers to aesthetic, affective and moral qualities; "needs" are seen not only as to be satisfied,

but to be stimulated by arts education. The need to be creative is recognised in all young people, and the duty of
schools to develop creative impulses and encourage pupils to
use their imagination is stressed. Development of the imagination, it is pointed out, has practical application, and
children should be encouraged in school to see its relevance
in, for example, scientific enquiry. "Creative activity", it
is also argued, is equally applicable in the world of work.

The Role of the Arts in Soviet Society

In the Soviet Union the arts have been harnessed in the
interests of "progressive" activity: they are to serve socialist society and help in the building of communism. They are
subject to the tenets of "Socialist Realism", the theory of
which was first propounded in the 1930s and which is principally attributed to Maxim Gorky. The criteria are that writing, painting and musical compositions must conform to the
three notions of *narodnost', partiynost', ideynost'*. *Narodnost'* means that an art object must represent the interests
of the people *(narod)*, *partiynost'* that it must further the
cause of the Party, and *ideynost'* that it must have sound
ideological content. It is hard sometimes to decide whether a
given literary work conforms; it is much harder in relation to
music.   In recent years there have been many well publicised
cases of writers who have suffered for publishing unsuitable
works and painters whose pictures have been confiscated. Composers too have often failed to satisfy the demands of society
even with purely instrumental music. They have been castigated for "formalism" - too great an interest in radical experiment; "subjectivism" - the suspicion that the music is expressing too personal a feeling rather than the collective
spirit; "pessimism" - failure to express positive aspirations
towards a bright future; "apolitical" content - refusal to
entertain socio-political aims.
    Soviet theorists deny the possibility of "pure" art. For
them, art is tendentious: perceiving it is not only a matter
of the experiencing of beauty, but a means to the formation of
ideas and to the choice of a specific attitude to life.

MUSIC EDUCATION

It is music which perhaps best of all exemplifies the new
spirit abroad in Soviet education. As recently as 1978 the
official syllabus strongly emphasised sight singing, musical
literacy and basic skills. While not excluding emotional
response, it uncompromisingly declared: "The children must
understand the practical necessity for musical literacy." But
an irresistible enthusiast, the composer Dmitriy Kabalevsky
(1904-1987), swept through the world of Soviet music teaching,

determined not merely to instruct children in techniques of singing or reading staff notation, but to enthuse them with a love of music. The resultant ructions are still echoing from the corridors of the Academy of Pedagogical Sciences to class-rooms in remote Siberia and Central Asia.

Current Problems

This is not to say that school music teaching in the USSR is without difficulties relating to material provision, supply of teachers or hostility and indifference from parents and even other teachers - so much at least is reported by correspond-ents to the educational press. Because of this, not every Soviet school is able to mount music lessons. Not enough teachers are trained. Parents of seven-year-olds, it is said, sometimes question why little Tanya or Serezha should have to do music in school at all, since "they have no aptitude for it". Would they say this about physics or history? musicians ask angrily. Nevertheless, we must not forget that the ser-iousness of official support for music is a very strong weapon in the fight for the cause, and Soviet teachers and heads are not free to neglect any area of the curriculum. However, music for all figures for only two forty-five minute lessons per week in the first year and one in each of the next six (under the new curricular arrangements described in this book), though it may be available as an option after that.

Kabalevsky and the New Syllabus

Kabalevsky was a prominent political figure - a member of the Supreme Soviet and holder of the Order of Lenin for his work in education. Until the day of his death in February 1987 he was a tireless publicist for the cause of music, author of several books, pamphlets and articles, composer of much music specially intended for children (adapting an aphorism of Maxim Gorky he stated that it has to be "like music for adults, only better"), and a broadcaster and maker of gramophone records about music education. He and his colleague E. B. Abdullin began trying out the new system in 1973 by teaching children themselves as they constructed it.

Kabalevsky valued many types of music: classical and modern, jazz, light music and folk. He was severely critical of avant-garde and way-out experimental music and abominated the second-rate, which is purveyed purely as a means of com-mercial exploitation (even, apparently, in the USSR). He had no time for people who want only easy listening: "spiritual beggary" is a real problem for music education.

Kabalevsky did not wish to put music education into a compartment of its own, believing strongly that teachers of one of the arts should feel able to talk to children about the others. He wanted teachers of all subjects to know what goes on in music lessons and why. He believed that composers should see it as a special duty to write music for young children, he believed strongly in the beneficial moral effects of music, and he wished to make it accessible to every child.

Kabalevsky opens the introduction to his syllabus for classes 1 to 3 by expressing the deep dissatisfaction with the earlier music syllabus felt by parents, teachers and pupils. The aim of the new syllabus is to develop musical culture in children as a part of their entire "spiritual culture". He rejects the traditionalist view that singing should remain the basic form of music education; music should be allowed to fulfil its aesthetic, cognitive and moral role in education. Motivation is a greater problem than teaching: pupils must be interested in music as a living art-form.

In 1979 Kabalevsky said: "I compiled the new syllabus as if I were writing a massive symphonic composition." The new scheme is based on musical "perception", which is seen as something much more than mere intelligent listening - for which it has been mistaken by some Soviet pedagogues. The ultimate aim is to develop mature musical thinking, or what the psychologist B. M. Teplov has called "musicality" - the ability "to experience music as content". Perception is developed by engaging in listening, performing and compositional activities. The first step is that children are taught to recognise three types of composition: march, dance and song. These are likened to the three whales on which in Slavonic mythology the world was supported, and recognition of march-like, dance-like and song-like style is children's way in to musical understanding. The three "whales" are the most widely known and "democratic" genres in music, and ones with which children all have some acquaintance before they ever enter school; teaching is therefore based on what is already familiar to them. Here Kabalevsky argued in a way which was unusually "child-centred" for a Soviet pedagogue. This basic understanding of the three "whales" is extended into much deeper experiences of music both in class and out of school; the children's interest will be retained if teaching is related to their everyday experience.

Kabalevsky stresses that a very important characteristic of his scheme is its thematic construction, whereby each quarter of the year has a theme which is gradually developed and extended. Musical literacy is almost excluded from the first year's course, but Kabalevsky argues that musical notation and theory must be introduced only after pupils have acquired a real love of music itself.

Singing is not excluded; ideally every class should become a choir. "Where available" class musical instruments should be used for performance. Improvisation, the continuing and completion of melodies begun by the teacher as well as the composition of tunes and rhythms in specific styles, is recommended, but this should not be compulsory. Kabalevsky warns that improvisation in the conditions of school can lead to dilettantism in the shape of the barren repetition of musical cliche. Otherwise, the creative activities he recommends are limited to verbalised response: the children should speak freely of their reactions to music they have heard.

Finally Kabalevsky reiterates certain points which he obviously anticipated would lead to controversy: he asserts that school music must not and cannot ever be a sort of watered-down professional training in music on one period a week. Music lessons should help to form children's musical taste. Fearing excuses, he insists that the new programme is not beyond the powers of any music teacher. At all costs boredom must be avoided, and given good will, the intellectual, moral and emotional aims of music teaching will be attained.

The Syllabus: Structure and Content

The syllabus places "perception" first. There is no rigid distinction between the listening and the performing activities: even listening to a movement from a popular piano concerto (Rakhmaninov's third) is followed by a performance of the main theme on classroom instruments. The syllabus for year 1 includes about ten Russian folk songs, rather more modern composed songs (three by Kabalevsky and eight by others), some popular marches and works by Tchaikovsky, Prokofiev, Shostakovich, Shchedrin, Glinka, and Beethoven. In the second year Russian composers introduced are Borodin and Rimsky-Korsakov; Grieg, Chopin and Schubert appear, and a children's opera by Koval´ figures prominently; folk songs and so on appear as in year 1. In year 3 the Soviet national anthem and other patriotic songs are taught, but as the themes for the year seek to show connections between Russian music and that of other nations, the music for listening includes folk songs from Japan, France, Italy, Poland, Czechoslovakia and Bulgaria, and "art-music" variations on folk songs by Mozart, Beethoven and Kodaly. How interesting that the correspondence columns of the educational press indicate that, of all things, the Lacrimosa from Mozart's Requiem seems to have struck home to the heart of children with tremendous force.

The four themes in class one are entitled "The three whales in music: song, dance and march" (identification, performance of examples of all three types); "What music speaks about" (the feelings and ideas which music contains and expresses); "Where the three whales lead us" (principally on the power of musical compositions to depict things outside themselves; programme music), and "What musical language is" (how a composer uses musical sounds - notes of different pitch, rhythms, types of melody, etc. - to convey certain impressions). Year 2 themes are: "Song, dance and march develop into song-like, dance-like and march-like" (pupils come to recognise these elements in more complex compositions), "Intonation" (how the character of a piece of music depends on the nature of the melodic phrases which make it up; expression in musical performance), "Development in a piece of music" (elementary appreciation of the structure of a composition), "The construction (form) of music" (repetition and contrast; binary and variation form). Topics for class 3 are: "The music of my people" (based on the folk music of whatever republic or national area the children belong to), "Between the music of my people and the music of others there are no uncrossable boundaries", "Between the music of all nations of the world there are no uncrossable boundaries", and "Composer - performer - listener" (to heighten awareness of the roles of the three participants in musical activity).

Class 4 begins study of the relationship between music and the other arts. The first half-year deals with music and literature, and the themes are "What would happen to music if there were no literature?" and "What would happen to literature if there were no such thing as music?". Music and art is treated in the remainder of the year: "Can we see music?" and "Can we hear painting?" The topics in year 5 begin with a double helping of "Music as a force for change". The opportunity here for working on revolutionary songs and the like is obvious, but in fact there is very much more to this theme than that: the power of music to bring peace of mind, inspiration or a sense of purpose receives powerful exposition. The whole of the second half of the year goes on "What does the power of music consist in?" Here children are introduced to many fine pieces by Bach, Glinka, Beethoven, Tchaikovsky and others, and are invited to consider how and why they are felt to be beautiful, powerful and impressive. Much development of previous ideas about the emotional content of music takes place in this topic.

Class 6 again has two themes, "The musical image" and "Musical dramaturgy". The word "image" is known to the children; they have encountered some already in music: revolution, war, outstanding people. Reinforcement of the concept leads on naturally to the study of music which contains a variety of related images, not, as the title seems to suggest, operatic music necessarily, but larger-scale works such as sonatas, overtures and symphonies which by their very nature unite contrasting elements. Class 7, the final year of mass music education, appears to be, but is not, concerned with modern music: "What is meant by modernity in music?", "´Light´ and ´serious´ music", "The mutual influence of light and serious music" and "Our great contemporaries". The message of the year, which becomes clear by the end of the course, is that our contemporaries are any composers who get through to us with their music, whatever century they lived in. The notes make clear their author´s desire to sensitise children to music itself, and to its form and style. A particularly interesting section tackles the problem of good and bad in music and the difference between light and serious music. To face these problems with younger secondary-age children is nothing if not courageous, but, as will be realised from our discussion of Kabalevsky's attitude to music in education, they lie at the heart of the new syllabus.

The music prescribed for listening, study and performance in the seventh class, in the order in which it appears, in the first quarter of the year is: Toccata and fugue in d minor (Bach), "We shall overcome" (Pete Seeger), "Moonlight" sonata (Beethoven), "Alyosha" (Kolmanovsky), Pizzicato polka (Strauss), "Das Wandern" (Schubert), part of Tchaikovsky's fourth symphony, an aria by Villa-Lobos, theme song from the film "I walk around Moscow", and Shostakovich's ninth symphony. The rest of the year contains works by various Soviet light music composers, Rakhmaninov, Lennon and McCartney, American folk blues, negro spirituals, Milhaud, Berkovsky, Glinka, Kabalevsky, Verdi, Dunaevsky, Gershwin, Russian folk songs, Shchedrin, Beethoven, Musorgsky and Prokofiev.

What is New?

Anyone who has ever been inside a Soviet school will realise how revolutionary this must seem. No longer can facts be dinned into the children; pupils must have maximum opportunity for enjoyment and, above all, emotional response. They are to be encouraged to offer, even without being asked, their own reactions to music. Teachers are to aim at what must seem to some like airy-fairy objectives – developing a love of music – and, horror of horrors, are to be held responsible if the children are bored and ill-motivated. The teachers' notes for one lesson in the fourth year suggest that Paustovsky's story "The Old Cook" be read to the class: Mozart meets a cook, who is on his death-bed. After the reading, which is to be accompanied by music, the notes continue, "It is difficult to tell how this lesson will end; all will depend on how deeply the children have taken Paustovsky's story and Mozart's music... The teacher will have to show great emotional sensitivity." Such advice has not often been found in notes for Soviet teachers. The scheme has its enemies, and some rank and file teachers are frankly scared stiff – so much is obvious from published reactions to the reforms.

Particular anger is reserved for the notion that singing is no longer the be-all and end-all of class music lessons. Opponents attack what they claim to be the vagueness of the requirements, the lack of training in musical literacy and the "incomprehensible" lack of the exercises to which Soviet music teachers always used to cling. What is objected to is stultifying repetitious exercises. The whole controversy erupted in the educational press when one B. Volkov, a passionate supporter of Kabalevsky, published a report in *Teacher's Newspaper*. He exposed the activities of some influential op-

ponents of Kabalevsky, and took delight in naming names -
among which were some important people. Acts of petty spite
and bare-faced intrigues are openly related. Even the APN was
criticised for failing to give the opposition, which is centred on the Academy's own NII for Arts Education, its come-
uppance. The Institute is accused of wasting huge sums over
fifteen years on useless projects. The article is entitled "A
million roubles' worth of obstruction".

Successes and Problems

Several recent reports reflect both a general optimism over
the new syllabus and concern over many details of organisation
and provision which are not going perfectly. The new syllabus
has given a significant impetus to music teaching, raised
standards and captured the imagination of teachers. Both motivation and professional skill have improved. Teachers had
been obliged to look in a new way at the subject. The new
syllabus is said to have proved itself and to be "actively
promoting the communist education of pupils", but the need for
improvement of oversight and control of the quality of work
done in schools was stressed. Teacher morale is improving
because children are enjoying lessons more and showing intensified interest in the classics of music.

What is Meant By "Creativity"?

It is probably the notion of creativity in its English meaning
which seems to be most obviously lacking in the Soviet classroom, except in the painting lesson. The composition of
poetry is still regarded as an occupation for out-of-school
circles and is only occasionally a classroom activity. Nevertheless, the words *tvorchestvo* [creation] and *tvorcheskiy*
[creative] are increasingly to be found in Soviet writing on
arts education. The value of such work is beginning to be
recognised, and it is well understood that the lack of it has
led to the overloading of syllabuses with far too much memory
work. Oddly, it looks as if creativity might come into Soviet
syllabuses as a way of reducing the work load.
    Kabalevsky was in no doubt of the importance of a "cre-
ative basis" to human personality. He vigorously attacked
parents or teachers who think that getting children to write
poems and draw pictures is a waste of time. But what of the
role of creation in the music lesson? Here there *seems* to be
an odd gap. "Creativity" seems most often to mean a quality
of *response* rather than making new musical compositions. The
syllabus contains little reference to musical composition by
pupils: there is some careful use of improvisation, for example of a second part to a tune, and suggests that pupils
might help the teacher to write simple tunes. One might have
thought that the type of co-operative "collective" composition

projects which British children increasingly engage in would have appealed to the Soviets. So why is the new syllabus so reticent and conservative on this issue? There is some evidence of a fear of "dillettantism" and cliche.

Discussion of this issue with Soviet educationists confirms that the concept "creativity" differs in the two languages. For a Soviet teacher creativity is "an attitude of mind, a flight of thought, feeling and fantasy; it should help the child ´to take off and fly´ alongside the music of the great masters". Creativity cannot be taught, but it is possible to teach creative working, the Soviets believe. Music lessons in schools cannot possibly give the child a grounding in the craft of composition. However, elements of creativity and compositional working are invariably used in the treatment of the music set for listening: accompaniments to melodies are improvised, children "conduct" or move freely to the music, they arrange it for voices and sing it. A Soviet educator argues: "To develop creative abilities, to help the spirit to learn to fly along with the great, to experience desire for and delight in flight - this is the essence of the attitude to creativity expressed in the pedagogical system of Dmitriy Kabalevsky."

LITERATURE

Is literature to be seen as aesthetic education, an extension of language study, or a vital element in ideological upbringing? Soviet educators see it as belonging to all these categories, but recent work suggests that it is regarded first and foremost as a most important branch of aesthetic education, the only form of teaching about the arts in the upper classes of the secondary school, and a subject which is taught throughout a child´s career. It develops and extends children´s experience of the world, the arts, human nature and the social environment; it is essential to their cognitive and communicative development, while opening the door to aesthetic experience.

A Disputed Rationale?

Not all teachers agree about the relative importance of these different elements. Some argue strongly for the aesthetic side to be emphasised, but some are reluctant to be shaken from the notion of literature as a means to foster correct ideological attitudes in children.

It is important for Westerners to understand this, if only because we are apt to draw wrong conclusions from the evidence about syllabus content. In early 1987 a British Secretary of State drew unflattering comparisons between Soviet literature teaching (which he approved of) and practice in British schools, on the grounds that the British were allegedly neglecting worth-while works of literature while the Soviets were reading our Shakespeare for us. It is as nonsensical to believe that the Soviet child's literary diet is made up entirely of masterpieces as to imagine that English children study nothing but trivia. Moreover, unless it is known how literature is taught in the USSR, it is not fair to draw any conclusion at all.

Traditional Classroom Practices

The main problem for Soviet educators who wish to improve the teaching of literature is the standard form of the lesson which they now seek to change. I visited classes in 1961 and again in 1984 and found lessons being conducted in very similar format even after this lengthy interval. Children had been set to "prepare" such topics as the life of Maxim Gorky or the Russian *byliny* (ancient folk epics). Much of the lesson consisted of reading out to the class what notes had been taken from the literary histories by individual children. Pupils were tested on their understanding of Gorky by being asked questions, to which they gave answers so stereotyped that the teacher was able to prompt them exactly, in several cases continuing in exact unison with the child for ten or fifteen seconds at a time. Once (in 1984) a child who described Gorky as a "representative" of socialist realism instead of its "originator" was devastatingly rebuked. When Tolstoy was mentioned in passing, the teacher went off at a tangent to discover what the children knew about him - and this was investigated in the same tedious fashion. The pupils were learning nothing. The teaching method actively prevented them from having the aesthetic encounter with the "living word" of which Russian educators write so eloquently, because literary study became a matter of the rote-learning of facts and judgements of no real relevance to the children at all. How regrettable that so little progress seemed to have been made in 23 years.

On the day these words were written English inspectors published a report castigating literature teaching in similar terms: too much teacher monologue, dreary reading round the class, use by the teacher of dog-eared old university lecture notes, and the tendency of pupils to "listen in dutiful and passive silence nearly all the time". The presentation of literature to school pupils is obviously a problem of international dimensions. The concern is quite obviously shared by a very great many Soviet authorities. A number of recent books express such views; one urges the necessity to have teachers of literature with human qualities, concern for the individual pupil, a love of literature, breadth of vision and a creative approach. Another underlines the need for the teacher to love literature himself or herself by quoting the results of a sociological inquiry into the personal tastes of over a thousand teachers of literature in 15 cities; only 54% were prepared to admit to an interest in high culture. Writers urge teachers to bear in mind the personality and interests of the child, and not to try to run an honours course in literary history. While literature teaching is seen clearly as a value-laden activity, undue stress on the socio-historical background of a book is thought to lead to a trivial response. Authorities are now suggesting that creative writing in the standard literature course would broaden children's perception of literature. Written essays are too often seen by many teachers, the authorities say, as nothing but a form of testing, whereas they play a most important creative educational role.

The Syllabus: Structure and Theory

Discussion of literature teaching by Soviet educators tends to be confined to the secondary phase of general education. However, as might be expected, some attention is paid to prose and poetry in the primary classes. For the most part, the objective is to develop children's ability to read fluently and to further the upbringing aims of the Soviet school: passages for reading are prepared and chosen specially to inculcate the values described in Chapter 3. Nevertheless, some really good literature is introduced in the form of poems by classic authors for learning by heart: Pushkin, Maykov, Pleshcheev, Fet, Tyutchev and Krylov are all represented, as are some of the better Soviet poets, such as Marshak, Tvardovsky, Mayakovsky and Mikhalkov.

Secondary literature teaching is based on the Marxist-Leninist principles of *nauchnost'* [scientific basis], *partiynost'* [Party content] and *istorizm* [relation to history]. Theory of literature is not taught in isolation, but always in direct relationship with specific works. The course is not free from moral and ideological issues - in Soviet terms, it must not be "subjective". It should be systematic and include works by Russian, Soviet and foreign writers of all ages.

The literature course falls into two parts: in classes 5 to 8 its purpose is to develop children's interest in reading and their experience of the world in general, to help in the formation of good literary taste and judgement about books and literary characters. In this stage there is an element of author-by-author study, but also some thematic organization. Certain theoretical concepts are introduced: structure, plot, character, the expressive and descriptive power of words, subject, idea and composition in prose works, and in poetry: the poet's expression of his feelings, musicality or "intonation", the feeling of a poem, its composition, descriptive power and the exactness of the language in which it is expressed. The second part, in classes 9 to 11, involves more liter-

ary-historical work, chronological study and the establishment
of links with the time in which the works were composed.

Syllabus: Literary Works Prescribed

In preparing this section I have used the syllabus issued as a
separate booklet in 1980 along with corrections and additions
to it published in educational periodicals since then. The
changes are not radical. In 1982 several works by Leonid
·Brezhnev were included, and it seems more than likely that
they have already been removed. The number of lessons for
each topic in the 1980 syllabus is given in brackets.

Class 5. Three Russian folk tales (5): patriotic feeling,
belief of the people in the triumph of good over evil, the
wisdom of ordinary folk, their dream of being freed from back-
breaking labour; language, structure and poetic nature of the
tales. Riddles (2) as embodiments of folk humour and wisdom.
Proverbs (2) - their moral standpoint, literal and metaphorical meaning, linguistic qualities. Literary theory: the concept of oral and written tradition.
    Two fairy tales in verse by Pushkin (4) and the "Snow
Queen" by Andersen (4) are used to introduce concepts of
poetic language, versification, moral issues - good and evil,
inner and outward beauty. Nekrasov's "Peasants' Children"
(2), Tolstoy's "Prisoner in the Caucasus" (3), Turgenev's
"Mumu" (5) and Lermontov's "Borodino" (2) introduce peasant
life, oppression of serfs, the depiction of historical events
and geographical settings in literature, moral issues of loyalty, bravery and the like. Literary concepts taught include
simile, dialogue and monologue. Descriptive sketches by Paustovsky and Rylenkov, geared towards the natural beauty of
Russia (5). Further Soviet works studied are Fadeev's "Snow-
storm" (3), Simonov's "The Artilleryman's Son" (2), Kataev's
"Son of the Regiment" (7), Tvardovsky's "Lenin and the Stove-
repairer" (2), poems by Vera Inber and Marshak about Lenin
(2), and Gaydar's "Timur and his Team" (4). Syllabuses since
1980 have been strengthened by the addition of more literary
treatments of Lenin. Patriotism, revolutionary commitment,
heroism, and veneration for Lenin go side by side with the
introduction of concepts such as a literary hero or character,
relationships between characters and the historical basis of
literary works.
    About eight poems or passages are set to be learned by
heart, and eight lessons are allocated for the discussion of
works read at home: five folk tales from republics of the
USSR, tales by Marshak and Andersen, a miscellany of poems and
descriptive pieces by Russian and Soviet writers, and four
pieces in patriotic or revolutionary vein or of Leniniana.

Class 6. Two of the Russian *byliny*,(3) and another tradition-

al tale (1), continue the theme of oral heritage and introduce
the concept of hyperbole. Four of Krylov's fables (5); alle-
gory. Some Pushkin poems (13), two of Lermontov's and one by
Nekrasov (2), chosen to illustrate patriotic, historical,
social and moral themes and natural description. Korolenko's
"Children of the Vaults" (5) - the misery of the poor in
Russia before the Revolution, but also character studies,
awareness of the dignity of man, etc. Kataev's "Lone White
Sail" (5) - a famous children's novel of the 1905 Revolution.
Isakovsky, "Thought of Lenin", Bednyy, "Snowdrops" (2) - poems
on Lenin as the embodiment of the hopes of Russia. Prishvin,
"The Sun's Storehouse" (4) - a tale of moral and human significance; personification as a literary device. Kassil', "Tale
of the Missing Soldier" (1) - heroism in war and gratitude of
the people to those who sacrificed themselves. Polevoy, "Tale
of a Real Man" (5) - a famous Soviet novel about an air force
hero. Literary theory includes elementary understanding of
narrative prose writing and of short stories and novels or
novellas. Homer: extract from the Odyssey: "Odysseus and the
Cyclops" (4) - to be treated as an adventure tale, to some
extent embodying the life of the ancient Greeks, and illustrating the hyperbolic style, epithets and repetitions of epic
poetry.

In class 6, nine poems are set for learning by heart.
Out-of-school reading adds two more *byliny*, several Krylov
fables, poems by Pushkin, Lermontov, Nekrasov, Nikitin, Maykov
and A. K. Tolstoy, and two stories by Grigorovich and A. N.
Tolstoy. Seven for the most part very minor Soviet authors
are represented in the "revolutionary" section of the private
reading syllabus; Homer's companions are Smirnova's "Heroes of
Hellas" and R. L. Stevenson's "Heather Ale".

Class 7 begins with Pushkin (3): "The Prisoner" and an extract
from "Poltava". These introduce the idea of metaphor. Next
come two by Lermontov (3), Gogol's "Taras Bul'ba" (7), two
poems by the Ukrainian nationalist Taras Shevchenko (2), "Be-
zhin Meadow" and the prose poem "The Russian Language" by
Turgenev (4), Nekrasov's "Red-nosed Frost" (5), Saltykov-
Shchedrin's "Tale of How One Peasant Kept Two Generals Alive"
(2) and Chekhov's "Chameleon" (2). The themes include: love
of country, yearning for freedom, hatred of despotism and
contempt for parasitism. Attention is paid to theoretical
matters: literary genres such as epic, lyric and dramatic
works, poetic and prosaic language, some elementary versification; humour and satire. Some simple appreciation of style,
structure and characterization in a prose work are taught.

Next comes Soviet literature: Gorky's "Childhood" (5),
Gaydar's "School" (5), chapters from Furmanov's "Chapaev" (3),
Sholokhov's "The Little Scoundrel" (2), Bagritsky's poem
"Death of a Pioneer Girl" (2) and A. N. Tolstoy's "The Russian
Character" (2). Themes prescribed include miseries of life

before the Revolution, the "humane beauty" of character of the Russian masses, Lenin, heroism in the Civil War and revolutionary struggle against ignorance, religion and out-of-date attitudes. The final work studied is "Don Quixote" (5) - extracts only, it is assumed: "Picture of seventeenth century Spanish life... Don Quixote´s selflessness, knightly acts, loyalty to ideals, spiritual greatness, nobility and naive simplicity..."

Nine or ten pieces are to be learned by heart; out-of-school reading includes poems by Pushkin, Lermontov, Nekrasov and Shevchenko, a short story by Chekhov, Gogol´s "Evenings on a Farm Near Dikanka", four revolutionary works by minor Soviet writers, and scenes from Schiller´s "Wilhelm Tell".

Basic Requirements in Classes 5 to 7

Objectives to be reached by this stage include being able to re-tell the story of prose works, to read or recite poetry expressively, to tell a folk tale from a literary one, a *bylina* from a fable, a short story from a novel or novella; pupils should be able to outline the character of a hero on a basis of his actions, etc., compare characters, point out some of the artistic resources of language on a basis of which character is portrayed, give an oral account of works read at home and use reference literature.

The Syllabus Continued: Class 8. The first lesson is an introduction on the figurative nature of literature, the artistic image, the relationship between artistic and scientific literature and between literature and other forms of art. Literary works prescribed are: Pushkin, "The Captain´s Daughter" (9), Lermontov, "Song of the Merchant Kalashnikov" and "The Novice" (6), Gogol´, "The Government Inspector" (7), Nekrasov, "Thoughts by the Front Entrance" and "The Railway" (4), L. N. Tolstoy "After the Ball" (3). Literary theory taught here includes the role of truth and fiction in a literary work, theme and idea, the concept of an epic poem, drama, comedy, plot, structure, antithesis and the epigraph. Study of the works listed is also intended to centre on the literary depiction of historical conditions and characters, moral and social criticism. Soviet works follow: two poems by Gorky, "Song of the Falcon", "Song of the Stormy Petrel" (3), three poems by Mayakovsky (4), Fadeev´s novel "The Young Guard" (9) and chapters from Tvardovsky´s "Vasiliy Terkin" (4).

Requirements for this year closely resemble those for years 5 to 8, but one or two points are added: the ability to distinguish the author´s attitude to the events described (the distinction between the author and narrator is not made), and to discover the theme and underlying idea of a literary work. Extra reading consists of more Pushkin, Lermontov, Gogol, Nekrasov, L. N. Tolstoy, Gorky, Mayakovsky, Tvardovsky and eight other minor Soviets - for the most part these works are short stories and poems of moderate length.

General Features of Study from Class 9

At this stage some new elements enter the literature course. As before, a number of poems and prose passages are set for learning by heart from the works studied. Lists are given of works not included in the programme by ten or twelve writers "for talks on Soviet literature". There is also a section "On Work With the Writings of Lenin in Literature Lessons".

In *Class 9* a "systematic course" in Russian literature begins with an introduction: literature as "an artistic reflection of the life of the people": its links with social and national life, its class basis. Introductory remarks on the theory of literature are: "The cognitive and educative significance of literature. The ideological content, figurative and emotional nature of the literary art. The content and form of a work."
 Themes and works to be read are firstly brief information on Russian literature before the nineteenth century; "The Lay of Igor's Host" (3) - the possibly doubtful authenticity of this ancient epic does not worry Soviet educators. Review of eighteenth century literature (6): extracts from Lomonosov, Derzhavin, Fonvizin and Radishchev. Literary theory: tendencies in literature, classicism, the socio-political stance of a writer. Foreign literature: Moliere's "Le Bourgeois gentilhomme" (3). Literature of the first period of the Russian liberation movement; an introduction (3) - including some account of the work of Krylov, Karamzin, Zhukovsky and Ryleev. Griboedov's "Woe From Wit" (8), the classic verse comedy of the 1820s. Thirteen Pushkin lyrics (22) - a biographical survey of the poet, his significance for Russian literature, the time in which he wrote and the themes of his work. Next, Byron's "Childe Harold", cantos I and II, and two other works (3) - Byron's problems with society, romanticism, political themes, the theme of disillusionment and solitude, the Byronic hero. This is followed by eight poems by Lermontov (14). Gogol, "Dead Souls" volume I (12) - its plot and structure, character types, the concept of *poshlost'* (shallowness of character), the central character Chichikov, Gogolian "laughter through tears", the people and their land in the novel, Gogol's positive ideals. Belinsky (3) and the concept of a literary critic. Herzen's "Past and Thoughts" -four chapters (3): the world portrayed, language and composition.

The course in *Class 10* is entitled "Literature of the second period of the Russian liberation movement" (the 1860s-70s): the period (4); Ostrovsky, "The Storm" (8), Turgenev, "Fathers and Children" (12), Chernyshevsky, "What Is To Be Done?" (8), four works by Nekrasov (12), Dostoevsky, "Crime and Punishment" (10), Tolstoy, "War and Peace" (22), Chekhov "Ionich" and "The Cherry Orchard" (11). Two lessons on the world significance of Russian literature follow this, and the year is brought to a conclusion with Shakespeare's "Hamlet" (4), Goethe's "Faust" (eight scenes) and Balzac's "Gobseck" (3).

Four lessons is clearly not enough for "Hamlet" or "Faust", and the syllabus makes it clear that an overview is all that is intended. However, at least the textbook contains the full text of "Hamlet" in the magnificent translation by Boris Pasternak and most of the same writer's translation of Part I of "Faust". It is doubtful whether "War and Peace" can be adequately covered even in 22 lessons - while 12 for "Fathers and Children" is much more possible. Some children will doubtless manage all 1600 pages of the Tolstoy. The notes indicate that there is to be some concentration on the socio-political importance of these works. Style, characterization, the non-political and moral ideals of the author, the imagery and symbolism also figure in the syllabus notes.

Class 11 is concerned almost entirely with Soviet literature. An introduction (4) characterizes the third period of the Russian liberation movement". The main theme is the emergence of Socialist Realism and the "struggle of progressive Russian writers against decadent modernistic writing", and "Party-orientation in literature" is dealt with.

Works prescribed for study are: Gorky, "The Lower Depths", "The Old Woman Izergil'", "Mother", "V. I. Lenin" (13); Blok, seven poems including "The Twelve" (4); a survey of the years 1917-1929 (2 lessons covering at least five prose writers and seven poets); nine Esenin poems (4); a dozen by Mayakovsky (12); Fadeev's novel "The Rout" (5); a survey of literature 1930-1941 (2); N. A. Ostrovsky's novel "How the Steel Was Tempered" (4); A review of A. N. Tolstoy's works (3), including "The Road to Calvary" and "Peter the First"; a review of the literature of the Great Patriotic War (5); a review of Tvardovsky's works (3), and one of Soviet literature of the 1950s-1970s (7). The latest syllabus inserts ten lessons on three contemporary Soviet works here: Astaf'ev's "Emperor-fish", Aitmatov's "White Steamer" and Shukshin's "Talks by the Light of the Full Moon". This is achieved by "lightening the load" of the old syllabus (that is, by removing one or two poems by Blok and Esenin - scarcely a very effective measure of alleviation!). There are two lessons on the world significance of Soviet literature (the importance of the heroic Soviet character as an educative force, the influence of Socialist Realism on progressive literature everywhere, Soviet writers and the struggle against imperialism and anti-democratism). Finally, three lessons are given on contemporary overseas writing, concentrating on those authors who are seen as allies in the cause: Hemingway, Fučik, Saint-Exupery, Seghers, Dimov, Brecht, Neruda and Tuwim.

Home reading in classes 9 to 11 includes eleven classical Russian and eight Soviet works, Moliere's "Tartuffe", Byron's "The Prisoner of Chillon", two lyrics by Goethe, two Shakespeare sonnets, "King Lear", "Romeo and Juliet", and five novels by Balzac and Stendhal.

Language Development

In each of the senior classes, 9 to 11, a specific number of lessons (8 or 10) is set aside for the "development of language". It will be remembered that this is regarded as a most important element in Russian language work, but in classes 10 and 11 it goes on in the literature classes. Extension of vocabulary is a primary task in class 9, and the taking of notes and making of summaries is also developed. In the senior classes the overall aim is to enable pupils to give, orally or in writing, in essays, discussions, debates or lecturettes, coherent, well-planned expression to their opinions and judgements about the literature studied. Another objective is to encourage "expressive reading" aloud, which is believed to be of some importance for general reading development.

Drama and Theatre

Drama as known in England is not practised in the core curriculum in the Soviet school, though experiments in the teaching of theatre have been going on in optional lessons. What is sometimes seen in the regular lessons is the "literary-musical composition", which is a formally presented poetry and prose reading (often the music is recorded) on a theme, given before a small audience - parents, visitors or another class. Extra-curricular theatre presentations are common enough.

Successes and Failures

Surveys of schoolchildren's attainment have revealed certain weaknesses: children lack "specialist knowledge and skills of analysis", "expressive reading" is poor, the links between works of literature are not appreciated, there is poor understanding of the distinctions between the different genres and types of literary work, pupils do not understand Socialist Realism, they have out-of-date ideas about characters as "representatives of something or other". Considering that these remarks refer to the whole range of ability in the secondary school, they are perhaps not very alarming. One can, for instance, forgive children for being vague about Socialist Realism when professional writers are not always very sure, and one might not expect the average child to have highly developed skills of literary analysis.

The successes are that children know the content of works studied better than they did, they are keener to discuss the moral implications of what they have read, they can argue about literature in society and discuss individual works in some depth. Older pupils are also, it is said, better informed of Lenin's views on literature and of Party decrees.

Overall Considerations Concerning Literature Teaching

Almost every classic Russian author is represented in the syllabus by important works, and so are many Soviet writers of major, minor and minimal talent. However, it is rather odd that, in a multi-cultural state, relatively few writers of non-Great-Russian origin are included; Shevchenko and Chingiz Aitmatov appear - and Gogol, if he is counted a Ukrainian, though he wrote in Russian. Foreign writers are present, but not over-represented. But any child who had followed the Soviet syllabus conscientiously would have read a very wide range of books - more novels and poetry than plays, it is true; more Russian than anything else, which is scarcely surprising.

If doubts remain, it is whether a syllabus in which every author and every theme is prescribed from age ten to age seventeen gives enough freedom to the individual teacher to communicate enthusiasm to the children about those works which grip her or him; or, for that matter, choice to the pupils to follow some of their own interests within the context of the compulsory course. Methodologists complain about poor teaching - might not one solution be to set teachers free in this respect? And is there enough in the syllabus, despite recent improvements and urgings from the experts, about artistic, aesthetic quality? Is not the socio-political import too prominent still? Whatever the answers to these questions, it is still true that one meets many Soviet people with a genuine interest in the enjoyment of books whose education has not hindered them from pursuing it.

ART

At the time of writing older syllabuses are in operation, and they will receive some attention here. However, since 1976 an experimental project has been running under the auspices of the Union of Artists of the USSR, the Institute of Art Education of the APN and Minpros RSFSR. The leader of the project is Boris Nemensky, to whom I am indebted for detailed information. It seems likely that this experiment will eventually form the foundation for art education in the future, so an account of it is included in this section.

Aims and Principles

Art education sets out to "foster labour and polytechnical training", to develop children's taste and "ability aesthetically to assess the products of industry", to motivate them to participate in the conservation of nature and the historical and cultural heritage, and to contribute to "the artistic enrichment of the environment". "Art in school is based upon the artistic specifics of realistic art, which reflects reality in artistic images. This determines the content and method of instruction". So reads a primary syllabus published in Belorussia in 1986.

An earlier syllabus (from 1980) for the secondary stage states the aims thus: "To develop the aesthetic perception of pupils as regards life around them, demonstrating the beauty of objects in relation to the material of which they are made, to develop more assured skills in drawing and painting from nature, ...to enable pupils to represent the relative position of objects in a drawing... on a basis of the observation of perspective... the means of conveying space (shade, light, etc.)...; elementary drawing of human figures, the proportions of the human body,... to develop the child's ability to select a subject... and carry our preliminary studies and sketches; to deepen children's understanding of decorative work,... and to perfect skills in the creative composition of patterns."

The demand for "realistic" representational art is in tune with Soviet prejudices. It conforms with notions of children's drawing revealed by a kindergarten head that her children's art work was informally assessed by inspectors to see if it "represented the subject matter" (apparently the only criterion applied). Soviet children are most certainly taught techniques which will be likely to enable them to "represent reality" in a manner satisfying to them as well as to their teachers.

Syllabus content: Primary Classes

Material taught in the four primary-age classes is divided into four sections: "Perception of art and of objects of reality" (12 lessons in year 1, 6 in class 2, and 7 in each of classes 3 and 4), "Representation on a flat surface" (28 + 15 + 12 + 12), Modelling (10 + 6 + 6 + 6), and "Decorative and applied activities" (14 + 7 + 9 + 7).

"Perception" involves looking at reality, life and art, discussing it with the teacher, and discovering one's emotional reaction to things seen, links between life and art, and the media through which the pupils' reactions can be expressed. "Representation" includes drawing and painting from memory and from life, subjects set by the teacher or left to free choice, sketches, applied graphic design and collage. "Modelling" with plasticine, gypsum, clay, polystyrene, wood or papier-mache is believed to have great significance for the development of the child and is stressed in the primary years. "Decorative and applied" art has the closest links with labour, and deals with architecture, planning and design as well as including work with natural materials - leaves, flowers, etc. The concepts and principles of composition, form and space are dealt with across the boundaries of these sections.

This syllabus is a far cry from that published in 1980, which has no section on "perception". It is true that the new one has 60 or 70 more lessons available for art, but this alone does not explain the difference in approach. The old syllabus divided the lessons up into "painting from nature", "painting on particular subjects", "decorative painting" and "talks on art". There were no talks on art until year 3. The works mentioned were confined almost entirely to standard classics of Russian painting and showed less variety in medium and subject matter than the newer syllabus. In 1980 a great many exercises were included - drawing books, classroom objects, household utensils, flags, toys, natural objects and animals.

Syllabus Content: Secondary Classes

In the old-style programmes this formula continued until year 6: painting from nature (more than half the lessons), painting on specific subjects (about 15%), decorative work (another 15%) and talks on art (the same). Thus class 5 under the old numbering system was still drawing a formidable list of utensils, tools, fruits, leaves, furniture, cones, pyramids, science laboratory equipment, sports gear, "half a water melon" and "two apples on a plate". The six lessons of subject painting look much more enjoyable with "Buildings around us", "School clubs", "Harvest", "Round the camp fire", "Spring outside". Decorative work included the design of a wall-newspaper and the cover and interior of a book. The talks on art (6 lessons) are on historical painting, portraiture, sculpture and architecture , the work of Repin and Surikov. Flemish, French and Italian masters appeared in the old class 6. Since this style of art education is clearly on the way out, we shall turn to the syllabus of Professor Nemensky.

A New Subject: "Graphic Art and Creative Labour"

Boris Nemensky is the Kabalevsky of Soviet art education, a well-known artist who has held exhibitions at home and abroad, a professor and teacher-trainer. He is dedicated to his task and writes of it with enthusiasm and commitment. He stresses starting from the child's enjoyment of art; his syllabus is thematically constructed, it emphasises perception, it stands on three legs like Kabalevsky's three whales.

Rationale

In the introduction to his project Nemensky writes of the interaction of art with the life of man and society. Technological progress necessitates fostering people's creative resources. The feelings aroused by works of art unite the spiritual experience of people in general with the personal experience of each individual, awakening "social responsiveness". The character-forming effect of art is realised not through a didactic approach, but in graphic form, deeply affecting a person's emotional and inner world. Art, moreover, is closely connected with productive activity (hence the title of the experimental course) - with the artistic transformation of the world of objects in which man lives. The formation of artistic culture in children is vital because it is an essential part of their general spiritual culture. Accustoming children to emotional encounter with art is important, because without enthusiasm there will be no real contact with art - and it will have no educational effect. The cognitive side is not absent and the course is concerned with "the development of the system of `eye-brain-hand`".

Three key tasks are enumerated for the art teacher. They are: the formation of "aesthetic and ethical responsiveness to the beautiful and the ugly", the "formation of artistic and creative activeness in the personality" - meaning making pupils able and willing to be original, "training for fantasy" and enabling them to discover things and to act "not according to standard". The third task is "to perfect the workings of the visual system as an active instrument of cognition and reasoning. The development of the system of `eye-brain-hand`. The development of colour and tone sense, spatial and compositional thinking and a feeling for harmony."

Course Structure

The new system was conceived in three stages. The first is for classes 1-3 and is entitled "Basis of artistic ideas"; it is subdivided into class 1: you and art, 2: the art around us, and 3: every nation is an artist. Stage two, "Basis of artistic thinking", consists of class 4: decorative arts, 5: representational arts, 6: constructive arts, 7: the link between these three types of art and "synthetic" genres (theatre, cinema, book design). Stage three extends beyond compulsory art lessons, but its title is "Basis of artistic consciousness (culture)" - classes 8 and 9: the historical development of art, and 10: you and art today.

The course bases itself on three fundamental forms of art: representational, decorative and constructive. Lessons each term have a specific theme. The four topics in class 1 are: how and with what artists work; representation, decoration and construction - three spheres of artistic activity;

what art speaks about; how art speaks or artistic language.
Class 2: art in your house and school; art in the streets of
your town or village; art and spectacle (theatre design,
posters, animated film); museums of art. Class 3: the art of
your nation; the art of the nations of the Soviet Union; every
people in the world is an artist; the ideas of all peoples
about the spiritual beauty of man.

The themes listed above for the remaining classes in
which art is studied by all pupils, 4 to 7, are treated according to a similar plan: each of the three forms of art (and
the synthetic arts in class 7) are discussed in relation to
their function in life and society; their forms and genres are
described, and so also are their "language" and structure.
Thus in class 5 the themes for each quarter are the language
of representational art, its relation to the world of nature,
the objects surrounding man and man himself, and looking into
people (portraiture).

Methods

Nemensky advocates independence of working, discovery, discussion and initiative. He seeks creative freedom within the
limits of the classroom situation; teachers should not provide
ready-made answers, but should formulate questions so that
children are likely to find out for themselves. Collective
working, discussion of completed work so that all may discover
their strengths and weaknesses, and display of work so that
children come to believe in their powers, are commended.
Assessment should take into account not only the objective
quality of the finished product, but the enthusiasm and engagement of the pupil.

These precepts will come to life when we examine examples
of the lesson notes provided. In class 1 there is a series of
six lessons concerned with representation and reality, representation and fantasy, decoration and reality, decoration and
fantasy, construction and reality, construction and fantasy.
An aim is to show that an artist may depict the real surrounding world (and represent it in two or three dimensions).
Slides are used as a first stimulus; children are given such
themes as "our games", "Mother in the kitchen", or "a bicycle
ride". A jointed cardboard human figure is used to demonstrate the body in movement and to show its proportions.
Music is used as stimulus. The children are to work in gouache (two colours). For homework they are to look everywhere
for examples of representational art and talk about it next
lesson. The following lesson introduces the depiction of "a
fantastic or imaginary world" (but one always based on the
real world). When it comes to decoration the children first
base their work on natural objects - spiders´ webs, snow-
flakes, twigs - in charcoal, chalk, Indian ink, and one·colour
of gouache. The following lesson concerns abstract pattern;

use is made of folk art and of rhythmic music as a stimulus. The first of the two lessons on construction again uses natural objects (beehives, honeycombs, tortoiseshell, snails) to illustrate the harmonic construction of beautiful non-man-made objects in real life; children model in paper and card. In the lesson on fantasy construction they are invited in groups to design fantastic houses of the future or a fairy-tale town, using paper, card and discarded boxes, tubes, etc.

Typical of the approach in secondary education is a short series of lessons in year 6: "Great themes of life - the artist as focus of his time". In the first lesson the teacher introduces art as controversy about what is good and what evil, and speaks about art as protest. Slides used include Brueghel's "Icarus", "Blind man", Goya's "Execution of the insurgents of 3 May 1808" and Picasso's "Guernica". The first lesson passes in discussion and analysis of these slides. The following three lessons deal with engraving as a means of disseminating the artist's views. The teacher supplies historical background and slides of such works, and this leads eventually to the production of engravings from waxed paper. The subjects of these are chosen by the pupils working in groups and in consultation with the teacher.

The last lesson in year 6 is held out of school time, is a "Festival of art" open to parents, and there should be at least one work exhibited from every pupil.

Concluding Remarks on Art Teaching

These lessons comprise a minute fraction of work done during the compulsory period of education, but they do none the less illustrate clearly certain features of the course. Children work in many different media; they are allowed quite a lot of freedom to choose subject matter for their own works of art. There are links with the other arts, particularly music; there is a distinct multi-cultural flavour. There is open discussion, a place for collective as well as individual work. It seems more likely that the children will enjoy these lessons and learn something both useful and satisfying from them than if they were drawing pots and pans and compositions of blocks and cones. If this course is indeed officially adopted, it will certainly join music as representing what is in Soviet terms an innovative programme of study, and not merely a superficial tinkering with what tradition has handed down.

Chapter 9

HISTORY AND SOCIAL STUDIES

A SOVIET participant in a recent international education sym-
posium, Professor Viktor Kumanev, quoted in his paper on the
"socio-educational role of history teaching" a Russian pro-
verb: "The truth likes delicate treatment; it cannot be re-
shaped and re-interpreted. As they say, you can't handle
truth as a barrel of herrings, it is more like a powder keg".
   When Soviet educationists speak of the truth in this way
in relation to history, it is important to remember that they
hold to the materialist conception of history. This means
that it is not based on ideas or abstractions, but on the
material facts of life: the conditions in which human beings
live and the resources they have at their disposal. At the
most basic level it depends on the sheer material need of
humans to feed themselves, and on their tendency to combine
into groups or societies in order to simplify and organize the
quest for food for survival. Since human societies have never
yet satisfied their every member, a second feature takes on
importance: the "dialectic". This is the process whereby the
contradictions and conflicts in a society are gradually syn-
thesised, and a new form of society emerges, containing some
of the features of the old and some new characteristics. The
new society in its turn contains contradictions, and the
conflict within it resolves into a new synthesis. Thus did
feudalism evolve from more primitive forms of societal organization; feudalism in its turn was replaced by capitalism, the
contradictions of which resulted (in some parts of the world
at least) in socialism. That in its turn will eventually be
(though has not yet been) superseded by communism. The historical process is *progressive*, since it is more efficient
forms of society which the dialectic process produces. Engels
wrote that "all successive historical situations are only
transitional stages in the endless course of development of
human society from the lower to the higher". Communists
believe, following Lenin, that the laws of historical development are scientifically discoverable and that when they have
been discovered, men become controllers of history and cease

to be at its mercy. The system of historical and sociological education is therefore claimed to be "profoundly scientific". The materialist basis of history and the dialectical process by which human society develops are to be revealed to the pupils.

The Aims

Kumanev saw the whole process of education as an integral part of the "complex and intricate process of the intellectualization of youth". Knowledge of the past stimulates the growth of social and labour activity and the "fact that cognition of human society is as important and necessary as the cognition of nature". Understanding of historical determinism, constant social change and the impermanence of all phenomena fosters historical thinking; understanding of cause-and-effect relationships leads to comprehension of the "laws of historical development". A case is made for history in that it extends pupils´ experience of life, and enables them to learn lessons from "instructive examples from the past". Historical studies contain both ethical and aesthetic elements and "have a certain emotional colouring". Kumanev´s paper has been summarised here since it gives an articulate official Soviet view of history teaching made acceptable to an international audience. For home consumption the flavour of statements is likely to be more in the style of this quotation from another leading history educator, A. G. Koloskov:

> "Knowledge of the past, present and future of social development reveals profoundly to boys and girls the greatness of the revolutionary reformative activity of our Party and of the whole Soviet people, the indisputable advantages of socialism, its genuine democratism and humanism. A knowledge of history is an important source of the formation of Communist ideology and morality, one of the vital indicators of the cultural level of a human being."

The social function of history teaching is therefore very important indeed, and this applies too, obviously, to the short course in social studies which is seen as relating closely to history lessons.

Party, Government and History Teaching

The present structure, content and methodology of history teaching date back to a government and Party directive of 1934. Highest authority has concerned itself with the matter a number of times since then, notably in 1965 when the Central Committee of the Communist Party and the Council of Ministers issued a new directive "On changes in the system of history teaching in the schools of the USSR". This resulted in the construction of a syllabus, the main new feature of which was its linear structure. History is studied chronologically, and not on a concentric plan whereby the same periods of history are covered more than once in a manner appropriate to the age of the pupils. The exception to this general rule is the introductory course in year 5, "Episodic stories from the history of the USSR". Another feature of the course is the separation of Soviet from world or, as it is termed, "general" history. Slightly more hours of instruction are devoted to Soviet history but there is very broad coverage of general history, which cannot in any sense be said to be neglected.

History teachers have a particularly rigorous training in political theory, and are usually members of the Communist Party (which teachers of most other subjects do not have to be). This reflects the importance attached to the subject in passing on to children "sound" attitudes.

History Teachers East and West

Unlike the educators quoted above, many western history teachers have lost faith in their subject as moral teaching, agreeing that "the lessons of history are never learned". Some teachers write of learning history as an "experience" which stimulates the imagination. Disquiet is expressed if history seems to be too content-based and not sufficiently concerned with concepts. Some wish to teach children about the way historians work in the collection of information and its interpretation. Both traditional and reforming teachers make increasing use of primary sources. The traditional method of testing - by extended essay, often in response to a dull and unstimulating title like "Write about Thomas Cranmer" - is felt in many quarters to be totally inadequate. Is history about famous men and battles, or about ordinary folk? What is the place of the history of the locality in which the child lives in school courses? Can all these differing concerns be integrated, and all represented in the classroom?

For the Soviet educator history has lessons for the pupils which can be taught. They speak of pupils' emotional involvement with the subject. Their history courses are very full of content, but the content is arranged to reinforce certain important notions. The main primary sources mentioned in Soviet syllabuses are Party documents; these are indeed important, but to use only one set of sources is surely not the way to teach how a good historian works. Children are not tested by extended essay, but by oral recitation; however, the questions are often as dry as "Write about Thomas Cranmer". The role of the working masses is heavily stressed in Soviet history courses. Local history is allowed for (in relation to national events). Finally, the whole course is highly organized, so the individual teacher does not have to worry about the integration of the many elements: that is done for him. Let us now see how the powder-keg is made as nutritious and desirable as a barrel of herrings.

The Latest Syllabus

The syllabus was published in mid-1986, and runs to about 19,000 words of Russian. The general plan does not appear to be different in any important respect from its predecessor. The introduction to the syllabus makes the usual claims that the new programme raises the ideological level, intensifies its moral and ethical aspects, strengthens inter-subject links, predisposes pupils to socially useful labour, cuts out superfluous material and does all the things new syllabuses are supposed to do. What does this amount to in practice? There has been restructuring of individual topics to avoid duplication and assist comprehensibility, there is a higher content of Lenin's works and Party documents, more opportunity for the study of the history of the republics, more explicit links between Soviet and general history and an increase in the supply of visual aids. Some of this may be formality. A recent article on the new syllabus criticizes several of the republics for overloading their share of the syllabus. However, obviously defensive about the Union syllabus which has clearly not gone in for as much unloading of superfluous material as it perhaps ought, the astounding statement is made that if children are motivated in class to pay closer attention by teachers who make greater cognitive demands upon them, they will master the same amount of material more easily.

Class 5. The 68 lessons are devoted to "Episodic stories from the history of the USSR". The course is clearly designed to have a propaedeutic function in relation to later years, to interest the children and engage their emotions. In the first section, 28 lessons are given to "Our land before the Great October Revolution". Great stress is placed upon the multi-national character of the USSR and friendship between the nationalities. Nevertheless, it would appear that the Slavs are the good guys and the Tatars the bad guys in medieval history - not the happiest message for the millions of descendents of the Golden Horde living in the Soviet Union. Russian military glory and initiative in exploration are featured, while others are "foreign aggressors". Expansion of the Russian Empire is not described as aggression. Ten lessons on Russia under capitalism, the Communist Party and Lenin conclude the section.

The second section contains 35 lessons on the "Great October Socialist Revolution and the Construction of Socialism in the USSR". The stress is on the heroism of the workers in putting into practice the first five-year plan and in defending their homeland from the Nazi invasion. The terms in which the outbreak of the Great Patriotic War in 1941 are explained in the textbook are of some interest: capitalists throughout the world hated the Soviet state and wanted to get rid of it, and Hitler was its worst enemy. There is no mention of the German-Soviet Pact of 1939. Stalin's name is mentioned only in passing and scarcely more than once. The flavour of this course can best be conveyed by the contents of the last three lessons: "The struggle of the peoples of our country against foreign aggressors. The struggle of the workers against their oppressors. Participation of Soviet people under the leadership of the Communist party in the construction of a new life; friendship and cooperation between the Soviet republics".

Class 6. The 68 lessons in this year are devoted to "General History, Part I: the Ancient World" and are divided up thus: introduction (1 lesson), life in primitive societies (7): hunter-gatherers and early agriculture (importance here is attached to the role of labour in the development of such societies). Next, the rise, development and fall of slavery in Egypt, Asia Minor, India and China (56). The revision lesson with which this concludes reads "The world by the beginning of the formation of the first class societies. Reasons for their emergence and decline. The contribution of the peoples of the Ancient East to the development of world culture". Greece (21) and Rome (18): the development of slavery as a form of social organization is a main theme, and its superiority over primitive societies is explained; slavery in the Roman Empire is described as superior in development to any other system in the ancient world. Nevertheless, a second important theme is that of science, education and the arts in Greece and Rome, and their contribution to world culture.

The syllabus for each year includes near the end a section entitled "Basic concepts and central ideas", and for class 6 they include the following: the concepts of history, historical sources; primitive society, the role of labour in human development, the tools of labour and its productivity; race, tribe. Slavery, private property, exploitation, class, peasantry, demos, the class struggle as an unavoidable feature of slave-owning society, just and aggressive wars, culture and "religion - a distorted reflection of nature and society" are further concepts which are to be mastered. The final note in this section is "The progressive nature of slave-owning society in comparison with primitive societies". Skills which the sixth-year course should train include the reckoning of time in years in historical contexts, perceiving the relative position in time of events, and using historical maps. The final list of instrumental skills which the pupils are to receive is worth quoting too (a similar list appears at the end of the syllabus for each year; space will not allow the reproduction of each one of these, but this one may be taken as typical, since it gives valuable clues as to the way pupils are expected to learn). It includes: working with the text and illustrations in a texbook, discerning the main points in a paragraph, using the documents reproduced in the book as a source of knowledge, summarising the contents of a text and composing an account on a basis of two or three sources, giving a comparative analysis of conditions in two countries: their labour resources, the classes of a society, its cultural achievements, characterising the situation of classes and individual historical figures on a basis of information in the textbook, the correct use and explanation of historical terms used in the textbook, and commenting orally on other pupils´ answers.

Class 7. The 68 lessons in this year are devoted to a general history of the middle ages. The overall theme is the establishment, development and decay of feudalism and the beginnings of capitalism. Ten hours go on western and central Europe from the fifth to the eleventh centuries, firstly the Holy Roman Empire and its organization, Charlemagne and such issues as church and state, the growth of landowning and the subjection of the peasantry. The Slavs, as one might expect, figure in this section too, and there are lessons on the essence of feudal society, the church, education and literacy. Two lessons are given to the Byzantine Empire, three to the Arabs, and the summary lesson includes "features of feudalism and its distinction from what went before; the different paths to feudal structure followed by various nations."

Under the development of feudalism, there are four lessons on the development of trade and crafts, three on the Christian church in the eleventh to thirteenth centuries (its division into Orthodox and Catholic, the Inquisition and the crusades), and seven on the formation of the feudal centralized powers in Western Europe (England and France). Further themes with numbers of lessons are the Hussite movement in Bohemia (2), the Ottoman Empire and the Bulgarian and Serbian resistance to it (2), the arts in Western and central Europe (2), China in the middle ages (2), India (2), America and Africa (1 each). The summary lesson stresses the superiority of feudalism over previous societies, and the differences in the historical development of various nations; children are to receive an impression of the economic, political, social and cultural changes undergone by these nations in the second part of the middle ages (eleventh to the fifteenth centuries).

The disintegration of feudalism is covered in 21 lessons. Voyages of discovery and colonial seizures (3), the birth of capitalism in England (3), The Reformation in Western Europe and the Peasants´ War in Germany (5), the bourgeois revolution in the Netherlands (2), absolute monarchy in France (2), and the culture of Western and Central Europe in the first half of the sixteenth century (6) make up the rest of the year´s work.

Class 8. The 68 lessons are devoted to history of the USSR up to the end of the eighteenth century. The course begins with a survey of the territory of the Soviet Union in antiquity (5 lessons), in which Central Asia, the Caucasus and the Scythians figure as well as the Slavs. After this, 48 lessons go on feudalism: the first feudal societies in central Asia and the Caucasus (1), Kievan Russia (5), feudal fragmentation (9), the formation and establishment of the Russian centralised state (9), Russia at the beginning of the seventeenth century (3), the economic, political and cultural development of the country in the seventeenth century (7), and Russia in the first half of the eighteenth century (Peter I) (10).

The year finishes with 11 lessons on the decline of feudalism and the rise of capitalism in Russia. The first theme is Russia in the second half of the eighteenth century (7); this is followed by the culture of the peoples of Russia (3) and five summing up lessons, which make particular points of the distinction between feudalism in Russia and elsewhere, the contribution of Russia to world culture, "the creative role of the labour of the working masses", the expansion of the Russian state, the historical importance of peasant revolts and the defence of Russia from foreign aggressors.

Class 9. There are two parts to the history course in this year, to which three lessons per week are now devoted. First comes general history from the seventeenth century (55 lessons), and its main theme is capitalist society. The two introductory lessons to the course deal with capitalism as a new stage in the development of society, and an attempt is made to put the various steps (slavery, feudalism, etc.) in this development into perspective. The growth of industry and the emergence of "bourgeois" revolutions are referred to, and the basic content of modern history is described as the "move to capitalism and its development". Specific themes are: the victory of capitalism in England (4) and the American War of Independence and the formation of the USA (2). Under a new sub-heading of "The establishment and development of capitalism: the development of the workers' movement and the establishment of scientific communism" (47 lessons) the themes are: the great French bourgeois revolution of the eighteenth century (8), Europe after the French revolution (3), national liberation revolutions in Latin America (2), the development of capitalism in Europe and the first manifestations of the workers as an independent political force, the emergence of scientific communism: Marx and Engels (6), the revolutions of 1848-49 (5), the formation of national states in Italy and Germany (2), England in the 50s and 60s (2), the USA in the first half of the nineteenth century: the Civil War - the second bourgeois revolution in the USA (2), the anti-colonial and anti-feudal movement in Asia and Africa (4), the First International (1), technology, science and culture in the eighteenth and first half of the nineteenth centuries (4). Remaining lessons go on revision and summary.

The second part of the ninth-year course (47 lessons)

returns to the Soviet Union and takes the story to the end of the nineteenth century. 23 lessons deal with Russia up to the end of the Crimean War, and the general theme is "The decay and crisis of feudalism in Russia; the beginning of the revolutionary struggle against tsarism and serfdom". Topics included are: the War of 1812 (4 lessons), the aristocratic stage in the Russian revolutionary movement and the Decembrist Revolt (3), the crisis in serfdom and the emergence of revolutionary-democratic ideology in Russia (10), and the culture of Russia in the first half of the nineteenth century (4). The revision lesson notes state: "The historical inevitability of the destruction of serfdom (seminar work possible)". This is one of the very few methodological suggestions worked into the text of the syllabus.

The rest of the ninth-year course goes on "The history of our country in the capitalist period". Other major themes are the revolutionary-democratic stage and the beginnings of the proletarian stage in the revolutionary movement (21). Topics are the fall of serfdom (6), the development of capitalism and the formation of the industrial proletariat (8), the proletarian revolutionary movement (2), and the culture of Russia at the time and its international importance (4). Three lessons (seminars are again suggested) of revision bring the course to a conclusion.

The basic concepts to be instilled in class 9 include "common experience in the historical fate of the peoples of our country, the progressive significance of the entry of the peoples of Central Asia, the Caucasus, Kazakhstan, Siberia and the Far East into [the] Russia[n Empire], the strengthening of revolutionary, military, labour and cultural traditions of our country, and the mutual enrichment of the national cultures of the peoples of Russia".

Class 10. 136 lessons (four per week) are allocated in year 10, 63 of which are concerned with general modern history and 73 with the Soviet Union.

General history begins with the Paris Commune (4) and is followed by a study of capitalist countries at the turn of the century (15) under these headings: basic features of capitalism (3), the economic development of Germany, Britain (or as the Russians call it, England), France, the USA and Japan (3), the political structure and internal policy of Germany, Britain, France and USA (3), foreign relations of these countries and Japan (2), and the workers´ movements there (3). Themes to be picked up here include technological advance, imperialism and colonialism, the growth of monopolies, the class nature of parliamentary democracy, corruption, conflict between workers and bourgeoisie, inter-capitalist rivalry, the arms race, and within the workers´ movement the struggle of revolutionaries with "opportunists". The remaining themes in general history are the Second International (3), popular liberation struggles in South-West and Central Europe (2), similar struggles in Asia, Africa and Latin America (5), the culture of foreign countries and of Russia at the time - in this topic mention is made of the class character of education, scientific discoveries, anti-democratic developments in bourgeois ideology, the growing strength of Marxism, proletarian strains and social realism in Western literature, liberationist ideals in Eastern literature, and the significance of Russian culture in a universal context - (4), imperialism as the highest and last stage of capitalism (3), and the First World War and the participation of Russia in it (6).

History of the USSR in class 10 begins with a study of Russia in the imperialist period and the overthrow of tsarism (25): Russia's participation in imperialism, "Russia - the birthplace of Leninism" (8), the revolution of 1905-1907 (9), Russia between two bourgeois-democratic revolutions, 1907-February 1917 (5), and the February Revolution (3). History of Soviet society then begins with the Great October Socialist Revolution and the victory of Socialism (48): the transformation of the bourgeois-democratic revolution into a socialist one (7), the victory of the socialist revolution and the establishment of the dictatorship of the proletariat in Russia; the beginning of the move from capitalism to socialism (13), the years of intervention by imperialist powers and the civil war of 1918-1920 (8), the establishment of a national economy in 1921-1925 (6), the struggle to put the Leninist plan for the construction of socialism in the USSR into practice in 1926-1937 - again it is interesting to note that Stalin's name appears once only in two substantial pages of summary of content for this theme, and then it is casually, as the last in a list of leading figures of the period - (14).

The tenth-year course ends with nineteen more lessons of twentieth-century general history: "The capitalist world between the two world wars". The first of the two themes is the emergence of a revolutionary movement in capitalist countries and the growth of national liberation movements in colonies and dependent countries after the October Revolution (6): attempts at revolution and the formation of Communist parties in China, Germany, Hungary and Mongolia, support for the Soviet Union in Britain, France, the USA and Italy, the League of Nations, the rise of Fascism, and the Communist International. The second theme is foreign countries in 1924-1939 (11), and topics to be covered include the establishment of Fascism, colonial liberation movements, bourgeois reformism in Britain (i.e. the rise of the Labour Party), the Civil War in Spain, the invasions of Ethiopia and China, and the worsening of relations between imperial powers in the 1930s. The last two entries are "the encouragement by Western governments of aggression by Fascist powers (the policy of "non-intervention" and the Munich agreement); the struggle of the USSR in defence of countries which suffered aggression". Basic concepts include the October Revolution as the "main event of the twentieth century", the proletarian "front" against Fascism, the general crisis of capitalism and the crisis in the system of imperialism.

Study of the history of the USSR culminates in *class 11* (3 lessons a week). A lesson entitled "International relations on the eve of the Second World War" acts as an introduction to the subject of "Strengthening and development of socialist society in the USSR" (28 lessons). Separate themes under this heading are the USSR in the pre-war years 1938-1941 (4), the Second World War and Great Fatherland War of the Soviet Union (17), post-war recovery of the Soviet economy and further development of socialist society 1945-61 (6); two consolidation lessons make up the numbers. The next section is on the USSR and the improvement of socialism and the general movement towards communism (15):- economic development (3), social development (2), socio-political life (2), science and culture (2); Soviet foreign policy (2) is studied along with the theme of international relations in general history later in the year. The XXVII Congress of the CPSU and its historic significance receives 4 lessons, and 15 are devoted to consolidation and revision for examinations.

The basic concepts to be mastered by pupils include the main reason for the Second World War ("the deterioration of inter-imperialist contradictions"), the Great Fatherland War as "a just war for the freedom and independence of the socialist homeland", the superiority of socialist state organization and ideology, the ideological and political unity of the Soviet people, the crucial role of the Communist Party in winning the war and as the avant-garde of the people, post-war recovery as a great exploit of the people, the Soviet people as a "new historic community" and as one "national-economic complex", and "Soviet culture as a fusion of the achievements of all the peoples of the Union". It would be interesting to go into the details of the syllabus at length, but space does not allow; however, the main directions are to stress the heroism of 1941-1945, the leadership of the Party, the unity of the multi-national Union and the rightness of Soviet policy (even when directed by long-discredited figures). Phrasing of the syllabus notes sometimes creates an impression of causality which Western historians would not necessarily accept: "Use by American imperialism of the atomic bomb. Entry of the USSR into the war against Japan. Defeat of the Kwantung army. Unconditional surrender of Japan."

General and contemporary world history is studied for 49 lessons. Section II (section I was studied in class 10) is the Second World War (5). Section III is the "formation and development of the world socialist system; the intensification of the crisis of capitalism; collapse of the colonial system; the struggle of the peoples of the world for peace, national independence, social progress, democracy and socialism and

against imperialism". Formation of the world socialist system
(14) covers the revolutions of the 1940s in Central and SE
Europe and the establishment there of the basis of socialism,
the socialist countries of Europe and Asia from 1960 to the
present, Cuba as the first Latin-American socialist country,
and the development of cooperation between socialist states.
Next, capitalist countries 1945 to the present (10) - USA,
Europe and Japan; the national liberation movements in Asia
and Africa (8); anti-imperialist struggles in Latin America
(2); the international communist movement since 1945 (2) -
communism as the most influential ideology in the modern
world, the struggle for the unity of working-class action
under communist leadership, the struggle for peace by all
truly progressive forces; international relations since the
war and peoples' peace movement (4); and finally the development of culture in the contemporary world (7).

A large number of "central ideas" appears in the syllabus, but those indicated as being particularly important for
the pupils to master are: socialist internationalism, the
general crisis of capitalism, state-monopoly capitalism, the
two types of international relations at the present time: that
between socialist countries which is of a new quality, and
peaceful coexistence with countries of different political
structures.

Teaching Method and Study Skills

The content of the whole school course in history is considerable, but how is it meant to be learned? It is clear from
methodological literature that the understanding of concepts
as well as the assimilation of facts is prominent in the minds
of educators. Fifteen years ago the introduction to a
seventh-year textbook addressed the pupils who would use it,
giving a set of instructions which amounted to little more
than how to swallow the text whole: read it in conjunction
with tables, maps and illustrations, learn the dates in heavy
print by heart, try to answer the questions at the end of each
section on a basis of thoughtful reading of the book, try to
re-tell the content of each paragraph in your own words, and
if you find that difficult, break it down into component parts
first. Now, it is certainly true that pupils need to be able
to extract the essence from the textbooks they use. But
effective and intelligent reading is not taught merely by
encouraging the paraphrasing of parts of one book; moreover,
the message which comes over is that historical truth resides
in these pages and that success in studying history consists
in remembering their content in detail. Much more recent
methodological literature, with its now customary emphasis on
creative learning, still none the less concentrates on discussion of how the content can be made more coherent, convincing,
comprehensible and easy to assimilate. There is talk of

getting pupils to seek information independently. Visual aids, supplementary reading matter, seminars, independent study of sources (almost exclusively Party documents), and "use of the pupils´ social experience" are all now recommended.

Prospects and Challenges

When the present syllabus was compiled there was controversy over a number of issues. There were those who would have incorporated the at present episodic fifth-year course into the desired linear structure, but this suggestion was not adopted: because that course was to prepare for work in future years, it was seen to have great value in moral education and fifth-year pupils were perceived to experience emotional involvement in the subject matter. (In any case the argument for a linear syllabus is not accepted by all.) Then there was a proposal to shift down some of the material into earlier years to cut down the overloading in the senior classes, where the problem is worst. Thirdly, there was tension between specialists responsible for individual units of the course, many of whom wanted more material included, and the educationists, whose task it was to cut down overloading. The demands of the specialists were rejected.

One possible future move may be to replace cultural studies by a thematic approach; cross-cultural treatment is felt in some quarters to be preferable to "one lesson, one country". The syllabus for class 11 has given some difficulty; a book published in 1985 described it as existing in several experimental variants, and the version described above may prove not to be the definitive one.

In assessing the Soviet history syllabus from a Western point of view, it is important to remember that the compilers of the Soviet syllabus have explicit moral and ideological aims and set out openly to convince children of certain points of view. It is this adoption of a viewpoint and the consequent perception of the subject as a body of scientific knowledge, rather than as a vehicle for ideas or as representing a set of skills, which causes the greatest misgivings . Nevertheless, if the notion of history as a content-laden subject is accepted, the Soviet syllabus has strong points. It is certainly not parochial: thirty countries appear in it and there is a creditable attempt to give a picture of world history as well as that of the territory of the Soviet Union. A child who had undergone the full course and mastered it would know a lot of facts about many parts of the world. He would know far less about battles and heroic leaders than about movements and changes in society, and he would also know not a little about the technology, science, arts and culture of many societies. The course is well-organized and thoroughly planned. Full understanding of many of the concepts would be beyond most average children, but at least it can be said

that a wide-ranging account of the Marxist-Leninist interpretation of history is systematically presented to the pupil.

SOCIAL STUDIES

This subject is closely related to the history course, and
conceived as the culmination of the political education of
schoolchildren, as "accelerating the socio-economic development of the country" and effecting "qualitative reconstruction
of all spheres of Soviet society" - staggering claims for a
syllabus taught only in the last two years of schooling.
    Compulsory courses in political theory for students in
all faculties are a feature of the higher education system,
and one which has not been without difficulties, the unpopul-
arity of any compulsory course being one of them. At least
one handbook for lecturers hints at occasional poor behaviour
and contains advice on improving relations with the students
and also their motivation. The school course in social studies has been criticised for "scholasticism and contemplative-
ness", for being divorced from real life and apparently irrelevant to the pupils' interests and personal experience.
The task of the subject is to convince pupils of the Party's
adherence to true Marxist-Leninist principles, the innovatory
and continuous nature of Party policy, the creative character
of revolutionary theory and the advantages of socialism, but
teachers should not shirk the need to display the "contradictions and difficulties of the present stage of the development
of society". The duty of teachers to motivate pupils both to
learn and actively to put Party policy into action is frequently mentioned.
    The effectiveness of the teaching of social studies is
giving cause for concern. The syllabus is in a state of flux,
and the most recent version available at the time of writing
(late 1986) is described as "projected". Since it is likely
that this version will be adopted in some form or other, it is
given most of the space here. However, comparison of this
with the 1983 definitive syllabus indicates the direction in
which political educators are moving.

The 1983 Syllabus

The 68 hours (2 fewer than under the new dispensation) are divided into three sections, after a two-lesson introduction on
Marxism-Leninism. The first is entitled "Dialectical and historical materialism - the basis of a scientific world-view"
(18 lessons) and has two themes: fundamental questions of
dialectical materialism and the materialistic understanding of
history. Section two is "Capitalism - the last exploitative
structure; from capitalism to communism" (9 lessons): the
characteristics of the capitalist organization of society,

imperialism as the highest and last stage of capitalism, and the era of the collapse of capitalism and the triumph of communism. The third section is the most substantial, consisting of 35 lessons on "Socialism and communism – two phases of communist formation; developed socialist society in gradual transformation into communist society". The six topics into which this is divided are: the economic structure of developed socialism, the socio-political structure of developed socialist society, the education of communist man, the socialist way of life, the Communist Party of the Soviet Union – the leading and directing force in Soviet society, and communism – the bright future for the whole of humanity.

Contents of the 1986 Syllabus Project

Introduction (2 lessons): Marxism-Leninism as working-class ideology; revolutionary doctrine and the foundation of a scientific world view. Section I, "Dialectical and historical materialism – the philosophic basis of a scientific world view" (20): principles of dialectical materialism (7) and principles of historical materialism (13). The central ideas listed in relation to this section include "Matter is primary, consciousness secondary... The materialist dialectic is the method of perceiving and transforming the world. Materialism and idealism, science and religion are irreconcilable. Social life determines social consciousness... The development of society is subject to laws... The laws of social development are manifested in the practical activity of people."

Section II, "Capitalism as the last exploitative structure" (11): "Basic features of the capitalist means of production" (4) and "Imperialism is monopoly capitalism; the general crisis of capitalism". The central ideas here are: "The requisition by capitalists of added value is the economic basis of the antagonism between proletariat and bourgeoisie. Capitalism is still powerful and dangerous, but... past its peak... At the stage of imperialism material conditions mount up for the replacement of capitalist economic relationships by socialist ones, and the objective and subjective preconditions for a successful socialist revolution become ripe".

Section III: "Socialism – the first phase in the formation of communism; guidelines for the perfecting of socialist society" (45 lessons) is made up of five topics: how the formation of communism emerges and develops (5), the economic structure of socialism (13), social relations under socialism (8), socialism as a political system; the Marxist-Leninist party as the leading force in socialist society (6), and the intellectual [actually: "spiritual", *dukhovnaya*] life of socialist society; the formation of a rounded personality (8). The central ideas of this section include: "...the creation of a new society... is the mission of the working class... Socialism... is the incarnation of humanism... `From each according to his abilities, to each according to his needs´ is a principle of communism. The present course of the CPSU towards the achievement of a qualitatively new state of society... An ever fuller discovery of the opportunities... offered by socialism... signifies a real movement... towards communism... Public property is a fundamental factor in the existence of socialism and the main source of its progress... The main motive force in progress is, was and will always remain the human being. An active role in the creative activity of the people is the patriotic duty of every Soviet person".

Section IV is "The struggle between the forces of progress and reaction in the contemporary world" (5). Its central ideas are: "The move from capitalism to socialism and communism is the basic content of the modern era. Socialist society is superior to capitalism as a stage in social progress. World socialism is a guiding force in the struggle for peace and social progress."

Teaching Method

The conceptual level of the content of the social studies course is certainly high, but many intellectually less strong pupils must find it hard to digest, while the brighter might sometimes be sceptical of some aspects of the philosophical standpoint. How is the subject taught? The accompanying literature recommends lectures as "popularization in the best sense of the word", seminars in which "formalism" and the repetition of answers learned by rote should not be tolerated, work with textbooks in which the pupils are to study them and extract the essence for themselves, and testing in which both oral and short written answers should be designed to test conceptual understanding of the issues. The 1983 syllabus suggests "research, analysis, generalization" and use of locally available material, as well as "conferences", disputations and meetings with local workers.

One does not have to read very many articles on the teaching of social studies to realise that present methods are not proving as effective as the authorities would like. By boring children silly with stultifying theory and propaganda, teachers are not getting very far. The Soviet reaction to this situation is that if teachers are not convincing the pupils or if they are not arousing much interest in the subject among pupils who yearn for Western popular music or imported goods, something must be wrong with the methodology. Since the Soviet position is demonstrably based on scientific principles, then the point will surely be got across by redoubled effort. What the Soviet educator does not do is shirk the issue - the content is presented whatever happens.

Chapter 10

GEOGRAPHY

GEOGRAPHY from classes 6 to 10 is conceived as a unified
course, linear and thematic in structure. In class 6 the
subject is entitled "Basic course in physical geography";
class 7: geography of continents and oceans; classes 8 and 9:
physical, social and economic geography of the USSR; class 10:
world economic and social geography. Two lessons a week are
devoted to the subject, except in class 7, when the period
allocation is three.

This structure is reported by Soviet educators to have
"stabilized" at the beginning of the 1980s, but the arrangement summarised here (from the syllabus published in January
1986) is innovative in at least two respects, while not in
fact being a radical departure from previous practice. Study
of the Soviet Union in years 8 and 9 used to separate physical
geography from economic, and the word "social" did not appear
in the title of that part of the programme. It therefore
appears that the new syllabus more closely reflects the Marxist triad man - nature - society, but when the content of the
programme is more closely examined, we discover that within
the overall title, physical and social-economic geography are
studied separately, and the innovation looks on the face of it
like little more than the insertion of eight lessons of social
and economic geography before the end of year 8. However, we
have discovered before that Soviet educational thought attaches great importance to the arrangement of the presentation of
information. A second innovation is the reorganization of the
tenth-year course on a regional basis, cutting out the duplication involved in studying several different countries of a
very similar type in detail, and replacing it by a partially
thematic approach, highlighting selected global problems and
the making of connections. The syllabus also provides for
more study of the child's own region than before. The whole
course is now said to be more logically constructed and better
graded than it was.

Moves in Geographical Education

Geography presents the image of a rather low-status subject, suspended uneasily between the sciences and the arts, and not receiving very much attention in the general educational forum. Soviet teachers express determination to put their subject on the map, so to speak; they probably show more awareness of what is going on in geographical education in other parts of the world than do teachers of other subjects. Along with educators in capitalist countries, as they say, they have been seeking to raise the intellectual level of geography in schools and to use the subject to develop the reasoning powers of pupils. The new syllabus does show a real attempt to cut down content and teach geographical concepts. Geography lessons begin in year 6 with a substantial introduction to the nature of geographical studies (which is certainly new) and a thorough grounding in the representation of terrain in conventional form on charts, plans, maps, and globes. There are attempts to get at principles rather than merely to convey vast amounts of information. Theorists declare they are now less interested in teaching "what is where", but in "the generalization and typologization of geographical phenomena".

Aims

It will be no surprise that geographers set out to form a dialectical-materialist world-view and to "convince children that socialist economic organization is best". However, two leading theorists write: "The teaching of geography is intended to form in pupils a favourable attitude to the workers of all countries, respect for the customs and traditions of the peoples of the world, and also to work out a sense of common purpose and common responsibility in social and economic matters, along with zealous concern for the natural resources of the homeland, pride in its economic success and responsibility for its developmental prospects." Bravo! For once we discover, moderately expressed, a truly internationalist and intelligently patriotic attitude.

Further, geography teachers declare that geographical studies should develop the imagination of school children (as well as their memory and their logical powers), but it is not claimed that the subject should be easy. To master geographical knowledge is "impossible without serious effort".

The Syllabus

Class 6. The course begins with an introduction (5 lessons), in which children are told what the subject is all about, how human concepts of the world have changed since antiquity, and the role of more recent exploration and modern research and investigation in establishing the subject. The rest of the year falls into four sections as follows, with numbers of lessons given in brackets. I: Charts and maps (15) - the representation of terrain in graphic form, types of maps; basic concepts of scale, conventional signs, latitude and longitude; maps local, national and universal. II: The earth's surface (39): the lithosphere (9) - rock strata, the earth's crust, volcanic phenomena, mountains, ravines, ocean basins; the hydrosphere (10) - seas, oceans and their depths, rivers, river basins, lakes; the atmosphere (12) - wind, precipitation, weather, climate; the biosphere (3); the interdependence of the components of nature (5). III: Human life on earth (5) - population, races and their equality, economic activity and way of life (including that of the local area), how centres of population are represented on a map. IV: Natural features and population of the area local to the school (a new topic in the 1986 syllabus).

Class 7 (three lessons a week), deals with the geography of continents and oceans. Introduction (2). I: Characteristics of the natural world (9): lithosphere and the earth's relief (2); the world ocean as the main manifestation of the hydrosphere (4); atmosphere and climate (3). II: Variety in natural features of continents and oceans (7): the variety of natural complexes (5) and natural zonality (2). III: Population and the political map of the world (3) - the interrelationship between natural characteristics and patterns of settlement. IV: Continents and oceans (73): Africa (13) - its physical characteristics, exploration, colonial history, population, and brief study of four particular countries: Algeria, Nigeria, Ethiopia and the United Arab Republic; the Indian Ocean (1); Australia (4); the Pacific (2); the Antarctic Continent (3); South America (10), studied much as Africa and where the particular countries featured are Brazil, Peru and Argentina; North America (11) - USA, Canada, Mexico and Cuba; the Atlantic (2); Eurasia (22) - its physical geography, climate, river systems, population, political position, and study of six countries - the Soviet Union, Britain, France, Federal Republic of Germany, Japan and India; the Arctic Ocean (2); comparison of the natural conditions of continents and oceans (2). V: The "geographical envelope" and natural complexes (8), including the characteristics and structure of the geographical envelope (8); the interaction of nature and man (2).

Classes 8 and 9: geography of the USSR. Class 8: Introduction (3) - the role of geographical science in the solution of economic and social problems; sources of geographical knowledge; specialised maps, reference materials. Part I, "Physical Geography of the USSR"; section I: general characteristics of the natural world (21), including relief, geographical structure and useful minerals (6); climate (5); lakes and water resources (4); soil and earth resources (4); plant and animal life (2). II: Variety in the natural complexes of the USSR, including division into natural areas (2); natural zones

(8); the main natural regions (12); the seas which surround the USSR (3).   III: Rational use of natural resources and the conservation of nature (8), including natural resources and the economy (6); fundamentals of the use and conservation of natural resources (2).

Pupils begin to study "Economic and Social Geography of the USSR" at this stage, a course of 64 lessons, which begins near the end of the eighth year with an introduction (1) on the general and political importance of the subject and its relationship with other parts of the course.   IV: Population of the Soviet Union (7) - a "united multinational state", the numerical strength of the population, and its distribution. By this time it is the summer holiday, and the course continues in class 9 with section V: general characteristics of the economy (26), including labour resources (2); the economy and the interdependence of its various branches (3); geography of the more important economic complexes and branches of the economy (21) - comprising engineering (2), fuel and power (4), processing of natural resources into building materials (4), the agro-industrial complex and land improvement (3), consumer goods and services (2), transport (2), general considerations and summary (4).   VI: Economic and social geography of the Union Republics and large regions (30), including the territorial organization of the economy and the division of the country into economic regions (3); economic zones of the USSR (21), subdivided into themes as follows: the western zone (10) - central Russia, the European north, west and south, the Urals and Volga region - general features and problems of the western economic zone (1), the eastern economic zone (5) and the south-eastern zone (5); the economics of the USSR - a unified national-economic complex (3) - a generalization section; the development of the economy and social progress of Soviet society (3).   The geography of the republic to which the school belongs (12)is a separate part of the course, studied in the light of the foregoing material.

Class 10 studies the economic and social geography of the world.   After an introduction (1) in the usual style, section I is entitled "general characteristics of the economic geography of the world" (18).   This includes the contemporary political map of the world (2) - related to Marxist-Leninist theory about social and economic development and typology of states, international relations and the peaceful Soviet foreign policy; a world geography of natural resources and ecological problems (4); the geography of world population (4) - the economic reproduction of population, demographic policies, urbanisation etc.; the geography of the world economy (7) - stages in the formation of the world economy, international division of economic labour; global problems of humanity (1) - summary and generalization: the prevention of another world war, natural conservation, regulation of the reproduction and movement of population, fuel resources and the use of the resources of the ocean as global problems of the modern age; means to their solution in countries of differing socio-economic types. II: the socialist economic system and socialist countries (12), including general characteristics (2) - the world socialist economic system, Comecon countries and the state of their economic development; the socialist countries of Europe (5); the socialist countries of Asia and America (3) - this covers, obviously very briefly as so few lessons are available, Korea, Mongolia, Vietnam and Laos, but China and Cuba are featured in greater detail. There are no critical remarks about China in the syllabus notes. Section II concludes with 4 lessons on the international socialist division of labour and socialist economic integration.

Section III: the world capitalist economic system and the development of capitalist countries (9), including general characteristics (2), the development of the capitalist countries of North America, Western Europe and Asia (6) - at least twelve countries feature in the notes for these few lessons, but the main attention falls on the USA, Japan and major West European countries treated together; international capitalist division of labour and capitalist economic integration (1) - "USA, Western Europe and Japan - the three main centres of imperialist contradictions". IV: the developing countries (9). This topic is sub-divided into general characteristics (3), the developing countries of Asia, Africa and Latin America (6) - this subject really is taken as a theme, not as a list of individual countries, and the only single country which figures prominently is India. V: universal economic relations (2). This concluding short section deals with the inequality in the economic relations of capitalist and developing countries, the struggle of developing countries for the establishment of a new world economic order, their relations with the Soviet Union, the principal industrial concerns set up in developing countries with Soviet help. Pupils are taught about economic relations between socialist and developed capitalist countries, economic cooperation between East and West, the "inevitability of the victory of socialism in this competition" and "the world on the brink of the third millenium".

Methods and Materials

If teachers are serious about using geography to develop the cognitive abilities of children, teaching methods will avoid heavy reliance on lecturing in class and factual recall in testing. The introduction to the syllabus writes of three stages in the mastery of geographical knowledge: the assimilation of ready-made information and data, the application of knowledge and skills in familiar situations according to a model, and thirdly the creative application of knowledge and skills in a new learning situation. "The attainment of this third level is usually connected with the creation in lessons of problem situations and the involvement of pupils in their solution. One of the forms of problem teaching with good prospects in geography is active games." The nature of these games is not described, but the type of activity intended will be familiar to most progressive western teachers of geography as of several other subjects. The use of micro-computers is suggested as one way forward.

The introduction to the syllabus is emphatic that "practical work" has an important part to play, but it may be found a little surprising that there is really very little field work. The early years include a reasonable amount of observation of the weather (which one imagines Russian schoolchildren are beginning to find a little tiresome after five years of it in primary and junior secondary classes in "Acquaintance with the world around" and nature study before the geography course ever starts). Class 6 has a few items of field work, such as orientation in the open, study of the surface of rocks, examination of a small sector of ground with a plane-table, and acquaintance with the physical features of the local area. In year seven children are to study the interaction of man and nature in their area, and that is an end to it. For the rest, practical work means map interpretation and the collection of evidence for reports and essays which, of course, is fairly innovative in a country where attainment has traditionally been tested by individual recitation of learned facts.

Apart from the textbook, a list of visual aids and other teaching materials is appended to the syllabus. For class 6 this consists of a familiar list of collections (minerals, ores), models of rock strata, maps and globes, a working model of the water cycle in nature, a tellurion, the necessary instruments for the outdoor observations mentioned above, pictures and tables, calendars for recording meteorological observations, various illustrated handouts, slides (5 sets), film strips (4 sets), film clips (9) and one film ("Why we study our earth"). A similar amount of material of the same type is specified for all the other years of the geography course.

Assessment

Testing is carried out under three headings, "knowledge", "practical skills" and "ability to carry out observations in nature and in a work-place". The knowledge norms are broadly comparable with those for subjects such as history. To be awarded a five pupils must give an answer in the oral test which is full, correct and a reflection of the course content, it must show correct understanding of geographical concepts, make correct use of maps and other sources of information, be independent and be based on knowledge received and additional information about the "geographical events of the present age". For a mark of 3 the pupil answers broadly correctly, but shows much weaker conceptual grasp and gives a less logical explanation, perhaps being unable to explain the interrelations of aspects of geographical data. On practical knowledge, for 5 the pupil should give a fully correct answer and a full interpretation of the physical characteristics of the area represented by the map, or be able independently to draw conclusions from his own practical activity, and present results acurately. For a mark of 3 some inaccuracies in the formulation of conclusions and the presentation of results are tolerated.

Observational work receives a mark of 5 if it is carried out fully "according to plan", the phenomenon observed is accurately described and represented in plans, maps or diagrams, deductions are correctly formulated and observations neatly presented. For 3, incomplete representation of objects observed, part inaccuracy, and substantial insufficiencies in the presentation are allowed. It will be seen that considerable leeway for discretion is granted here.

Geographical Education East and West

The shift from the "capes and bays" tradition of geography teaching towards concept-based work and problem solving which this new syllabus illustrates is familiar enough to Western geography teachers. The Marxist basis with its stress on the means of production and world political systems has its counterpart in the "humanistic geography" which is to some extent established in British higher education, but which is still a source of educational and political controversy in schools. Recognition of the ecological dimension represents a coming-together of Western and Soviet school geography. British teachers are, however, very far ahead of their Soviet colleagues in field work and assessed independent inquiry - though it has taken the compulsory introduction of the General Certificate of Secondary Education to ensure that such practices have become general.

Chapter 11

THE FOREIGN LANGUAGE

IT IS NOT immediately obvious why any child in the Soviet Union should want to learn a foreign language. The number of Soviet citizens who ever leave their native country, however briefly, whether for professional purposes or for holidays, is very small indeed. Yet motivation and achievement among pupils appears high. Research by Soviet sociologists confirms that children show a high level of interest in foreign languages, but indicates that enthusiasm falls off in the senior classes – a fact very likely due to the small number of lessons at that stage and the inevitable consequent frustration at lack of perceptible progress. Soviet society attaches importance to foreign languages in education. Learning a foreign language clearly contributes to all-round development and assists the child to develop an understanding for the native language. Soviet educators believe that there is a "linguistic mode of thought" which an educated person should experience. The state perceives a need for linguistically proficient personnel in a wide range of jobs: in industry, technology, science, teaching, translating, librarianship and the mass media.

Psychology of Foreign Language Teaching

A key principle is the "unity of consciousness and action". The "conscious-practical" method advocated by B. V. Belyayev most closely enshrines this principle, and a fairly recent influential survey of language teaching defends the method vigorously and affirms that the basis of the conscious-practical method is "the Marxist theory of cognition... which has been borne out by the experience of teachers of Russian as a foreign language". Soviet experts are now convinced that attempting to teach a foreign language without attention to grammar gives poor results and that the method of inviting pupils to deduce grammar rules for themselves is wasteful of time. The child must be able to operate the rules of a language consciously. A sound method should ensure abundant practice in speaking, so that application of the rules becomes automatic for the pupil. The need to "maintain an optimal balance between theoretical knowledge and practical skills" is regularly referred to in official statements on foreign language teaching, and the Soviet style of applying audio-visual and audio-lingual methods contains elements of conscious-practical principles. There is no faith in the Soviet Union in the idea of speaking a foreign language as behaviour learned without an understanding of the structures of the language.

The Languages Taught

Russian is, of course, the principal language taught to non-native speakers. In all schools one foreign, non-Soviet, language is taught compulsorily to all pupils. In about 50% of the schools that language is English, in 20% German and in another 20% French. Spanish and other languages account for the remaining 10%; an exhaustive list cannot be given, but certainly Italian, Chinese, Hindi and Urdu are included in small measure. Not all local authorities stick to these centrally planned percentages; those in charge of some local offices had their fingers rapped a few years ago for allowing too much English to be taught, thus causing an awkward shortage of English text-books.

Organization

All pupils study a foreign language from class 5 until the end of their school career with a lesson allocation of 4 + 3 + 2 + 2 + 1 + 1 + 1. The single period in years 9 to 11 is regarded with particular disfavour by linguists. Some children may choose to start a second foreign language in class 10 by dropping the first and adding two of the periods allocated to options to the one saved, always assuming that the school is able to offer this.

The most impressive achievements in language teaching probably proceed from classes in schools with a special profile in a foreign language. Languages in the mass schools have a lower priority and less prestige. Nevertheless, one aim of foreign language methodologists is to use the special schools as laboratories to try out new methods in the eventual hope of raising standards of language teaching in all schools.

Content of the Syllabus

In view of the limited time available in the mass schools, goals set are modest. The course is seen partly as a basis for further study after school. The entire secondary school course teaches 850 lexical items for active use, which is held to be enough for basic conversational purposes, and 100 more for reading purposes. International and easily guessable words are added to this. Skills taught and tested are speaking, listening and reading. Children write in class, but are tested orally. The main problem is how to keep syllabus content to a minimum while ensuring that content taught is "sufficient" - one may ask, for what? Sufficient, perhaps, to make pupils and teachers feel the exercise is worth while. In the last three years the demands of the course in listening and speaking are identical with those of class 8; the one lesson per week is only sufficient to develop reading skills while marking time on the rest.

The published syllabus is arranged so that the thematic content and the practical requirements, which are the same for all languages taught appear first, followed by the linguistic content of each language separately. We shall follow a similar plan here, but shall follow each skill - understanding, speaking and reading - through the whole school course; this procedure will aid both brevity and clarity. The exact linguistic content will be given for English only, but that for the other languages is very similar.

Themes.   Two lists appear, the first for years 5 to 8 and the second for 9 to 11. These will be given here in full to illustrate the moral and social content, and it should be assumed that they are built upon and extended as the course progresses. The first of three themes in classes 5 - 8 "for oral speaking and reading" is "the pupil and his immediate surroundings": the person, his appearance, character, how he feels, his clothes, possessions, life; the family, its life, occupations; flat, house, community, household; shopping; school life and learning of the foreign language; Pioneer work and socially useful labour; leisure, cultural activities, sport; health. Theme 2 is "our country": the USSR, Moscow, hero-cities; life and activity of Lenin; national holidays and celebrations (eight are listed - five more than previously), the coat of arms, anthem, and flag (another new topic in the latest syllabus); town, village, home area; farm and agricultural work; nature, animal and plants, seasons; travel, local sights. Theme 3 is "countries where the language learned is spoken": various information (no further details given).

The themes (for reading only) in classes 9 to 11 are two, firstly "our country": cultural, social and sporting life of young people; choice of a profession; the Communist League of Youth, its history and activities; the Constitution of the USSR; the peaceful Leninist policy of the USSR, the struggle for peace and the reduction of tension, current political events; industry and agriculture, the building of communism; heroism in labour; scientific and technical progress, the conquest of space; nature conservation. The second is "countries where the language studied is spoken": geographical position, the economy, social conditions; "sights" and points of interest; life and activity of Lenin in the countries concerned; important historical events and famous people; struggle of the workers for peace and for their economic and political rights; youth organizations; science, literature and art; school life and educational system.

Requirements in terms of skills. Listening. Pupils should be able to understand language texts spoken by the teacher or recorded, based on the linguistic material for the year in question. In class 5 these are very short, in class 6 they may take up to one minute to deliver, in class 7 two minutes - and 1% of unknown words may be included, in class 8 - 2% of new vocabulary, in class 9 - 3% (still limited to two minutes).

Speaking is divided into "dialogue" and "monologue". For the former, pupils are to learn to ask and answer questions and issue commands within the framework of the material learned. The pupil should be able to produce at least three correctly formulated, coherent and complete responses or utterances in the course of a conversation (class 5), four such (class 6), five (class 7) and six (class 8). In class 6 pupils must be able to hold a conversation, issue requests, instructions and amplification of earlier remarks; these may be based on something "heard, seen or read". In class 7 new points are exclamations, expression of agreement or refusal, and cross-questioning. In class 8 additional requirements are the communication of information, expressing objections and exchanging opinions.

In class 5 pupils should be able to produce a short "monologue" or talk without preparation on any subject in the syllabus, and it should be at least 5 sentences long. In class 6 the requirements are more specific: it must be at least 7 sentences long, be "logical and consecutive" and may involve re-telling the content of a text heard or read (a popular and educationally very useful procedure with Soviet language teachers). In class 7 the talk should be 9 sentences long; in class 8 ten sentences are required, and pupils should be able to express their attitude to the information conveyed.

In classes 9 to 11 the requirements for speaking and listening are exactly the same as for class 8, and the one lesson per week is devoted mainly to improving reading skills. These are not, however, neglected in the early years. In class 5 knowledge of the alphabet, ability to read simple texts silently with undertanding and to read aloud with division into phrases by sense are required. In class 6 the content of reading passages may include 2% of unknown words (supplementary information helps the pupils with comprehension) and a reading speed of 250 printed signs per minute is suggested; in class 7 the speed is 300 per minute aloud and 350 silently, in class 8: 400 for both - and use of a translating dictionary is to be taught. In class 9 adapted texts are supplied to be read for pleasure and information on socio-political and popular science topics. Speed is still 400 printed signs per minute; 2% new words (for guessing without dictionary) and 4% with dictionary is allowed; texts of not less than 1500 printed signs are set for study in one 45-minute lesson. In classes 10 and 11 the figures are 3%, 6% and 1700 signs, and in the last three classes texts adapted from artistic literature are supplied.

Taking English as the example, the linguistic content of the syllabus is as follows. Class 5 deals with phonetics: all the sounds of English and the intonation of narrative, imperative and interrogative sentences. Vocabulary: in the first four years of the course lexical items are to be assimilated for active use in the following amounts - 350, 550, 700 and 850 respectively (totals are cumulative, of course). 100 more items are added in the reading course in classes 9 - 11. Word-formation in class 5 involves the suffixes -teen, -ty, -th; in class 6 division of words into syllables; in class 7 -er, -tion, -y, -ly; class 8: -ment, -ness, -ful, -able, -less and prefixes un- (etc.), re-; class 9: suffixes -ic, -ical, -al, and prefixes dis-, mis-; class 10: -ist, -ism, -ize, -ate, -ify and anti-; class 11: -ant, -ent, -ance, -ence, -(i)ty, -ous, -ive, and -en.

Grammar and Syntax. Class 5: verbs to be, to have, impersonal "there", present continuous and present indefinite tenses, auxiliaries can, may and must; affirmative, negative and interrogative statements and affirmative and negative commands. Plural of nouns, marking the possessive, use and non-use of definite and indefinite articles [which are lacking in Russian]. Personal, demonstrative, interrogative and possessive pronouns; cardinal numerals to 100, use of ordinals, use of prepositions and conjunctions. Class 6: The present perfect, past indefinite, and future definite tenses; verb "to let", "to be going to", structures with infinitive (it's hard to, I want to, I want you to); sentences with subordinate clauses; use of indefinite pronouns, numerals beyond 100 and adverbs.

Class 7: passive verbs, present and past indefinite tenses (for passive recognition only - an attempt at reduction of overloading of the syllabus, since active use was earlier required); adverbial clauses; comparison and superlative of adjectives; present indefinite tense after if and when referring to future time [Russian uses future tense in such cases].

Class 8: past continuous and past perfect tenses (for recognition only - more reduction of overloading). Class 9: present perfect passive voice, future indefinite tense, the future in the past; sequence of tenses. Class 10: conditional clauses; the infinitive and infinitive expressions. Class 11: the gerund; present and past participles and their use.

Teaching Styles and Methods.

Teachers are urged to use the foreign language in the classroom (and observation indicates that very many of them do so), always to introduce new material orally, never in the early stages to allow children to read without oral preparation, to use visual and technological aids every lesson, to use group work and pair work as well as class teaching, to plan their lessons carefully, and to make the children participate actively instead of merely sitting and listening. Many teachers encourage a good deal of participation, and though most of the questioning flows one way - teacher to pupil. - use of pair work (which is now welcomed by more inspectors than it was a few years ago), role-play and improvisation shows that this slight weakness is recognised.

Striking features often to be observed in foreign language lessons include wide use of the language being learned for both teaching and management purposes. This is not pedantically insisted upon, and pupils in difficulty are allowed to use Russian occasionally. Activities are changed every few minutes. In junior classes activities rarely last longer than five or six minutes. Teachers move briskly from reading aloud to asking questions, reading silently, summarising a passage, doing a grammar exercise, listening to a text read aloud, acting out everyday situations. Work cards appear from files, visual and audio-visual aids are regularly used. Classes are not usually divided into groups by ability; differentiation comes in the activities organized by the teacher, some of which are less demanding than others.

It must be said that many Soviet foreign language lessons are more interesting, more effective, more educational (in the sense of developing cognitive processes), more professionally competent and more marked by pupil participation than those of any other arts subject, except, perhaps in some respects, the native language. Uncritical and sometimes mindless rote-learning can be seen in some subjects, but not usually in foreign language lessons. An in-service trainer of modern language teachers, writing recently in the journal for foreign language teachers *Inostrannye yazyki v shkole* was enthusiastic about an improvement in language teaching which she claimed to have perceived; she was pleased to have seen more group work, more independent working, the use of the foreign language to discuss ethical and other problems, and teachers getting away from "standard, stereotyped exercises" and mindless lesson beginnings like "what is the weather like today?"

Textbooks

Until a few years ago books were unattractive and dull. With the introduction of somewhat more colourful printing techniques, they now look a good deal better than they used to.

More audio-visual aids have been appearing and are widely used by teachers. The contents of textbooks are extremely thorough, but give next to no information about the countries where the language is spcken, even if they are socialist states. We have seen in examining the syllabus that the stress is cn "our" country rather than the foreign land. The lamentable failure to present the foreign country is rationalized by referring to the need to give children the language in which to speak about their own lives. It must be said that Soviet authors have little or no first-hand experience of the countries whose languages they are presenting, to the extent of writing (according to one informant) "If, in London, you wish to know the time, ask a militiaman" - insisting, in the teeth of British protests, that this was correct, and apparently believing that there was something suspicious about the objections. The actual English language printed in many textbooks, it will be gathered from this, is often stilted and uses turns of phrase which are un-English.

Assessment

The 20 oral examination tickets for 1987 all consist of two questions, the first of which is "talk on a topic" and the second "reading of a text" - sometimes with and sometimes without a dictionary - followed by giving a summary of it. The summary will normally be in the foreign language, though traditionally weaker pupils were allowed to do it in Russian.

In early 1985 the 1977 "Norms for assessment in foreign languages" were withdrawn and replaced by a much tighter document, which was obviously designed to create the impression that assessment in languages mattered. It refers to testing at all stages in the school career of a pupil, and it requires assessment to be carried out in all three skills. The tests are still oral. To be awarded an excellent mark of 5 in listening, total comprehension of the passage heard must be demonstrated by success in a communicative activity associated with it. For a good mark of 4, one or two details may be less than perfect. A 3 is awarded if only the basic sense of the passage is understood. Failing grades are given if the sense of the passage is not comprehended. In speaking, 5 goes to the candidate whose answers fully meet the requirements laid down in the syllabus in terms of number of utterances, content and correctness; for 4 a few mistakes in the language are allowed. For 3 more serious mistakes are tolerated provided the answer is still comprehensible; failing marks are given if "discourse does not take place" or if the language is so poor that comprehension is affected. In the reading section, the criteria for the various grades closely correspond with those for listening, except, of course, that the text is a printed one.

Concluding Remarks

What are the reasons for the success of Soviet foreign language teaching? One probable reason is historical and concerns motivation. Study abroad or with foreign professors was, in the eighteenth and nineteenth centuries, a very common feature of a Russian education (and not exclusively with the gentry). Knowledge of several languages was essential for trade, study and indeed acceptance abroad. It may well be that the notion that languages were an essential part of education percolated through to the whole of society and is still uncritically accepted - and opportunities to learn foreign languages fiercely demanded.

Secondly, in considering reasons for Soviet success in language teaching, it would be a mistake to underestimate the benefits of central planning, regular compulsory in-service training. the setting of clear goals and the exact definition of the content of syllabuses in terms of skills, lexis and grammar. The teacher who receives booklets suggesting plans for every lesson in the school year, who knows exactly what has to be covered in the time available and how it is to be taught, has only one thing to worry about: putting on a good professional performance in the classroom.

Some will object that this is an idealized picture of Soviet foreign language teaching, and indeed it may well be so. There is, however, little sign of self-satisfaction among methodologists in the USSR. Reservations remain, but the conditions exist for success: clear aims, a sound agreed methodology, oversight, carefully compiled teaching materials and good pupil motivation. If teachers are committed and well trained, success within limits carefully set is assured.

Chapter 12

PHYSICAL EDUCATION AND ELEMENTARY MILITARY TRAINING

ONE OF the characteristics of the "new Soviet person" which
education seeks to create is physical fitness. To be fit is
not optional, therefore, but a political and moral obligation.
There are several reasons for this. Health and social services are less likely to be overburdened if citizens are fit
and active (especially in a climate which is severe for much
of the year). Physical activity is traditionally believed to
have beneficial psychological effects, and games-playing students and employees are likely to be more contented and successful in their work. Fit young people are well equipped to
defend the fatherland in times of national emergency, perhaps
unexpected emergency. Athletes and sports teams who are successful in international competitions bring prestige to their
native country. Athletic pursuits constitute a focus for the
energy and enthusiasm of players and spectators young and old,
which, properly channelled, should be conducive to civil peace
and friendly international relations - at least, many people
used to believe this, before recent examples of hooliganism by
spectators and obsessive fanaticism by players. Few would
disagree, least of all in the Soviet Union, that it is the
duty of schools to see to the physical fitness of pupils and
to introduce them to sport as an enjoyable, healthy and morally and physically improving activity.

Controversies in Physical Education

What form should school physical education take? Should it be
the mindless "up, two, three, four" of the army instructor (or
the modern equivalent, disguised as "aerobics", "swing into
shape" and the like)? The enthusiastic team game player, the
middle-aged man trying to "run away from a heart attack", as
the Soviet slogan has it, or the woman seeking to lose a few
pounds may all be sufficiently motivated to go in for repet-
itive routines which may have the desired result, but will
children in school do so when the teacher is not actually
loking at them? What is the role of competitive sport in the

school P.E. lesson? In the 1920s Soviet authorities were of the opinion that team and combat sports had a bad effect on mental and physical health. Should the school be more concerned with widening every individual´s social opportunities by introducing a range of sports? Is it the duty of the school to identify and encourage outstanding talent? Do certain sporting activities have such special qualities for developing the body and the personality that they should be made compulsory for all? Should prowess in P.E. be noted on the school-leaving certificate, as it now is? Is a further certificate of proficiency (or, for that matter, of excellence) needed as a goal to work for? These questions have received a variety of answers in the Soviet Union, as elsewhere, in the last half century or so.

The Concept of Physical Culture

So far the term "physical education" has been used. The Soviet phrase is actually *fizicheskaya kul'tura* literally "physical culture", which would seem to imply more than a course of mere instruction in sports and bodily fitness. To be physically cultured means to be sports and fitness-oriented, to go in for sport and at the same time to know about it, to do morning exercises regularly and to be conscious of the need for physical fitness - perhaps also to seek new sporting experiences as opportunities present themselves. In line with this, it is worth noting that school lessons are reported by observers to be formal with an emphasis on skill rather than fun. Homework is set, two periods of fifteen minutes per week on the theoretical side, and the syllabus provides for instruction in theory. All of this reinforces the seriousness with which the subject is regarded.

Physical culture for children is not the sole responsibility of school. The family is supposed to see to it that children (and the parents themselves, for that matter) perform fitness exercises at home, learn to swim, skate and ride a bicycle. Sociologists have discovered that 40-50% of school-children do their morning exercises at home, which on the face of it appears to be a very good figure; it is, however, regarded as rather poor. For the highly gifted, sports boarding schools exist. For the child who is keen but who does not necessarily show outstanding talent, there are several possibilities: to join the school physical culture collective, to become involved in the sporting activities of the Pioneers, or to attend an after-hours sports school. The mass school fosters interest in fitness generally and in the G.T.O. Sports schools tend to cream off the better games players, with the result that inter-school sport is not strong in many places. These schools often have no premises of their own, but use municipal sports halls, factory or school facilities. It is clear, then, that opportunities do exist for schoolchildren to extend their physical culture outside lessons. Premises and equipment are often basic rather than lavish but are usually adequate for good work to be done.

A National Fitness Programme : the GTO

The letters represent *gotov k trudu i oborone SSSR* which means "prepared for labour and the defence of the USSR", and the GTO lies at the basis of the school syllabus. The GTO is a programme of proficiency in the theory and practice of physical culture. The theory includes knowledge of the rationale of PE and sport, some first aid, what might elsewhere be called "health education" and basic civil defence. Practical activities mean proving competence and showing stamina, skill, courage and energy in various ways. The goals set are not beyond normally fit people who have prepared themselves adequately and the idea is to encourage children and adults to take regular physical exercise by recognizing their achievements in the award of certificates. There are seven stages altogether. The first five are for children of school age: (1) age 6 to 9, (2) 10 to 11, (3) 12 to 13, (4) 14 to 15 and (5) 16 to 17. Stage six is for people aged 18 to 39 and stage seven for men of 40 to 60 and women of 40 to 55; above these ages a doctor's certificate must be obtained in order to participate. The GTO, therefore, is an interest which can be maintained throughout youth and middle age. Figure 3 shows examples of the standards children are expected to reach.

The Syllabus

Children receive two lessons a week of PE for their whole school career. In years 1 to 3 the 68 lessons are apportioned as follows: 28 for gymnastics, 24 for children's "movement" games, and 16 for skiing, skating or cross-country training (depending on the climate of the region. In class 4 gymnastics receive 28 lessons, athletics 10, movement games 14 and ski training (etc.) 16. For years 5 to 11 the programme is the same: 16 lessons of gymnastics, 20 athletics, 16 sports (volleyball, basketball, handball, football) and 16 ski/skating/cross-country. In classes 5 to 7 the school may choose two of the sports mentioned, and one from year 8 onwards. In class 4 swimming may be introduced for 28 lessons; in classes 5 to 11 fourteen may be given up to it at the expense of time taken from the other activities. If the school has access to a pool, swimming may be introduced as early as class 2. Its presence in the curriculum is a recent innovation and represents part of a national campaign to teach everyone to swim.

The syllabus is divided into four sections; the second is the most substantial and deals with the content of PE lessons. Section three describes extra-curricular PE and sport, and Section four occasional all-age sporting festivals.

The first section consists of instructions for "Physical-cultural health-related measures during the school day". For children in the first four classes these include "generally developmental" exercises before lessons begin, very short bursts of physical activity as a break during lessons, movement games, skipping, exercises with a ball, elements of dance, skiing, sledging or cycling during the longer playtime breaks. The movement games referred to often involve singing and dance-like steps: one occasionally sees a Russian version of the hokey cokey. In classes 5 to 8 the exercises before school and during lessons continue, and in the long breaks there are similar activities as for the younger children plus elements of rhythmic gymnastics and dance; cycling is also mentioned, and the boys are permitted to exercise with dumbells. In classes 9 to 11 six to eight exercises before lessons are prescribed, in the breaks boys and girls may exercise with various equipment: weights, hoops, Indian clubs and the like. Elements of sports and rhythmic gymnastics are mentioned for both sexes.

Section two is the hard core of the school PE syllabus. Each topic will be followed through from its introduction to the end of the pupil's school career, but first we shall summarise the "fundamentals of knowledge" for each class - these are short paragraphs indicating the assumptions on which the course is based and the theoretical knowledge the pupils are to receive.

Class 1: "Rules for behaviour in the gym and on the sports ground. Information about daily routine and personal hygiene. The importance of physical exercise for health." Class 2: "The importance of morning exercises and open-air exercise. Hygienic rules when engaging in physical exercise, rules for water, air and sun bathing." Class 3: "Active routine. The influence of physical exercises on health and bearing. Breathing while running and skiing." Class 4: "The meaning of hardening the organism; natural factors affecting hardening - air, water and sun." Class 5: "Rules for independent exercising... breathing while exercising. Safety rules. Diet and active routine."

Class 6: "The importance of physical exercise for maintaining fitness for work. Safety rules in the gym, school sports ground and pool." Class 7: "The reaction of the body to various physical stresses. Self-control. Safety precautions, first aid for sports injuries." Class 8: "The significance of physical culture for the all-round development of personality. Safety rules for carrying out exercises designed to develop speed and strength. The dangers of smoking and alcohol." Class 9: "The effect of physical culture on the organism and constitution. The role of medical oversight of sports players."

In class 10 separate syllabuses are given for boys and girls, and the way basic knowledge is formulated differs slightly. That for girls reads: "Physical culture and sport - one of the means to the all-round development of personality, the preparation of girls for labour and social activity, the harmonious development of the organism of the future mother. Girls´ hygiene during physical exercises. Engaging in out-of-school activities with younger schoolchildren." Boys on the other hand receive "preparation for military service", and another phrase is added: "physical exercise - a means to improve fitness for work"; apart from these and the omission of the reference to motherhood the paragraph is the same. In class 11 the paragraphs are identical for both sexes. "Physical culture in the country of developed socialism. The Soviet system of physical education. The influence of life-style upon health. Physical culture in the family. Fatigue and excess fatigue, how to recognise and prevent them. The control of training loads by pulse measurement."

In reading the paragraphs below, it should be remembered that not every school will offer every activity described in the syllabus, and that schools have discretion to use time as seems best to them bearing in mind the staff and facilities which they have or lack. This explains why, in the senior classes especially, more periods appear to be allocated in the syllabus than exist. Space does not allow every exercise and activity to be listed here, since they are specified in considerable detail. In Gymnastics every aspect of running, jumping, climbing, throwing, balancing and acrobatics which the children are to master at every stage is given. This applies even to six-year-olds, at which age in Western educational practice a very large measure of free activity is encouraged. Thus, in class 1 "Exercises to improve bearing: walking in a circle, in a column, over obstacles, on tip-toe, on the heels, half-squatting. Running up to one kilometre. Jumping and hopping on the spot, while moving forward, standing long jump, long and high jumping with a run up, jumping from a height of not more than 30 centimetres..." and so on. By class 11, boys are expected to perform exercises on parallel bars and the horse at a height of 120-125 cm., and for an "excellent" mark must be able to pull themselves up to a beam 12 times (boys) or sit up from a lying position with hands behind the head 25 times (girls). Girls do not seem to be allowed near the horse or the parallel bars, though they perform various support and pulling-up exercises.

A marked feature of the gymnastics course throughout the Soviet school is the presence of all sorts of marching and drill activities, and the use of a military style of communication: "Attention, stand at ease, quick march" and many others. From the age of six children are taught to line up, move smartly from one formation to another, dress ranks, break ranks and reform, march and countermarch, turn, wheel, mark time and so on. Visitors to lessons have commented on impressive displays of drilling. The purpose of this, according to the introduction to the syllabus, is to prepare pupils for military service, and instructions are given that every lesson should include practice in responding to military commands.

Ski training is provided for in every class. By class 5 children should be able to trek for up to 2.5 kilometres, and by class 8 the length of their maximum trek is 3.8 km. Further details are given in Figure 3.

Athletics training begins in class 4 with 60 metre running, high jumping with a straight or diagonal approach, throwing a ball for distance, and running up to 2.2 km. In the following years they are taught techniques of starting, methods of long and high jumping, throwing a ball at a target, hurdling and steeplechasing, relay racing, throwing a grenade in class 9 for distance (500 grammes for boys, 300 for girls) and later (class 10) a heavier one (700 for boys, 500 for girls) at a target, putting the shot, and racing finishes.

Swimming begins in class 4 or earlier. As well as the usual confidence-building exercises, the front and back crawl are taught first. In class 5 the breast stroke is introduced, and pupils are taught turning and starting from a pedestal. By class 7 pupils are expected to build up their speed, be able to swim using leg stroke alone and carry articles in the water. Life saving is taught in classes 8 to 10, and by 11 pupils should be able to administer artificial respiration.

Cross-country running is taught in areas where opportunities for skiing are fewer. It begins in class 5 with alternate walking and running over broken terrain, and is developed in the succeeding years by instruction in crossing obstacles, running on hard, soft, grassy or sandy ground, coping with changes of direction, and building up stamina.

Elements of sports, two chosen from basketball, football, handball and volleyball, depending on the staffing and facilities of the school, are taught from class 5 onwards. All that needs to be said about this is that the emphasis in this part of the PE course as in others, is on strict training: the syllabus specifies exactly what moves, passes, skills, manoeuvres, strokes and are to be taught. Actual games of volleyball and the others are not often mentioned in the syllabus, and sometimes the word "game" is qualified by the adjective "instructional". Teachers therefore give pupils a sound foundation in the techniques of the games, and pupils consequently should possess a knowledge of the basic skills.

Wrestling for boys, where it can be offered, appears as a separate element in classes 10 and 11, though the eighth and ninth-year gymnastics syllabus contains a simple introduction to single combat. In years 10 and 11 ways of falling, holds, escaping from holds and safety rules are taught.

Extra-curricular School Sport is the subject of the third section of the syllabus. For the primary classes the clubs which children should be offered are "groups for general preparation for the GTO", gymnastics, swimming, table tennis, skating and badminton. For years 5 and 6 other sports are added: basketball, volleyball, football, ice hockey, handball, athletics, skiing, training for outdoor activities (hiking, camping and map-reading). In classes 7 and 8 the same activities are available at a more advanced level, and in classes 9 to 11 there are further additions: wrestling, rhythmic gymnastics and "applied military training" (throwing the grenade, air rifle and small-bore shooting, route-marching and orientation in the open). In a good school which can offer these activities a child would apparently have excellent opportunities to extend his or her repertoire of sporting activity.

Section four of the syllabus lists special occasional events, such as school "health and fitness days", sports festivals, "spartakiads" - inter-school competitions run on a city or regional basis, and mass sporting festivals for school children such as fun runs and ski days.

The Standards

Space does not allow reproduction of all the assessment norms for every year in the school PE course, but three representative examples are given in Figure 3. The standards to be reached for the marks of 5 (excellent), 4 (good) and 3 (satisfactory) are shown. In every case, achievement of a mark of 5 would qualify the pupil to receive the gold badge in the GTO and 4 a pass certificate in the exercises assessed, but actually to receive the GTO there are additional weekly requirements, such as running, skiing or swimming a certain distance and performing set exercises a stated number of times.

General Remarks on Physical Culture

School PE is, then, a significant part of a national system of sports, fitness and health education. Children are prepared for a lifetime of opportunity for sporting pursuits, and are supported by every social and political agency. A significant intervention by government, which is still frequently referred to by Soviet specialists, was an order issued in 1981 by the Central Committe of the CPSU and the Council of Ministers entitled "On further increase in mass participation in physical culture and sport". It is true that schools face difficulties, in that many of them have no indoor or outdoor sports premises, and many simply have to use any open space they can find inside or outside the school building. (The figures in 1984 were 44% of schools lacking a sports hall and 60% outdoor sports grounds.) There is a shortage of teachers, and some schools, especially in country areas, cannot offer the subject; recent orders on certification of school leavers indicate that the possibility exists that pupils will not have attended physical culture lessons. Visitors to the USSR give mixed reports of lessons observed, sometimes commenting on the

CLASS 3/GTO Stage 1
[age 6–9: "Ready for the start"]

	Boys			Girls		
	5	**4**	School mark: **3**	**5**	**4**	**3**
	GTO gold	pass		GTO gold	pass	
3 x 10m. shuttle run (sec.)	9.1	9.8	10.4	9.6	10.4	11
or high start 30m. run	5.7	6.2	7	5.8	6.3	7.2
1500 m. run	any time allowed					
8 jumps, total distance (m.)	12.5	9	6	12.1	8.8	5
ball thrown at target from						
6 m., hits from 5 throws:	4	3	1	4	3	1
chin ups on high bar	4	2	1			
pull ups on low bar				13	8	6
skiing, 1 km. (min., sec)	8	8.30	9	8.30	9	9.30
or 2 km.	any time allowed					
swimming 25 m.	any time allowed					

CLASS 9/GTO Stage 4
[age 14–15: "Sporting reserve"]

	Boys			Girls		
60 m. run (sec.)	8.4	9.2	10	9.4	10	10.5
2 km. run (min., sec.)	9.20	10	11	10.20	12	13
or 3 km.	any time allowed					
long jump (cm.)	430	380	330	370	330	290
or high jump (cm.)	130	125	110	115	110	100
throwing 150 g. ball (m.)	45	40	31	28	23	18
chin ups on high bar	10	8	7			
sit ups, hands behind head				20	15	10
skiing, 3 km. (min., sec.)	17.30	18	19	19.30	20.30	21.30
or 5 km.	any time allowed					
cross country run (in snowless						
regions), 2km. (min., sec.)				11.30	12.30	13.30
3km.	16	17	18			
swimming (m.)	50	50	25	50	50	25
time required (sec.)	43	any time		65	any time	

Figure 3a *Standard Performances for the award of certain marks in school and of GTO gold badge and pass certificate.*

apparent failure of teachers to promote the subject or show much interest in any but the keener pupils (usually boys), but sometimes praising the very high level of fitness shown by whole classes. The system has notable successes too. Physical culture is popular among the population at large. Reports in the educational press give glowing accounts of massive success in school physical culture in towns as far apart as Kiev (Ukraine), Kaunas (Lithuania) and Barnaul (Siberia), where 70,000 pupils out of a total school population of 80,000 are said to have taken part in a town "ski day" and in a separate "day of the runner" in 1984/85. Strenuous efforts are being made in many places to remedy the lack of resources and teachers. Whatever the problems, the Soviet Union has a coherent national policy which can carcely fail to maintain public health and fitness and a relatively high level of interest in sporting activities of all kinds.

CLASS 11/GTO STAGE 5
[age 16–17:
"Strength and courage"]

Tasks	Boys			Girls		
	School mark					
	5	4	3	5	4	3
	GTO gold	pass		GTO gold	pass	
100 m. run (sec.)	14.2	14.5	15	16	16.5	17
2 km. run (min., sec.)	.	.	.	10	11.30	12.20
or 3 km. run				any time allowed		
3km run	13	15	16.30			
or 5 km. run	any time allowed					
long jump (cm.)	460	420	370	380	340	310
or high jump (cm.)	140	135	120	120	115	105
throwing grenade 700g.(m.)	38	32	26			
500g.				23	18	12
circles on high bar (times)	4	3	2			
or chin ups on bar	12	10	8			
sit ups, hand behind head				25	20	15
press ups	12	10	7			
skiing 3 km. (min., sec.)				18.30	19	20
or 5 km.				any time allowed		
5 km.	25	27	29			
or 10 km.	any time allowed					
cross-country run 2 km.				10.30	12.10	13.10
3 km.	14	16	17			
swimming: distance (m.)	50	50	25	50	50	25
time (sec.)	41	any time		60	any time	

FIGURE 3b. *Standard Performances (continued from Figure 3a).*

ELEMENTARY MILITARY TRAINING

Aims

This subject is related both to physical education and to other parts of the curriculum. It is closely linked with that side of upbringing which deals with patriotism, its theoretical aspect has an affinity with the syllabus for Soviet government and law and, for that matter, with sociology and history. In so far as future career soldiers might be recruited from school pupils it could be seen as an extension of labour training and professional orientation.

The stated aims of NVP, as the subject is known by its Russian abbreviation, embrace all these matters. Since most young men will be conscripted into the armed forces within a few years after leaving school, NVP includes fitness training in preparation for service. The subject is a culmination of the work in military-patriotic education. Interest is aroused in military matters by some stress on the sporting and adventure side of training - war games, shooting and military technology. Through drill instruction discipline, order and obedience are to be instilled. All of this, however, taught in two weekly periods for the last two years of compulsory education, is not intended as any more than a mere introduction to the real thing which young men will encounter on military service.

Teaching

Not a great deal of information about the content and teaching of NVP reaches the general educational press. In recent years the same type of dissatisfaction has been expressed as about most other school subjects. A particular problem has been the supply and training of teachers. NVP in each school is in the hands of a *voenruk* [military instructor], invariably a man, and ideally an officer in the reserves. It is said that 75% are reserve officers, but that in the rest of the schools the instructor is a retired non-commissioned officer. (At least he is a man, and his inevitable presence on the staff guarantees some male representation in a predominantly female profession.) Emergency short-term training has been set up, and under a new scheme run by the Ministry of Defence and Minpros a four-year course gives a qualification to teach both physical culture and NVP.

Facilities are said to be variable. City schools are likely to have a better-trained instructor and they are more likely than rural schools to have access to a shooting range or an "instructional complex".

Complaints reach the press that the ideological content of the course is not well taught - or, at least, not well learned. It is thought too abstract; pupils do not receive a clear impression of Soviet foreign policy, and they remain indifferent to such issues. They do not feel threatened by the international situation at present; they cannot be persuaded to drill properly, stand up straight, or keep their hands out of their pockets when talking to a superior.

The course is differentiated quite radically between boys and girls. During the Second World War the Soviet Army was unusual in that women were employed in active combat roles. In peace-time, on the other hand, very few women serve in the forces. This is reflected in the syllabus for NVP.

Recent (1987) correspondence in the press expressed constructive wishes for the improvement of NVP teaching. Apart from the usual pious hopes that Lenin's works and materials from the 27th Party Congress would receive intense and animated study, there was talk of the need for a modernization of the material basis for NVP. The need for active, creative, problem-solving activities; role-playing as commander, duty officer, NCOs, etc. in military simulations was recommended to inject some life into the subject.

As with most other school subjects, out-of-school and Pioneer activities are run to reinforce and encourage interest in NVP. The war game *zarnitsa* is played by Pioneers, and older teenagers engage in a more sophisticated game called *orlyonok*. In 130 cities of the USSR school pupils, boys and girls, wearing military uniform, form guards of honour for fifteen-minute periods over war memorials. *Sledopyty*, "scouts" or "sleuths", engage in research to discover veterans and heroes of the War and interview them about their experiences. Schools sometimes set up "museums of military glory", exhibitions of war photographs and memorabilia to recall the events of 1941-45.

Syllabus Content

It has not proved possible to obtain access to the most recent syllabus, but it can reasonably be assumed that the content described here closely resembles that of the latest course. It begins in class 10 with a few theoretical lessons on the Soviet armed forces in defence of the motherland - the "sacred duty" of the citizen to serve, the role of the armed forces in the contemporary state, the history of Party policy on the services, army personnel, the oath and unit banner, the law on military service; military regulations and discipline. Both boys and girls attend these lessons, though boys have more lessons on the regulations which girls do not attend in the last year.

Not a great deal of time is spent on drill (about 8%) and it is done by boys only. Weapon training is undergone by both sexes (though the girls do rather less of it) - it includes the maintainence, operation and firing of small-calibre and Kalashnikov rifles, and throwing hand grenades. Twenty-four shots of small-bore and nine on the Kalashnikov are all that is allowed to each pupil (but it is scarcely less than the amount allocated to British national servicemen in the RAF thirty years ago!)

Tactical training is undergone by both sexes for a few lessons in class 10 and for slightly more by boys only in class 11. Nearly fifty pages of the textbook are devoted to this, despite the mere ten lessons allocated in one recent syllabus. Topics covered include the organization and function in combat of a motorized rifle company, modern combat involving all three services, marching and battle order, conditions ensuring successful achievement of military objectives, supply, command, obligations of the soldier in battle, the arms and tactics of motorized infantry, action against tanks, action against low-flying aircraft, engineering defences (mines, dugouts, trenches, etc.), movement on the battlefield under fire, the soldier in action in attack, defence, observation and reconnaissance.

A quarter to a third of the girls' lesson time in both years is taken up by first aid (not covered in the textbook), but the boys - to whom this would surely be equally vital - have only two lessons on "military medical training". The boys receive two lessons of military topography - orientation in the field without a map.

A little less than half of the first year's work is on civil defence, and about 60 pages of the textbook are devoted to this. Pupils study its organization before going on to nuclear explosions and fall-out, and chemical and bacteriological weapons. This is followed by information on protection from these horrors - respirators, shelters, dug-outs. Rescue work, protection of food supplies and farm animals from infection and contamination, evacuation of the civil population, disinfection and decontamination, and the use of scientific instruments for reconnaissance of areas attacked by nuclear, chemical or biological arms. There is also a section on handling the consequences of natural disasters.

Half of the lessons in class 11 are devoted to "military technical training". This, despite its substantial representation in the course, does not figure in the textbook available to me, but it is clear from other literature that the expression means any branch of technology which is useful to the military. Pupils apparently concentrate on one branch of it. In particular, communications and signals are felt to be of importance and interest. This area is regarded as a good one for extra-curricular activities; pupils also may be found constructing models - and actual apparatus. This section of the course is studied by both boys and girls.

Chapter 13

VARIATIONS ON THE MAIN THEME

NOT EVERY Soviet child follows exactly the programme of study
described in this book, and the purpose of this short chapter
is to summarise the possible variations in the curriculum
allowed within the system. Two of these "variations" are, in
fact, scarcely that, as will be seen in due course. The
differences arise for four reasons. These are, firstly, the
case of disabled or handicapped pupils; secondly, the right
possessed by the union republics to publish syllabuses for use
within their own boundaries; thirdly, the different choices
any given pupil may make when it comes to optional courses;
and fourthly the possibility of attending a school with a
"special profile". Some of these variations fall, strictly
speaking, outside of the scope of this book, which is what the
Russian child is taught in the mass school; the summary here
is intended merely to outline the rest of the picture.

Handicap and Disablement

This is a vast subject, and the problem is treated very differently from Western practice. For example, the Soviets make
fine distinctions between categories of handicap and develop
special methods of handling children with each one. Such
children are very rarely taught in "mainstream" schools; special institutions are established for them. As for the curriculum, if children can possibly master the standard syllabuses, they are enabled to do so. Deaf children, for example,
are given an extra year or two to complete secondary education, depending on the degree of their deafness. Some categories of mentally retarded children complete primary education in eight years. Minpros publishes adaptations of the
syllabuses for specific types of disabled pupil.

Syllabuses in the Union and Autonomous Republics

The Ministries of Education of the Union republics are responsible to the central Minpros in Moscow. They can either
use the union syllabuses, or organize their own, or supplement

and adapt the union programmes. The situation is further complicated by the existence of 20 autonomous republics (ASSRs), 8 autonomous regions and 10 "national areas" within five of the union republics (the RSFSR, Uzbekistan, Georgia, Azerbaidjan and Tadjikistan). The autonomous regions and national areas have very little power or authority; their existence simply recognizes the presence of a body of people of a particular ethnic origin in the republic in which they are geographically situated. The ASSRs (of which Yakutiya is the largest) have their own ministries, but in practice tend to pass on decisions from the republic ministry to which they are directly responsible. They do, however, often organize schools in the language of the people they represent.

Conversations with leading figures in the republics usually reveal fierce local pride and a desire to impress upon the visitor that "our republic is not run from Moscow". "I know you think I´m always on the phone to Prokof´ev [the USSR Minister of Education at the time], but I´m not! Half the time I don´t even ask him," said one minister in 1984. For example, Belorussia claims to have been doing especially good work in moral education, and to be well ahead of many of the rest in the efficient organization of labour education. The Georgian minister in 1984 was proud of having had a fifteen-year start in educating six-year-olds; he also claimed to have been ahead in the implementation of professional training. Nevertheless, he admitted that the reform Guidelines were enabling him to knock a few heads together and to get things moving even more quickly. The same republic had adjusted the school year to fit the agricultural needs of the economy (that is, so that children could be free to help on the collective farms when most needed). Estonia, along with other Baltic republics retains one extra year of compulsory education: it was eleven years previously and will be twelve from now on. Reasons given for this, other than tradition, include the difficulty for Estonian children in learning Russian and the cultural need to include more music in the curriculum.

But what differences are obvious in the curriculum? Of prime importance is the teaching of Russian. The problems here vary enormously, depending on the nature of the pupils´ native language. In Belorussian 70% of the vocabulary is the same as Great Russian, and children often forget which they are speaking; they are not always quite sure which words differ and which do not. If they become confused it is because the languages are so similar, whereas in Estonia they are so different as to have hardly any points of contact at all. Gender, for example, is non-existent and Estonian children often have problems distinguishing between "he" and "she". It is clear, then, that the teaching of Russian and foreign languages must be in the hands of the republics. A Moscow-based institute holds a watching brief.

The history, geography and literature of the republic are

matters decided locally, usually by adaptation of the union syllabuses. The local language is, of course, wholly a matter for local initiative and decision, though it has to be taught within the narrow confines of the lessons allocated. The curriculum illustrated in Figure 2 applies in the republics too, where "First language and literature" is replaced by the same number of lessons on "First and Russian language and literature". The arts, and in particular music, have their syllabuses adapted in the republics. Finally, each republic is responsible for publishing textbooks in the local languages, and these vary from straight translations of the central courses to entirely fresh works.

Options

Options are not really "variations on the main theme", but a niche within it where pupils can follow their own interests. The authorities see the options as falling into four basic categories. Some give pupils the opportunity to extend their knowledge of subject which they are learning already. A second type of optional course enables a pupil to start a new subject altogether, one which is entirely fresh to the school curriculum or which is related peripherally; examples occasionally quoted include logic, psychology, education, a second foreign language, cartography and geology. Thirdly, there are aesthetic subjects: music, painting, theatre. Finally, the more practically-minded pupil may choose applied studies sometimes of a vocational character: car mechanics, plant or animal breeding. The existence of all these courses is in tune with Marxist-Leninist notions of allowing the individual to develop his own aptitudes. They are regarded as an enrichment of the curriculum and as an alternative to the schools with special profile. As is seen from Figure 2, the number of lessons available for such studies is small. Authors of the mass syllabuses, however, often show that the enrichment offered by optional courses in their subject is regarded with particular favour.

Many such courses are planned centrally, but schools may suggest their own courses which the ministry of the republic may decide to confirm. Hundreds of such courses are available. Tallinn in 1980 claimed to know of 130 options in the city. One Moscow school at the same time was offering eight, but it was held that a reasonably well-run school of average size might expect to offer about fifteen different ones.

Schools and Classes with Special Profiles

Schools with curricula which place a certain emphasis on one particular subject are a matter of controversy in Soviet education. Foreigners are often taken to visit the special English schools, and will know the high standards achieved in them. On successive visits to the Soviet Union I have myself visited a mathematics school, one with a bias towards appled art, a sports boarding school, several special English schools, one with intensified study of Russian (where the children's native language was another), and a school with a speciality in wood carving and crafts. There are schools with a bias towards history, geography, music, physics and car mechanics. Minpros reports that there are about 750 special language schools in the USSR and about 1,000 schools with other specialisms. It should be remembered that in many of these schools only some of the children will be following the special programme; perhaps only one class in three. They tend to be smaller schools than the average.

Do these schools infringe the comprehensive principle? In his 1977 book John Dunstan concluded that the number of such schools was very small - about 2.9% of the total. We are not speaking of a powerful system of selective schools for the very able; if entry to them, or some of them, is controlled by aptitude, the means by which this is done remain shrouded in mystery. Nevertheless, it is obvious that the Soviets too regard their presence if not as an anomaly, then as a curiosity which needs to be explained. The 1984 reform declared that the number of such schools would not be increased - but it is not to be decreased either. At a meeting in the USSR Ministry of Education in 1984 one speaker spent a great deal of time justifying the existence of schools with a special profile.

The justification ran along the following lines. The problem is the need to ensure the full development of all types of personality. The special profile schools made a contribution to this. However, the special profiles amounted to no more than a regular mass-school-type curriculum in which all periods available for options were devoted to the specialism. Such schools do not infringe the principle of the single unified school, because every element of the mass curriculum is present, and the specialism is no more than an intensification of one side of it. Pupils from special schools are not favoured in university entrance because questions in the entrance examinations are asked only from those parts of the syllabus which are common to all. It should be added that there are a very few real elite boarding schools for senior pupils only, attached to major higher education establishments, such as the school at Akademgorodok in Siberia. The local special profile schools are not in this category.

This concludes our study of the content of the official curriculum of the Soviet general-education school. We began, afte preliminary surveys with the explicit moral content of Soviet education. The concluding chapters deal with the implicit or hidden curriculum and the directions in which Soviet education is moving in the last years of the twentieth century.

Chapter 14

THE ETHOS OF THE SCHOOL AND THE "HIDDEN" CURRICULUM

THE CONCEPT of the hidden curriculum is not a new one, and the notion is very well known. It refers to all those matters which are in some way taught in school, especially moral values and the pupil's understanding of authority and the structure of society, but which do not appear in any subject syllabus. So, for example, teachers wearing gowns, as they once regularly did in Britain, act as an unspoken reminder to pupils that academic learning and diplomas were a good and important thing. When the head teacher stood on the platform at morning assembly surrounded by senior staff and prefects, the image presented reinforced the leadership and authority of those concerned. All educational establishments have rituals and ceremonies which clearly convey a message, but it is very doubtful whether such messages can be considered "hidden". David Hargreaves (in C. Richards, *Power and the Curriculum*, Driffield, 1978, pp. 97-108) has therefore renamed the notion "paracurriculum". It scarcely needs to be said that in the Soviet Union schools have a very strong paracurriculum, much of which is not hidden, but which is explicit. Nevertheless, there are elements the paracurriculum there which are less obvious, and the purpose of this chapter is to look in partic- ular at the Soviet lesson and try to see what messages are conveyed about the nature of learning and knowledge by the way in which it is carried on. The style of the remarks which follow will be somewhat subjective, but the personal judge- ments are based on systematic observation.

It is not so easy to do this today as it might have been fifteen or twenty years ago. In some subjects more than others the classroom ethic is changing. As is obvious from the reform "Guidelines", a new approach is now expected of teachers. The spirit of the classroom is a subject of contro- versy and interested discussion. Traditional teachers are complaining that the new manner in foreign language and arts teaching, for example, is undermining authority and discipline in other subjects. It is not unlike the complaints one used to hear in English secondary staff rooms that all discipline problems stemmed from the fact that primary-age pupils were no longer ruled with a rod of iron and taught to pay attention.

School Premises

Before considering lessons, let us look at the school environment. Most schools are well kept and lacking in the graffiti that have begun to take over in some schools in many Western societies. The main entrance often bears welcoming notices to the visitor. Information boards are usually well maintained and tidy, and they proclaim the rules for pupils, responsibilities of parents and goals for the teaching staff with praiseworthy openness. Prominent in many schools are photographs of the *otlichniki,* the pupils who have achieved top marks in all subjects. Symbols of the state and the republic often appear on corridor or classroom walls. Slogans, political exhortations, quotations and pious wishes appear on walls; their authors may be leading politicians, artists, writers or thinkers of any country or period, but Lenin is the most commonly represented in this way. Flags and regalia of Communist youth organizations are to be seen in open spaces inside the buildings. Members of the staff who have served in the armed forces are often honoured in special displays. Schools sometimes maintain a museum in honour of war or resistance heroes.

There is a certain standard appearance about the classrooms, which is not totally unwelcome. Visitors often comment on the ubiquitous pot plants. Portraits or busts of Lenin are everywhere. Other political leaders are also represented. Most schools now operate on the "subject-room system" (most lessons are taught in a room intended for that particular subject). Consequently, relevant displays ("Lenin in London" in the English room, "USSR - our Motherland" in a primary class) are commonly observed. Children's work is often seen on classroom walls, but in very much smaller quantities than in English schools. Classroom notice boards bearing the list of duties to be performed by each "detachment" or small group of pupils are often very attractively presented. The building is not manned during breaks by prefects, but by a duty class.

Readers will draw their own conclusions from all this. It is obvious that the premises are seen as more than the empty space in which learning is intended to take place. The context in which that learning goes on owes something to the arrangement of the buildings. It may be that the omnipresence of slogans and good advice builds up a resistance in the minds of those who see them, or that they are just not noticed. However, the intention is clear: to convey messages, ethical, patriotic, academic, political and social through the appearance and administration of the building.

Lessons

It is through the conduct of instruction that the nature of the paracurriculum becomes most obvious, especially as regards the concepts of learning and knowledge. Simple notions such as "school" and "lesson" as understood differently in the Soviet consciousness - and sub-conscious. There has been controversy over the lowering of the school starting age to six, and educationists remarked in 1984 that the majority in favour of this aspect of the reform was not overwhelming. Why should this be so? The reason can be illustrated by a short extract from a lesson to six-year-olds witnessed in 1980 in a kindergarten. Now let it be said that this is several years ago now, and it is intended to illustrate an approach which the better Soviet pedagogues wish to get away from.

Teacher: There are some interesting pictures on your desk. Look at them and try to make up a sentence.
Pupil: Shura is on his bicycle.
(The teacher corrected the pronunciation of "bicyc-le" *(velosiped)*, which was giving the child consid-erable difficulty. Six more pupils then gave sen-tences they had made up.]
Teacher: What have we done?
Pupil: We have made up some sentences.
Teacher: What does our speech consist of?
Pupil: Our speech consists of sentences.
Teacher: What do sentences consist of?
Pupil: Words.
Teacher: Now give me a proper answer.
Pupil: Sentences consist of words.
Teacher: How many words are there in the sentence [This is a house]?
Pupil: There are two words in that sentence.
[The teacher asked two similar questions.]
Teacher: How many syllables are there in the name "Masha"?
Pupil: There are two syllables in the name Masha.
Teacher: How do you know that there are two syllables in Masha?
Pupil: I know there are two syllables in the name Masha, because when I put my hand under my chin and say it, my chin hits my hand twice, like this - Ma-sha [demonstrated].

It is perhaps clear from this why a specialist in primary education commented: "School is no place for six-year-olds". The fact is that until very recently the idea of "school" was inseparable from this stilted manner of interaction, not to mention the content, some at least of which would not be considered appropriate to infants by Western teachers. Many parents, in the words of a recent article, "fear to deprive their children of a year of childhood" (childhood, in their eyes, is presumably ended by lessons such as this).

In 1984 I pressed some leading figures in a union republic to say how they reacted to these ideas. Many asserted that children, when they come to school, expect to learn by sitting behind a desk and being told what to do; "informal" methods were not appropriate to real learning. When pressed further, they admitted that there was one experimental school running on informal lines in another city. In a different republic, Georgia, an innovative primary teacher, Professor Shalva Amonashvili, has been carrying out experimental work on more humane and flexible teaching methods for young children. One of his books sold 300,000 copies (in Russian), so unusual did the ideas seem to Soviet teachers and parents. Its sequel was selling like hot cakes in March 1987. Primary teachers from all over the Union beat a path to his door, but surprisingly he was a prophet without honour in his own republic. According to *Teachers' Newspaper,* his compatriots knew less of his work than did teachers in Russia, and the book had still not been issued in Georgian by early 1987.

Nevertheless, the teacher in charge of primary work in a Moscow school demonstrated that she had a new attitude when she was asked to sum up the methods used with six-year-olds: "Play, constant play". An article in the press by an adviser in Gatchina referred to the psychological barrier in many parents´ and even teachers´ minds, and stressed the need for specially designed rooms, equipment and methods. Children should spend at least two hours a day in activities involving movement, there must be an easing up on the strict regimentation of behaviour and instruction. Teacher training was vital in creating new attitudes; the timetable had to be carefully constructed with an easy Monday and Friday, more intensive work mid-week, and Saturday devoted entirely to sports and active pursuits. Some preference is noted for teaching six-year-olds in the kindergarten (though supervised by the neighbourhood school), and there is some hesitation as to how to handle the youngest children in small schools. Vertical grouping does not come easily to Soviet teachers.

It is clear from all this that things are changing at primary level as regards the atmosphere of the classroom, but that the nature of the changes is not yet assented to, fully appreciated or understood by all teachers and parents.

Native and Foreign Language Lessons

Attendance at a number of other native language lessons and several where a foreign language was being taught indicates that a fairly wide variety of teaching styles operates, but that the relative "creativity" or freedom of approach does not seem to depend on the age of the pupils. As noted in Chapter 6, native language lessons place great stress on grammar and technical matters concerning the use of words. There is a good deal of drilling in grammar, and the children are often asked to compose sentences exemplifying particular language structures. As far as our study of the classroom ethic is concerned, these matters are neutral; of greater interest in this context are other features of the lessons. Teachers make great use of the arts: reproductions of famous paintings and recordings of music are discussed, poetry naturally makes a frequent appearance. Sometimes these stimuli are used in a similar way to that common in Britain: as an imaginative stimulus to free composition. At other times, however, they have the purpose merely of suggesting to the pupils pieces of technical language which the teacher uses to exemplify her theme. For example, in one lesson witnessed by me a teacher played a recording of Tchaikovsky's piano piece "The Snowdrop" and asked for adjectives which appropriately described the music. She received several very good ones from the young pupils, which, to be sure, she accepted with praise, but did not allow herself to be sidetracked into aesthetic discussion: she used the adjectives offered to hammer home the point (which the children obviously completely understood and scarcely needed teaching) that an adjective in Russian qualifying a feminine noun requires the ending -aya. In another lesson with children of the same age a different teacher used a painting to get the pupils to produce verbs. However, in this lesson the teacher actually talked about the painting and related the verbs to the way the painter had suggested movement in his work; she also made a point of stressing the need to "speak beautifully" when talking about works of art. From all of this pupils might be expected to sense the values subscribed to by the teacher and receive some impression of the cultural heritage of their own country, and from some of it they would doubtless pick up the feeling that the arts mattered and could figure as a subject for fruitful and intelligent discussion. The teaching was fairly straightforwardly didactic, but room was left for individual response.

It is in foreign language lessons that I have observed the greatest freedom, and in which I have seen children asked to take the most initiative in recent years. Fifteen years ago or less, a visiting British exchange teacher reported that when he asked a senior class to act out a short play in the classroom, they claimed that they had never before been asked to move the desks or even come out from behind them other than to go to the board to be tested on their homework. However, this has changed. In line with the current stress all over the world on "communicative" language teaching, one sees role-playing, acting out of sketches and spontaneous language use in Sovet classrooms. In 1987 I saw ten-year-olds perform with great gusto in English a parody of a television magazine programme. As recently as 1980 group and pair work in foreign language teaching was disapproved of by at least one older inspector (in whose company I visited what I held to be an excellent lesson) on the grounds that the teacher was not in full control of what was going on. In another school a head teacher apologised for the fact that children were "playing" in class; what they were actually doing was acting out in Russian (not their native language) a scene at the doctor´s - they were practising the language and learning from the experience. But it looked like "play"!

Beneficial elements in the paracurriculum of good Soviet foreign language lessons are that pupils learn the necessity of taking responsibility for their own progress - at least sometimes - and they discover that learning can be fun.

History, Ethics, Social Studies

Fun is a word one would scarcely ever apply to Soviet lessons in history or social studies. I have witnessed a social studies lesson of unparallelled tedium, in which pupils were called upon to do little other than read out lengthy passages from the textbook in answer to the teacher´s questions; no attempt was made to check understanding, and very little effort was made to make the pupils think about the potentially very interesting issues in political theory which were being dealt with. Interesting they might have been if the approach had ever got away from pure abstraction expressed in impenetrable jargon. History can similarly be ruined, of course, but it does at least deal more immediately with people and events. There is real opportunity for discussion and analysis. In history lessons, one does hear searching questions being asked: "What were the characteristics of Russian imperialism at the end of last century?", "What contributions did the working class make to the revolutionary movement?" and "Describe the industrial development of Russia at the turn of the century". However, one quickly realises that the pupils are being asked to recite learned facts, often in a set form of words, that "think" means "try to remember what you have read" or that "discuss" means "paraphrase the textbook". In this, Soviet history teachers may be no worse than some of their British counterparts. The paracurriculum is clear: history and social studies are learned from books. Differing views are judged correct or incorrect. Historical knowledge is assessed according to how closely its expression conforms to a standard set of answers; success in history is achieved by swallowing the book whole.

How deeply this attitude is or was ingrained in Soviet education is illustrated by an incident in a lesson which I attended a few years ago. The subject was an optional course in ethics for fifteen-year-olds, and the aim was to "teach the pupils to reason". Nevertheless, the teaching style adopted gave little real opportunity for discussion of ethical issues, and included many rhetorical questions asked and answered by the teacher herself. The significant incident occurred not long after the start. The theme for discussion was considerate behaviour towards others and the stimulus for this particular part of the lesson was a cartoon drawing of a man in a telephone box talking, while a queue of others waited their turn in the falling snow. The conversation ran as follows:

Teacher:	What principle is infringed here?
Pupil:	He's keeping them waiting.
Teacher:	But perhaps he needs to talk?
Pupil:	He should keep it short.
Teacher:	How long should you talk on the telephone?
Pupil:	[slight pause for thought] Two minutes.
Teacher:	No! Three minutes, three minutes.

This exchange is very revealing for our understanding of the nature of discussion in this teacher's lesson. She first provided an interesting stimulus in the shape of the cartoon and the question. She kept the pot boiling by the remark "perhaps he needs to talk" - (the only remotely provocative utterance in the whole lesson). The pupil was disposed to respond to the provocation. The teacher then tricked him into exercising his judgement; when he did so, she closed the trap - it was not an invitation to express an opinion, but a factual question, which has a correct answer: three minutes. The boy gave an incorrect answer and was firmly put right.

Overall Considerations

It would be as well once again to emphasise that the lessons and incidents described here are not intended to prove that all Soviet lessons are like these. The situation is changing, and the lessons mentioned are intended as an indication of what the system is changing from. Nevertheless, the regular visitor to Soviet schools quickly comes to realise what a lesson is meant to be like, and it rapidly becomes clear what the teacher feels he or she must show to the visitor as being "typical". The following summary may seem like a caricature; the reader is free to take it or leave it.

Most Soviet lessons are serious affairs. Smiles and laughter are not absent altogether, but some feel them to be inappropriate to the business of education. Pupils occasionally apologise to visitors for laughing during a lesson. The seriousness is intensified by minor rituals and the formality of classroom organization: posture, set ways of raising the hand, standing to answer a question. Because of the formal atmosphere, spontaneous response or intervention by a pupil are unlikely to occur often. Strict discipline is insisted upon. There are, of course, occasional disruptive pupils as in any country, but in general behaviour is very good for reasons which have as much or more to do with the societal context as with any techniques practised by teachers. Strict discipline has great advantages, but many disciplinarians would not wish their control to inhibit discussion. In 1987 a leading educator in Belorussia expressed the view to me that "authoritarian teachers must change their ways".

When tackled about ways to introduce a new classroom spirit, Soviet educators often mention the questions asked of the pupils. By this, they tend to mean the questions for discussion printed in the textbooks, but this must obviously have a "backwash" effect on questions asked by teachers orally. In a small research project carried out by me in 1980, which focused on teacher questions, it became clear that most questions required factual recall, sometimes of a whole series of facts in order. Very few asked children to work out an answer from first principles, present an argument or be devil's advocate. Some questions which appeared to do so were in fact requesting recall of an argument which had been learned as fact. The hidden curriculum here, which is very well learned by many average Soviet children, is that there is a certain answer to everything and little room for differing opinions in human affairs. The brightest products of the system are, needless to say, as critical as anywhere in the world - but they certainly do not learn their questioning attitude at school, unless it is a reaction against the "certainties" with which they are presented there. For education in the Soviet Union is very much a matter of the conveying of information and values by directly didactic means. Until recently there has been little exploration of the ideas or insights of the child, only the measuring up of the norm possessed absolutely by the teacher.

Conclusions

Small incidents are often of the greatest significance in illuminating attitudes to education. A year or two ago a group of Soviet teachers were visiting an independent boys' grammar school in a Northern English industrial city. A Russian lady teacher took one of the masters by the arm at the end of the visit and said, "Thank you very much for letting us come. We have seen several state comprehensive schools in England, but your school is like a real Soviet school." It can not have been the all-male atmosphere of the place which was familiar to her, nor the residually Anglican muscular Christian ethos, the Victorian classrooms or the middle-class pupils. What the schools share is a strong sense of achievement-orientation and academic purpose and the belief that learning matters. A great strength of the Soviet school is that, in concert with the society it serves, it has got across the message to the mass of the population that study and the acquisition of knowledge are a good thing.

Chapter 15

THE DIRECTIONS OF CHANGE IN THE SOVIET CURRICULUM TODAY

THIS BOOK has devoted a good deal of space to the details of the most recent subject syllabuses. It may be that the wood is no longer visible for the trees. The purpose of this concluding chapter is to consider the overall picture of current curricular change. Are Soviet children likely to get a better deal from their schooling now in view of present and projected reform, particularly as regards the content of education?

Is the Mould Really Being Broken?

Though the present changes appear conservative on the surface, they are aimed at breaking the mould in at least one important way: leading educators feel that a rigid and authoritarian spirit which has been present in the classroom for too long must be changed. An official of Minpros at a private meeting in 1984 declared that a principal purpose of the new syllabuses was to stop teachers teaching by simply turning over the pages of the textbook, and to make them think about what they were doing. The new syllabuses show a significant move from the former almost exclusive concentration on content to a format which expresses their aims in terms of concepts and skills too. The degree of change here is undoubtedly on the cautious side. It seems to be proving very hard to change the attitudes of those who formulate the syllabuses. They still contain a very great amount of sheer information, and sometimes the "skills" listed for mastery include factual recall in disguise: "Pupils should be able to give an account of..." Moreover, the examination tickets published for 1987 do not seem to have gone far in breaking the mould either. *Teachers' Newspaper* for 14 April contains an eloquent protest by a literature teacher that the exam questions are "in howling contradiction to the underlying principles of restructuring". The reform aims also to move towards a more pupil-centred approach. The phrase "pedagogics of cooperation" has become a slogan. There is a genuine desire in many quarters to move from rote learning to "creativity", from factual mastery alone to the arousal of interest, and genuine engagement with the subject matter. It is clear both that many Soviet teachers welcome the prospect and regard it with delight, and that many conservative ones see no need for change and are actively obstructing it. What is new in 1987 is that these controversies are surfacing more openly in the press than ever before.

Other aims of the reform of direct relevance to curricular change are the intention to bring the syllabuses up to date; in terms of their factual content, this has undoubtedly been done. Efforts have been made to make them relevant to modern life in all its forms, and most particularly to the world of work. The moral content of Soviet education has always been highly important, and is certainly no less so now. It is difficult to visit a lesson without hearing the teacher take opportunities to underline moral values.

The intensification of the purposefulness of labour education and careers guidance stresses a feature of the system which has always been strong in theory, but at times weak in practice.

The Mechanics of Change

Let us remind ourselves again of some of the reasons for the restructuring. The USSR is in need of workers for the economy and has recently become keenly aware that they must be creative and adaptable in order to be of any real use. As any rational nation would, they seek civil peace by trying to ensure that the work force enjoys job satisfaction through adequate training and careers counselling. The state wishes to protect its young from "ideological pollution" from influences from without. This comes in addition to the natural need in the modern world to compete with other nations in economic, political and indeed military fields. And in order to achieve these aims, talent must be fostered.

Comparative educationists in the 1970s expressed keen interest in the processes of educational change, in particular the reasons for the success or failure of educational innovation. The view is widely shared that effective changes in education are unlikely to occur in isolation from changes in society at large. Educational innovation in Russia has never, before or since 1917, been thoroughly successful if significant sections of society (including "public opinion", in so far as that could be estimated) showed resistance to it. The World Bank formulated six questions (in *Education*, 1974) which were intended to illuminate educational change in a society. In summary they were:- (1) Who designs and provides education? (2) Who administers provision, controls standards and monitors performance? (3) Who receives education and to what level? (4) Who pays for it? (5) Who appears to benefit most and least from education? (6) Who wishes to change the system or parts of it and why?

For the USSR the answer to questions (1) and (2) is: the state, under the leadership of the Communist Party, which has delegated the task to trusted professionals of proven political rectitude, but which keeps a very close eye on their handling of it. The answer to (3) is: everyone, with free access at least to age 15, but with certain restrictions operating after that age. (4): the state. (5): This is an interesting question which is not entirely relevant to our theme. However, it is probably true that successful people in the Soviet Union are those who have worked through the meritocratic educational system, and have succeeded academically without transgressing politically. Question (6) is of the greatest interest to the subject of this book, and the answer in relation to the 1984 reforms would appear to be: a leading group in the Communist Party who feel strongly about education and are trying to take the educational world and its "establishment" along with them. What difficulties are they facing and to what extent do they appear to be succeeding three years after the reform guidelines were promulgated?

Soviet education has never, perhaps, been very adept at handling innovation. "Experimentation with children is wrong" sounds a very noble slogan, but it can be no more than the excuse for sloth and reaction. The simplest innovation, after all, could be said to involve some degree of experimentation with pupils. The word "innovation" and its derivatives are to be read everywhere these days in the educational press, heard at meetings and used in schools. Those who oppose the concept are already saying they are tired of hearing about it: for them, a very little would seem to go a long way. Nevertheless, while the system may seem to be restrictive, there is a machinery for dealing with the ideas of resourceful and creative teachers: when reported or recommended, their ideas are taken up by inspectors and local authorities, investigated, and, if it seems desirable, experimentation authorized and the results disseminated. The problem arises in attracting the attention of authority outside the school - a hostile inspectorate might suppress an idea they did not like. But at best, knowledge of good innovative practices could very quickly become widespread in the highly centralized system.

Resistance to Change

Other difficulties encountered in the implementation of the reform include resources, especially for labour education. Links with industry, which were a problem under Khrushchev in 1958, are proving difficult today.

The real problem at present would appear to be that of carrying public (not forgetting teacher) opinion along with the changes. When visiting Soviet schools and reading the press a spirit of optimism and positiveness is encountered which will not be easy to vanquish. But the press prints news of opposition, sometimes vehement, to anything new; refusal to show initiative and sheer inertia are frequently referred to. Proponents of advanced study in the upper classes of schools have not been silenced, and there are some who appear to be calling for a system resembling the selective English grammar school with its specialist sixth-form. At a teachers´ conference in Vilnius a deputy education minister of the USSR sneered at the "pedagogics of cooperation", declaring that he neither understood nor accepted the phrase and asserting that far too much attention was being paid to innovative teachers. "Contrary to his expectations", writes the correspondent of *Teachers' Newspaper*, [4 April 1987], "he did not please anyone by these remarks." We have seen that academicians sometimes vehemently disagree about curricular change and are not above stabbing each other in the back when they get the chance. On the "overloading" of syllabuses, an eminent senior Soviet educationist, M. I. Kondakov, was provoked by a correspondent of *Literaturnaya gazeta* into exclaiming that he thought far too much fuss was made about overloaded syllabuses: children were not prepared to work and teachers were creating "a generation of loafers". Meanwhile, complaints are also made about poor teacher attitudes to children who do not achieve the best marks. They are said to pour insults and humiliation on pupils who are awarded the mark of 3 ("satisfactory") - which is regarded as a pretty poor show. This failure to respect the difficulties of the average and less able pupil is reprehensible, but illustrates an attitude which has to change if full secondary education really is to be for all. Exhortations are still common to "improve upbringing work". This is an area in which success could never be anything like 100%; none the less, upbringing is not felt to be presented satisfactorily yet.

Changing Attitudes

The state of the debate about education in the Soviet Union is very healthy. It is being carried on openly in agreement with the principles of the Gorbachev regime. All of a sudden the whole world has learned the Russian word *glasnost'*. The aims of the reform are mostly praiseworthy. However, it must seem to many parents that young people are being directed at 15 into SPTUs perhaps against their will, and perhaps into a course of training which will benefit the economy rather than satisfy the young person concerned. If this is what will happen, it may not work for at least two reasons: firstly, because if young people really do not like the job they have been trained for they can leave it after the short period of direction is over, and secondly, because in the good old Russian tradition parents will mobilize every scrap they possess of influence, "connections", threats and perhaps even bribery to have their children allocated to the educational institution they want.

As to whether the reform will succeed, it will depend entirely upon the ability of the leaders of opinion to change attitudes - especially among teachers, whom the authorities regard as the vital element in the process of change. It is not merely teachers who see education, in the memorable phrase of one Soviet journalist, as being like "stuffing a goose with nuts". One has only to visit the Soviet Union and watch how uncritically gaggles of Soviet tourist-geese follow their excursion-leaders around the historical sights, eager to be stuffed with the often irrelevant and unmemorable nuts which she dispenses so liberally. This common "museum attitude" is probably what the general public thinks of as education, and if creative, adaptable workers are to be formed, it will have to change. Assessment too is a major problem for Soviet education, and it has not yet been solved. Anyone knows that the way children are to be tested profoundly influences the way they are taught and the way they can be persuaded to learn. *Teachers' Newspaper* for 14 April 1987 again declares: there is "no profound assimilation of the principles of the new syllabuses; the quality of knowledge is still assessed at times formally":.. or the marks are raised afterwards. A literature teacher complains bitterly that she cannot persuade her pupils, who suffer from examination nerves for the last six months of the last year at school, to do anything but learn by heart "stereotyped jingoistic views"... "School literature is mindless repetition of a few unconnected formulae which can be made to fit anywhere... When are pupils going to learn to seek the truth, argue with each other, form their opinion and learn to defend it, when are they going to build themselves, their own personal `I´?"

Summary and Concluding Remarks

The curriculum of the mass school in the Soviet Union has many virtues. Nations seeking to construct a national curriculum for their own schools would do well to look at it, while - of course - avoiding the "pitfalls" of "misconceived" comparative education and resisting the temptation to imagine that aspects of it could necessarily be transferred wholesale from the Soviet system to another.

The curriculum of the Soviet school is standard: all the subjects in a very substantial "core" are offered to every child. All children receive a balanced programme of study, and though a little specialization is possible through the options, no one is allowed to drop basic subjects until he leaves school.

The content of the subject syllabuses is serious and of high quality. It does not pander to immaturity. It is not anti-intellectual and it affirms the values of "high" culture.

If teachers are unsuccessful in conveying it to their pupils, they have failed, honourably one hopes, to teach something worth while. Children are not introduced to a new subject without being told why it is important and why people study it - a simple matter which teachers in Britain often fail to observe.

Syllabuses still go for broad coverage of the subject matter, and despite efforts to lighten the load, attempt to convey a general knowledge of the subject. They none the less often have a unifying theme and seek to convey fundamental concepts (though sometimes less successfully than the factual content). The syllabuses are carefully planned, continuous and "linear". There is little duplication or waste of time. Soviet theorists still complain, however, of failure to ensure logical liaison between subjects. This is a shortcoming in a system which insists on non-integrated single-subject teaching while placing great emphasis on inter-subject links.

Syllabuses pay great attention to the practical, applied uses of the subject matter taught. Children are systematically made aware of the relevance of what they learn at school to the economy and to the wider world.

The moral, cultural and scientific values conveyed through the explicit and implicit curriculum do not for the most part conflict with the values of official society, those expressed by the media, mercantile interests, youth organizations or other agencies which overtly influence young people. The child's home or the peer group may, of course, not fully support this ethos, or he or she may rebel against the ideas conveyed at school. The wariness in Soviet society about Western influences and the existence of unofficial young people's clubs and gangs clearly demonstrate that they are subject to opposing forces. But they are not pulled in many directions at once, or presented daily with values that blatantly fly in the face of what they are taught at school.

The reader of this book will, it is hoped, have arrived at some impression of the educational experience undergone by the Soviet child at school. Knowledge of this experience is vital for our understanding of the nature of Soviet society. It is an orderly, well-planned, organized experience, in which traditionally a great deal of information is conveyed and consolidated by formal teaching in fairly large classes. Though the present reform seeks to modify this, a feeling of certainty and confidence is imparted by the methods used. Clear-cut definitions of difficult concepts are presented and opposing views are "settled" by the teacher conveying the official viewpoint as correct established fact. The consequences of all this are more complex than might be expected. It would be naive to imagine that the best minds in the country are taken in by it. At the highest levels of scientific and intellectual activity people are as independent-minded and genuine-

ly creative as anywhere else in the world - and as critical of
the education they have received. But on a lower level there
is much less awareness of uncertainty, much less caution in
the expression of judgements, and sometimes genuine surprise
that the foreigner regards some issue as contentious. The
much publicised television confrontation between the British
Prime Minister and Soviet journalists in March 1987 illustrated nothing so clearly as that the Soviets had not been
trained to debate so much as to utter cliches; moreover, the
reaction of the public who saw them trounced was indignation
that they had not been able to produce the arguments to troun-
ce *her.* That such arguments existed was not doubted, their
power to win the day even less so.

Now, however, leading educators are saying with great insistence: "We must get rid of authoritarian teaching", "A
teacher must be a friend and counsellor", "We wish to teach
pupils to think", "We need to teach young people to work crea-
tively and show initiative". This is very similar to what
British teachers were saying in reaction to the educational
practices of the Gradgrind era. German educators have been
fighting similar traditions in their own educational ethos
since the Second World War, and in many other countries the
trend has been the same. Progress towards the fostering of
initiative and independent working in these countries is slow,
but it has taken place. There is no reason to believe that it
will not happen in the Soviet Union. Nevertheless, the significance of such a change if it were to succeed would be considerable. A genuine desire to teach children to think for
themselves goes along with an apparent reluctance to encourage
them to do so - or is it a real inability to snap out of
ingrained classroom habits? The wish for creative thinking
and working, for discussion and debate, is accompanied by the
requirement that certain specific political and social views
should be instilled. If the spirit of the recent curricular
reform is allowed to win out, if creativity gains the upper
hand over intellectual orthodoxy, if children learn to reason
rather than to replicate, then the average product of the
Soviet education system of tomorrow will be of a very different quality from that of today.

RATHER than overload this book with many thousands of foot-
notes, they have been dispensed with altogether. The main
sources of each section are indicated by reference to the
bibliography which follows, and which has been kept within
manageable bounds by strict selection.

General

Principal Soviet educational periodicals which have been used
include the newspaper for teachers, *Uchitel'skaya gazeta*
[Teachers' newspaper], the monthly *Narodnoe obrazovanie* [Edu-
cation], the academic journal *Sovetskaya pedagogika* [Soviet
pedagogy] and *Byulleten' normativnykh aktov Ministerstva prosveshcheniya SSSR*, which contains notification of all new leg-
islation, instructions, orders and regulations relating to the
running of the school system. The daily and weekly press have
also been useful, especially *Literaturnaya gazeta* [Literary
newspaper]. It is possible to keep abreast of educational and
social issues in English through the *Current Digest of the
Soviet Press*. *Soviet Education* has in 1987 begun to publish
English translations of the more important mathematics and
science syllabuses.
    The stance adopted towards comparative studies in this
book involves keeping at least one eye on the theoretical
frameworks described in recent academic works, especially
[95], [115], [153] and [203]. [115] also contains a useful,
but now dated chapter on the USSR. Other publishers too
should allow authors to bring their very useful books up to
date: [73], [88]. [135] deals knowledgeably with an earlier
period; [201] is more recent and very informative.

Preface and Chapter 1

Visits to Russia mentioned in the Preface are described in
[71], [74], [94] and [144]. General history of Russian education is the subject of [43], [103] and [134]. Outlines of the

system and its administration may be found in [115], [73] and [88]. Though by no means recent, [114] is still useful for theoretical principles. On research see [118]. Recently revised rules for pupils appear in [199]. On examinations and assessment: rules for final exams [198], the published questions [57], [58], [59], remarks on specific subjects [154], [157], [158], [172]; assessment of behaviour [97], and some recent news [133].

Chapter 2

For the Reform Guidelines and comment on them, see [93], [79], [195]. On curriculum theory in the west, [96] is invaluable. The Marxist basis of Soviet curricular theory emerges from [67], [136], [171] and psychological issues from [167] and [187]. The history of Soviet curricular practice can be discovered from [128] and [165], general information on curriculum philosophy from [77], [183], [210] and especially from [220] and [122-3]. Accounts of Soviet programmes of study from the early 1960s are [56], [137], [202] and to a limited extent [68]. Apart from the syllabuses themselves, the most informative source of all in the preparation of many chapters of this book has been [222].

Chapter 3

Some of the material in this chapter was used in [149] and is shortly to be expanded in [148]. The best general works in English are [50] and [80]; also useful are [47], [130] and [132]; on the political aspect [126], [142]; Soviet pedagogues' views are typified by [61] (from which the Pioneer "meeting with the older generation" was taken), [63] and [64]. The Soviet Constitution may be consulted in [69]. [99], [120] and [138] comprise but three examples of the hundreds of popular Soviet works related to upbringing. On sex education see [113], [112], [220]. I have no official syllabus for "Acquaintance with the world around", but [191] contains almost every detail. For the other syllabuses see [10] and [37]. [82] and [89] concern [10]; [72] and [99] relate to [37]. The journal devoted to upbringing is *Vospitanie shkol'—nikov* [Upbringing of pupils] and parents as well as teachers read *Sem'ya i shkola* [Family and school].

Chapter 4

The journal for labour teachers is *Shkola i proizvodstvo* [School and production]. Syllabuses for labour training are [15-18]. A general article in English on several aspects of work training is [48]; on the polytechnical principle [169], [184] and [189]; on "socially useful" labour [161]. Vocational training and professional preparation are dealt with in

[52], [155], [163], [164], [200], while [180] deals specifically with careers guidance. On technical drawing, [38] is the
syllabus; [65], [66] and [190] provide valuable background.

Chapter 5

Of the two syllabuses [20] was very promptly superseded by
[21] in the course of 1985. Recent instructions on the conduct of examinations are typified by [157], [158] and [162].
Though [174] purports to contain the school syllabus in English, it is - despite the newness of its appearance - out of
date. [186] is brief, but useful; [213] and [214] are of the
greatest interest.
[14] is the computer studies syllabus and [156] is a
supporting directive. [215] is brief and general; [185] expresses both the keen interest in the new course and current
reservations about progress in its introduction. The general
Soviet educational press is at present full of articles on
computers in schools.
The journal for mathematics teachers is *Matematika v
shkole* [Mathematics in school], and for computer studies *In-
formatika i obrazovanie* [Information science and education].

Chapter 6

Teachers of Russian communicate through the periodical *Russkiy
yazyk v shkole* [Russian in school]. Multi-lingual, multi-
cultural issues are dealt with in many publications, particularly [60], [75], [87], [124], [131], and [166]. On the
development of Russian speech by young children, [40] may be
found of interest. Syllabuses for primary Russian are [32]
and [33]. [34], dated 1983, is brought up to date by [159]
and [192] and to some extent by [160]. On assessment, see
[154] and [172]. [51], [83], [173], [193], [196] and [197]
are treatises on methodology; [76] a western commentary.

Chapter 7

Official journals for science teachers are *Biologiya v shkole*
[Biology in school], dealing also with nature study, *Fizika v
shkole* [Physics in school], comprising astronomy too, and
Khimiya v shkole [Chemistry in school]. The primary teachers'
periodical *Nachal'naya shkola* covers science lessons at that
stage. For details of the "Acquaintance with the world
around" course, see [191]. Syllabuses are: nature study [25]
and [24], biology [7]; physics [28] and [29]; astronomy [29]
and [6]; chemistry [9] and [8]. [174] is in English, but out
of date. Examination questions are contained in [57] and
[58]. The content and rationale of the various courses are
discussed in [150], [174], [175] and [205]. Typical supporting articles are [92], [101], [102], [194] and [216].

Chapter 8

Music and literature teachers receive the periodicals *Muzyka v shkole* and *Literatura v shkole*, but there is no eqivalent for art teachers at present. Educational articles appear occasionally in *Tvorchestvo* [Creation] and *Iskusstvo* [Art]. A substantial Soviet study of aesthetic education is [85], see also [209]; [143] is a most informative book in English.

Syllabuses are, for art, [1-5], music [22-23], literature [19] - the last corrected by press announcements of very recent origin. General principles of music education are best studied in [108], while general background is supplied by [46]. Polemical and apologetical articles include [106], [107], [168] and [204]; [42] is by an alleged opponent of Kabalevsky who is attacked in [208]. The theoretical principles of the new syllabuses and their practical application are dealt with in [105], [217], [204], [207] and [39]. [212] is a somewhat superficial western account of the new system.

Nemensky's approach to art education is best understood by his introductions to the syllabuses and in an interview [152]. Support for or commentary on the innovative work is provided in [41], [81], [84] and [129].

A great deal of methodological, theoretical and support material accompanies the literature syllabus; on its history see [181], rationale [54], on the present state of the art [90] and [91], and on the preferred methodology three of the many works must suffice: [53], [218] and [219].

Chapter 9

History and sociology teachers read the journal, *Prepodavanie istorii v shkole* [Teaching history in school]. The history syllabus is [13]. Of particular help in preparing this chapter were: on the Marxist view of history [179], on the overall rationale [127], [116] and [117]. The Soviet approach to local history is seen in [170]; the methodological handbooks, typified by [210], and a selection of textbooks not listed in the Bibliography were illuminating, as always. The social studies official syllabus is [35], and the experimental syllabus project [36]; the spirit of the teaching of both subjects may be gauged from [116] and of social studies from the introductions to the syllabuses and from such material as [62].

Chapter 10

Little reference to geography teaching was found outside the pages of *Geografiya v shkole* [Geography in school]: it does not seem to figure much in general journals at present, despite the vigorous style in which specialists promote their subject. The syllabus is [12]; [86] is an example of relevant support material, and its rationale is described in [121].

Chapter 11

This chapter uses material compiled, lessons viewed and teachers (British and Soviet) interviewed for two articles: [146] and [147], and on more recent observation of teachers and reading of their journal, *Inostrannye yazyki v shkole* [Foreign languages in school], which has recently contained numerous pieces bringing the slightly elderly syllabus [11] up to date. [55] gives an excellent understanding of Belyaev's work on psychology and [110] shows how favourably it is regarded in the USSR in more recent years. [140] and [141] are examples of western studies of the subject. [109] illustrates teachers' present ways of working. [98] is a few years old, but is revealing on the conduct of examinations.

Chapter 12

The most recent syllabus [26] is found in *Fizicheskaya kul'tura v shkole* [Physical culture in school] - the previous syllabus is [27]. Riordan, [178] and [176], is the standard authority in this field; he kindly provided [177], which contains the GTO standards. [188] is also available to the non-Russian speaker. [206] is a limited, but none the less useful piece based on a study visit and interviews with Soviet PE teachers. [119] is an inspector's instructions to teachers, and a typical example of such communications. Very little published information is found on NVP; the syllabus did not actually emerge, but it was possible to reconstruct a fairly recent version from an invaluable study of the Soviet army, [104], and from the school textbook [151]. [49] illustrates the importance attached to NVP.

Chapter 13

This chapter is pieced together from numerous sources, such as interviews, especially some carried out in Union republics. On non-Russian schools, see especially the works referred to under Chapter 5 above; on the able child [78] is still the standard work; on what we in Britain call "special needs" little detail is available in English; a number of conference papers which are likely to appear in a volume edited by Riordan in 1988 were helpful.

Chapter 14

This chapter relies on classroom observation research carried out for [145], on more recent visits and interviews, and on the vast amount of polemical material on teaching methods now appearing in the Soviet educational press. [44] and [45] and the controversy surrounding them are of particular interest.

The view of Soviet education today expressed in this chapter
is based on an overview of all the material covered in this
book. [79], [195] and [111] typify British and American
accounts of the 1984 reforms. The text of the chapter cites a
wide variety of Soviet response: [182] is typical of a certain
type of hostility with which the authorities are having to
contend.

SELECT BIBLIOGRAPHY

All monographs and articles of which extensive use was made in the
preparation of this book are listed in this Bibliography. To make
the most rational use of space it was decided to exclude the titles
of the many school textbooks which were examined, specialist Russian-
English dictionaries; most encyclopedia articles and most standard
works in English on the curriculum. On the other hand, as many as
possible of the works in English of direct relevance to the Soviet
curriculum are included for the guidance of readers without a knowledge of Russian, since they will presumably form the majority of the
readers of this book. None the less, linguists should find listed
here the principal documents through which they may pursue study of
the subject. To save space, certain abbreviations are found in the
bibliography in addition to those used in the text:-

BNAMP	Byulleten' normativnykh aktov Ministerstva prosveshcheniya SSSR
Ed.	Education
ed.	edited by, editor
edn	edition
CDSP	Current Digest of the Soviet Press
Jnl	Journal
kl.	klass, klassy
L.	London
M.	Moscow
NO	Narodnoe obrazovanie
NSh	Nachal'naya shkola
obshch.	obshcheobrazovatel'naya
Pr.	Prosveshchenie
Russ.	Russian
Sov.	Soviet

Syllabuses

[1]   [Art] Programmy vos'miletney shkoly na 1980/81 uchebnyy god:
       izobrazitel'noe iskusstvo (IV–VI kl.). M., Pr., 1980.
[2]   Izobrazitel'noe iskusstvo i khudozhestvennyy trud. Proekt
       programmy dlya 1–10 kl. obshch. shkoly SSSR.   Materialy k
       provedeniyu eksperimenta. M., Soyuz khudozhnikov SSSR i APN
       SSSR, 1976–79.
[3]   Programma (proekt) 'Izobrazitel'noe iskusstvo, I klass' dlya
       obshch. shkoly (eksperimental'naya). M., Soyuz khudozhnikov,
       NII khudozhestvennogo vospitaniya APN SSSR, Min. pros. RSFSR,
       1981.
[4]   Programma 'Izobrazitel'noe iskusstvo i khudozhestvennyy trud',
       III klass (eksperimental'naya). M., Soyuz khudozhnikov, TsIUU
       Min. pros. RSFSR, 1983.
[5]   Programma 'Izobrazitel'noe iskusstvo i khudozhestvennyy trud'
       V i VI kl. obshch. shkoly (proekt). M., Soyuz khudozhnikov
       SSSR i NII khudozhestvennogo vospitaniya APN SSSR, 1985.

[6]   [Astronomy] "Programma 11-letney shkoly. Astronomiya." Fizi-
       ka v shkole, 1, 1986, pp. 60–64.

[7]   [Biology] "Uchebnaya programma po biologii." Biologiya v
       shkole, 6, 1985, pp. 36–60.

[8]   [Chemistry] "Programma po khimii." Khimiya v shkole, 6,
       1985, pp. 22–38.
[9]   Programmy 8-letney shkoly. Khimiya. M., Pr., 1983.

[10]   [Ethics and psychology of family life] "Etika i psikhologiya
       semeynoy zhizni. Tipovaya programma..." Vospitanie shkol'ni-
       kov, 6, 1984, pp. 42–49.

[11]   [Foreign language] "Programma sredney shkoly. Inostrannye
       yazyki (angliyskiy, nemetskiy, frantsuzskiy, ispanskiy) IV–X
       klassy." Inostrannye yazyki v shkole, 1, 1981, pp. 8–20.

[12]   [Geography] "Programma po geografii dlya sredney obshch.
       shkoly." Geografiya v shkole, 1, 1986, pp. 24–48.

[13]   [History] "Programma po istorii dlya sredney obshch. shkoly".
       Prepodavanie istorii v shkole, 3, 1986, pp. 32–86, & 4, 1986,
       pp. 47–62.

[14]   [Information science and computer technology] "Programma
       kursa 'Osnovy informatiki i vychislitel'noy tekhniki' X–XI
       klassy." Matematika v shkole, 3, 1986, pp. 49–53.
[15]   [Labour] "Tipovaya programma kursa 'Osnovy proizvodstva.
       Vybor professii' v VIII–IX kl. obshch. shkoly." Shkola i
       proizvodstvo, 7, 1986, pp. 24–28.
[16]   "Programma professional'nogo obucheniya uchashchikhsya VIII–IX

kl. sredney obshch. shkoly." Shkola i proizvodstvo, 8, 1986, pp. 45-49.

[17] "Programma professional'nogo obucheniya uchashchikhsya X-XI kl. sredney obshch. shkoly. Professiya - stolyar [stroitel'nyy] [razryad-2]." Shkola i proizvodstvo, 8, 1986, pp. 49-55.

[18] "Programma trudovogo obucheniya v V-VII kl. gorodskoy i sel'skoy shkoly." Shkola i proizvodstvo, 1, 1986, pp. 13-34.

[19] [Literature] Programmy 8-letney i sredney shkoly 1980/8 uchebnyy god: literatura IV-X kl. M., Pr., 1980.

[20] [Mathematics] Programmy 8-letney i sredney shkoly [1985/86]. Matematika. M., Pr., 1985.

[21] "Programma po matematike dlya sredney obshch. shkoly (V-XI kl.)" Matematika v shkole, 6, 1985, pp. 7-26.

[22] [Music] Programma po muzyke dlya obshch. shkoly (s pourochnoy metodicheskoy razrabotkoy) 1-3 kl. M., Pr., 1982 & 1985.

[23] Programma po myzyke dlya obshch. shkoly (s pourochnoy metodicheskoy razrabotkoy) 4-7 kl. M., Pr., 1983 & 1985.

[24] [Nature study] "Programma po prirodovedeniyu sredney obshch. shkoly." Biologiya v shkole, 4, 1986, pp. 41-44.

[25] Programmy 8-letney shkoly. Prirodovedenie IV kl. M., Pr., 1983.

[26] [Physical education] "Kompleksnaya programma fizicheskogo vospitaniya uchashchikhsya I-XI kl. obshch. shkoly." Fizicheskaya kul'tura v shkole, 1985, 6, pp. 19-32, 7, pp. 30-35, 8, pp. 53-57.

[27] Programma 8-letney i sredney shkoly. Fizicheskaya kul'tura dlya uchashchikhsya IV-X kl. M., Pr., 1982.

[28] [Physics and astronomy] "Programma 11-letney shkoly. Fizika VII-XI kl." Fizika v shkole, 6, 1985, pp. 21-37.

[29] Programma 8-letney i sredney shkoly. Fizika. Astronomiya. M., Pr., 1983.

[30] [Pre-school] Kurbatova, R.A. & Podd'yakova, N.N. (ed.), Tipovaya programma vospitaniya i obucheniya v detskom sady. M., Pr., 1984.

[31] Programma vospitaniya v detskom sady. Minsk, Narodnaya asveta, 1986.

[32] [Primary] Programma I kl. 11-letney obshch. shkoly s russkim yazykom obucheniya na 1986/87 uchebnyy god. Minsk, Narodnaya asveta, 1986.

[33] Programmy sredney shkoly. Nachal'nye klassy. M., Pr., 1980.

[34] [Russian: native language] Programmy 8-letney i sredney shkoly. Russkiy yazyk. M., Pr., 1983.

[35]   [Social studies] Obshchestvovedenie.   Programma dlya sredney
        obshch. shkoly i srednikh spetsial'nykh uchebnykh zavedeniy.
        M., Pr., 1983.

[36]   "Programma po obshchestvovedeniyu dlya vsekh tipov srednikh
        uchebnykh zavedeniy (proekt)." Prepodavanie istorii v shkole,
        5, 1986, pp. 31–44.

[37]   [Soviet government and law] "Programma kursa 'Osnovy sovet-
        skogo gosudarstva i prava'."   Prepodavanie istorii v shkole,
        6, 1985, pp. 3–13.

[38]   [Technical drawing] "Programma po chercheniyu sredney obshch.
        shkoly." Shkola i proizvodstvo, 12, 1985, pp. 51–55.

General Works

[39]   Abdullin, E.B., (ed.), Muzyka v 5 – 7 klassakh. Metodicheskoe
        posobie dlya uchitelya. M., Pr., 1986.
[40]   Adshead, D., "The Russian Child's Acquisition of Morphology".
        Jnl of Russ. Studies, xxxvii, 1979, pp. 21–24.
[41]   Alekseeva, V., "Programma iskusstva - programma truda".
        Tvorchestvo, 2, 1986, pp. 15–16.
[42]   Aliev, Yu., "Uluchshat' muzykal'noe vospitanie shkol'nikov".
        NO, 2, 1984, pp. 51–54.
[43]   Alston, P.L., Education and the State in Tsarist Russia.
        Stanford (University Press), 1969.
[44]   Amonashvili, Sh.A., Kak zhivete, deti? M., Pr., 1986.
[45]   Amonashvili, Sh.A., Zdravstvuyte, deti!. M., Pr., 1983.
[46]   Archazhnikova, L.G., Professiya – uchitel' muzyki. M., Pr.,
        1984.
[47]   Attwood, L., "Gender and Soviet Pedagogy". Unpublished con-
        ference paper, L., 1986.
[48]   Atutov, P.R., "Polytechnical Education, Labour Training and
        the Vocational Guidance of Pupils". Sov. Ed., xxvi, 4, 1984,
        pp. 40–57.
[49]   Averin, A., "Train Reliable Defenders of the Homeland".
        CDSP, xxxiv, 34, 1982, p. 19.
[50]   Avis, George (ed.), The Making of the Soviet Citizen. L.,
        Croom Helm, 1987.
[51]   Babaytseva, V.V., Obuchenie russkomu yazyku v 7–8 kl.
        Metodicheskoe posobie. M., Pr., 1983.
[52]   Batyshev, S.Ya., "Vocational and Technical Education". Sov.
        Ed., xxvi, 5, 1984, pp. 44–54.
[53]   Belen'kiy, G.I., "Predislovie" in [218], pp. 3–11.
[54]   Belen'kiy, G.I. & Snezhnevskaya, M.A., "Soderzhaniya obuche-
        niya literatury" in [222], pp. 65–85.
[55]   Belyayev, B.V., The Psychology of Teaching Modern Languages.
        Oxford, Pergamon, 1963.
[56]   Bereday, G.Z.F. et al., The Changing Soviet School. Bos-

ton, Riverside Press, 1960.

[57] Bilety dlya vypusknykh ekzamenov za kurs 8-letney shkoly na 1986/87 uchebnyy god. M., Pr., 1987.

[58] Bilety dlya vypusknykh ekzamenov za kurs sredney shkoly na 1986/87 uchebnyy god. M., Pr., 1987.

[59] "Bilety po russkomy yazyku i tematika ekzamenatsionnykh sochineniy dlya vypusknykh ekzamenov za kurs 8-letney shkoly na 1985/86 uchebnyy god". Russkiy yazyk v shkole, 1, 1986, pp. 104-110.

[60] Bilinsky, Y., "Expanding the Use of Russian or Russification?" Russ. Review, xl, 1981, pp. 317-332.

[61] Bogdanova, O.S. et al., O nravstvennom vospitanii podrostkov. M., Pr., 1979.

[62] Bogolyubov, L., "Prepodavanie obshchestvovedeniya". NO, 1, 1985, 39-44.

[63] Boldyrev, N.I., Klassnyy rukovoditel'. M., Pr., 1978.

[64] Boldyrev, N,I., Nravstvennoe vospitanie shkol'nikov. M., Pedagogika, 1979.

[65] Botvinnikov, A.D., Puti sovershenstvovaniya metodiki obucheniya chercheniyu. M., Pr., 1983.

[66] Botvinnikov, A.D., Cherchenie v sredney shkole. M., Pr., 1979.

[67] Carew-Hunt, R.N., "Marx's Materialism and his Theory of Knowledge" in The Theory and Practice of Communism. Harmondsworth, Penguin, 1963, pp. 54-60.

[68] Chapman, J.V., Education in the Soviet Union. L., College of Preceptors, 1962.

[69] Constitution (Fundamental Law) of the USSR, in Institute of Marxism-Leninism, CPSU Central Committee, Leonid Ilyich Brezhnev: a Short Biography. Oxford, Pergamon, 1977, pp. 191-240.

[70] Dalin, P., Limits to Educational Change. L., Macmillan, 1978.

[71] Darlington, T., Education in Russia. L., HMSO, 1909.

[72] Davydov, G.P., & Golovatenko, A.Yu., "O programme 'Osnovy Sovetskogo gosudarstva i prava'". Prepodavanie istorii v shkole, 2, 1986, pp. 33-37.

[73] Denisova, M.A., Lingvostranovedcheskiy slovar'. Narodnoe obrazovanie v SSSR. M., Russkiy yazyk, 1978.

[74] Dewey, J. Impressions of Soviet Russia. New York, New Republic, 1929.

[75] Dickins, T., "Multi-lingualism in Soviet Schools. The Lessons for British Education." Unpublished paper, University of Nottingham, 1986.

[76] Downing, J., "Reading Research and Instruction in the USSR". Reading Teacher, xxxvii, 7, 1984, pp. 598-603.

[77] Dunstan., J., "Curriculum Change and the Soviet School". Jnl of Curriculum Studies, ix, 2, 1977, pp. 111-123.

[78] Dunstan, J., Paths to Excellence and the Soviet School. Windsor. NFER, 1978.

[79] Dunstan, J., "Soviet Education Beyond 1984: a Commentary on the Reform Guidelines". Compare, xv, 2, 1985, pp. 161-187.

[80] Dunstan, J., "Soviet Moral Education in Theory and Practice".

Jnl of Moral Education, x, 3, 1981, pp. 192-202.

[81]   "Eksperimental'naya programma 'Izobrazitel'noe iskusstvo i khudozhestvennyy trud'". NO, 12, 1985, p. 100.

[82]   Feltham, A., "Education for Family Life in the USSR". **Sov. Ed. Study Bulletin**, iv, 1, 1986, pp. 1-11.

[83]   Fomicheva, G.A., "Soderzhaniye i metody obucheniya russkomu yazyku. Shkola I-IV". **NSh**, 7, 1986, pp. 17-21.

[84]   Fomina, N., "Nravstvennoe i esteticheskoe vospitanie v shkole". **Iskusstvo**, 12, 1985, pp. 47-49.

[85]   Gerasimov, S.A., **Sistema esteticheskogo vospitaniya shkol'nikov**. M., Pedagogika, 1983

[86]   Gerasimova, T.P., "O novoy programme nachal'nogo kursa fizicheskoy geografii". **Geografiya v shkole**, 2, 1986, pp. 24-27.

[87]   Grant, N., "Linguistic and Ethnic Minorities in the USSR: Educational Policies and Developments" in [201]. pp. 24-49.

[88]   Grant, N., **Soviet Education**. Harmondsworth, Penguin, 1979.

[89]   Grebennikova, I.V. (ed.), **Etika i psikhologiya semeynoy zhizni. Probnoe posobie dlya uchiteley**. M., Pr., 1984.

[90]   Gromtseva, S., "Programma po literature dlya shkol RSFSR". **NO**, 8, 1982, pp. 48-50.

[91]   Gromtseva, S., "Sovershenstvovat' prepodavaniya literatury". **Literatura v shkole**, 4, 1985, pp. 20-25.

[92]   Gudoshnikov, S.V. et al., "Izuchaem i obsuzhdaem programmu po biologii". **Biologiya v shkole**, 3, 1986, pp. 58-63.

[93]   "Guidelines for Reform of General and Vocational Schools. Approved by the plenary meeting of the CPSU Central Committee on April 10 and by the Supreme Soviet on April 12 [1984]" in **USSR. New Frontiers of Social Progress**. M., Novosti, 1984, pp. 50-78.

[94]   Hans, N., "The Moscow School of Mathematics and Navigation (1701)". **Slavonic and East European Review**, xxix, 1950-51, pp. 532-536.

[95]   Holmes, B., **Comparative Education: Some Considerations of Method**. L., Allen & Unwin, 1981.

[96]   Hooper, R. (ed.), **The Curriculum: Context, Design and Development**. Edinburgh, Oliver & Boyd, 1971.

[97]   "Instruktsiya ob otsenkakh za povedenie, za prilezhanie k obshchestvenno poleznomu trudu uchashchikhsya obshch. shkol". **BNAMP**, 8, 1985, pp. 34-37.

[98]   "Itogi ekzamenov po inostrannym yazykam v 1978/79 uchebnom gody". **Inostrannye yazyki v shkole**, 1, 1980. pp. 19-21.

[99]   Ivanov, M., **Roditeli, podrostok, zakon**. M., Pedagogika, 1980.

[100] Ivanova, I., "Inostrannye yazyki v shkole". **NO**, 10, 1980, p.60

[101] Ivanova, R.G., "O novoy programme po khimii (VIII-IX kl.)" **Khimiya v shkole**, 1, 1986, pp. 24-29.

[102] Ivchenkova, G.G., "O novoy programme kursa prirodoveniya IV kl." **Biologiya v shkole**, 4, 1986, pp. 45-46.

[103] Johnson, W.H.E., **Russia's Educational Heritage**. Pittsburgh, Carnegie Press, 1950.

[104] Jones, E., **Red Army and Society. A Sociology of the Soviet Military**. Boston, Allen & Unwin, 1985.

[105] Kabalevsky, D., "Osnovnye printsipy i metody programmy po myzyke dlya obshch. shkoly". In [22] (1985), pp. 3–30.

[106] Kabalevsky, D., "O tvorcheskoy svobode uchitelya (otvety na tri voprosa)". **Myzyka v shkole**, 4, 1984, pp. 7–9.

[107] Kabalevsky, D., "O tvorcheskom nachale" in [108], pp. 47–51.

[108] Kabalevsky, D., **Vospitanie uma i serdtsa. Kniga dlya uchitelya.** M., Pr., 1981 & 1984.

[109] Kalinetskaya, Yu.A., "O nekotorykh itogakh raboty uchiteley inostrannykh yazykov v usloviyakh shkol'noy reformy". **Inostrannye yazyki v shkole**, 3, 1986, pp. 55–60.

[110] Kapitonova, T.I. & Shchukin, A.N., **Sovremennye metody obucheniya russkomu yazyku inostrantsev.** M., Russkiy yazyk, 1979.

[111] Kaser, M., "The Economic Imperatives in the Soviet Education Reform of 1984". **Oxford Review of Ed.**, xii, 2, 1986, pp. 181–5

[112] Khadzhinov, K.A., "Iz opyta raboty po polovomu prosveshcheniyu i vospitaniyu shkol'nikov". **Biologiya v shkole**, 5, 1985, pp. 45–49.

[113] Khripkova, A.G, et al., "Sex and Hygiene Education in the Soviet School". **Sov. Ed.**, xxvi, 1, 1983, pp. 3–6.

[114] King, E.J. (ed.), **Communist Education.** L., Methuen, 1963.

[115] King, E.J., **Other Schools and Ours.** L., Holt, Rinehart & Winston, 5 edn, 1978.

[116] Koloskov, A.G., "Soderzhanie obucheniya istorii" in [222], pp. 93–111.

[117] Kiloskov [sic: presumably Koloskov], A.G., "Teaching History in the Soviet Secondary General-education School". **Teaching History**, 37, 1983, pp. 12–17.

[118] Kondakov, M.I., "Research, Theory and Practice in the USSR". **Prospects**, xiii, 3, 1983, pp. 275–298.

[119] Korbut, O.V., "Obuchenie fizicheskoy kul'tury v novom uchebnom gody". **NSh**, 9, 1986, pp. 48–52.

[120] Kotyrlo, V., **Rastet grazhdanin.** Kiev, Radyans'ka shkola, 1980.

[121] Kovalevskaya, M.K. et al., "Soderzhanie obucheniya geografii" in [222], pp. 208–224.

[122] Kraevsky, V.V. & Lerner, I.Ya., **Teoreticheskie osnovy obshchego srednego obrazovaniya.** M., Pedagogika, 1983.

[123] Translation of [122]. **Sov. Ed.**, xxvii, 8–9, 1986.

[124] Kravetz, N., "Education of Ethnic and National Minorities in the USSR: a Report on Current Developments". **Comparative Ed.**, xvi, 1, 1980, pp. 13–24.

[125] Kreindler, I. (ed.), "The Changing Status of Russian in the Soviet Union". **International Jnl of the Sociology of Language**, [whole issue], xxxiii, 1982.

[126] Kuebart, F., "The Political Socialization of Soviet School-children". Conference paper, University of Bradford, 1987.

[127] Kumanev, V., "The Socio-educational Role of History in School Education". Unpublished typescript, c. 1982.

[128] Kuzin, N.P., "Studies in the History of the School and the Pedagogical Thought of the Peoples of the USSR 1917–1941". **Sov. Ed.**, xxv, 1 & 2, 1982.

[129] Kuzin, V., "XXVII s'ezd KPSS i zadachi esteticheskogo vospita-

niya shkol'nikov". NSh, 8, 1986, pp. 30-35.

[130] Lawler, J., "Collectivity and Individuality in Contemporary Soviet Education Theory". Educational Psychology, v, 1980, pp. 163-174.

[131] Lewis, E.G., Multilingualism in the Soviet Union. The Hague, Mouton, 1972.

[132] Long, D.H., "Soviet Education and the Development of Communist Ethics". Phi Delta Kappan, lxv, 7, 1984, pp. 469-472.

[133] Louis, J., "More Testing Times Under Glasnost". Times Educational Supplement, 24 April 1987, p. 14.

[134] McClelland, J.C., Autocrats and Academics. Chicago, University Press, 1979.

[135] Matthews, M., Education in the Soviet Union: Policies and Institutions Since Stalin. L., Allen & Unwin, 1982.

[136] Matthews, M.R., The Marxist Theory of Schooling. Brighton, Harvester, 1980.

[137] Medlin, W.K. et al., Soviet Education Programs. Washington, U.S. Office of Education, 1960.

[138] Mikhalkov, S., Vse nachinaetsya s detstva. M., Pedagogika, 1980.

[139] Monakhov, V.M., "Normalizing the Work-load at School: Elements for Reform". Prospects, xv, 2, 1985, pp. 173-187.

[140] Monk, B., "Foreign Language Teaching in the Soviet Union: Continuing the Trend". Jnl of Russ. Studies, 50, 1986, pp. 28-37.

[141] Monk, B., & Fitzgerald, M., "The Search for Authenticity in Soviet Language Teaching". Modern Languages, xlvi, 4, 1985, pp.253-262.

[142] Morison, J., "The Political Content of Education in the USSR" in [201], pp. 143-172.

[143] Morton, M., The Arts and the Soviet Child. The Esthetic Education of Children in the USSR. New York, Free Press, 1972.

[144] Muckle, J., "Alexander I and William Allen: a Tour of Russian Schools in 1819 and Some Missing Reports". History of Ed., xv, 3, 1986, pp. 137-145.

[145] Muckle, J., "Classroom Interactions in Some Soviet and English Schools". Comparative Ed., xx, 2, 1984, pp. 237-251.

[146] Muckle, J., "The Foreign Language Teacher in the Soviet Union". Modern Languages, lxii, 3, 1981, pp. 153-163.

[147] Muckle, J., "Modern Language Teaching in the Soviet Union". Perspectives, xii, 1983, pp. 65-80.

[148] Muckle, J., "The New Soviet Child: Moral Education in Soviet Schools" in [50].

[149] Muckle, J., "Questions of Moral Upbringing and Character Training in Some Recent Soviet Educational Publications". Jnl of Russ. Studies, 45, 1983, pp. 41-49.

[150] Myagkova, A.N., "Soderzhanie obucheniya biologii" in [222], pp. 191-208.

[151] Naumenko, Yu.A., Nachal'naya voennaya podgotovka. M., Izdatel'stvo DOSAAF SSSR, 1983.

[152] Nemensky, B., "Mudrost' krasoty". Kul'tura i zhizn', 6, 1982,

pp. 21-22.

[153] Nicholas, E.J., Issues in Education: a Comparative Analysis. L., Harper & Row, 1983.

[154] "Normy otsenki znaniy, umeniy i navykov uchashchikhsya po russkomu yazyku." Russkiy yazyk v shkole, 6, 1984, pp. 112-117.

[155] "O poryadke i srokakh vvedeniya ob'yazatel'noy professio-nal'noy podgotovki shkol'nikov." BNAMP, 11, 1986, pp. 36-44.

[156] "O metodicheskom pis'me 'O prepodavanii kursa Osnovy informa-tiki i vychislitel'noy tekhnike v 1986/87 uchebnom godu'." BNAMP, 11, 1986, pp. 44-47.

[157] "O provedenii v 1985/86 uchebnom godu pis'mennogo ekzamena po algebre v 8-kh kl. shkol RSFSR." Matematika v shkole, 1, 1986, pp. 32-34.

[158] "Ob ekzamenatsionnykh biletakh po geometrii v 8-kh kl. obshch. shkol RSFSR." Matematika v shkole, 1, 1985, pp. 28-30.

[159] "Ob izmeneniyakh i utochneniyakh, vnesennykh v programmu po russkomu yazyku dlya IV-VIII kl...." Russkiy yazyk v shkole, 5, 1984, pp. 103-104.

[160] "Ob opyte raboty po russkomu yazyku v obshch. shkolakh RSFSR po usovershenstvovannoy programme v 1984/85 uchebnom godu." Russkiy yazyk v shkole, 5, 1985, pp. 3-6.

[161] "Ob organizatsii obshchestvenno poleznogo proizvoditel'nogo truda..." BNAMP, 3, 1986, pp. 2-5.

[162] "Ob ustnom ekzamene po geometrii v 8-ykh kl. obshch. shkol RSFSR." Matematika v shkole, 2, 1985, pp. 34-36.

[163] O'Dell, F., "Vocational Education in the USSR" in [201] pp. 106-142.

[164] O'Dell, F., "Vocational Training in the Soviet Education Re-form". Conference paper, Cambridge, 1985.

[165] Ognyov, N. [pseudonym of Rozanov, M.G.], The Diary of a Communist Schoolboy. L., Gollancz, 1928.

[166] Panachin, F.G. (ed.), "The Soviet Multinational School Under Developed Socialism". Sov. Ed., xxviii, 5 & 6, 1986.

[167] Petrovsky, A.V., "Basic Directions in the Development and Current State of Educational Psychology". Sov. Ed., xv, 15 & 16, 1973, pp. 92-109.

[168] Petukhova, N., "Radost' tvorcheskogo truda". Muzyka v shkole, 3, 1985, pp. 32-35.

[169] "Politekhnicheskoe obrazovanie" in Bol'shaya sovetskaya entsiklopediya, M., 1970, xx, pp. 216-217.

[170] "Prepodavanie istorii rodnogo kraya v shkolakh Rossiyskoy federatsii." NO, 9, 1986, pp. 101-102,

[171] Price, R.F., Marx and Education in Russia and China. L., Croom Helm, 1977.

[172] "Primernye proverochnye raboty po russkomu yazyku i matematike za 2 polugodie 1985/86..." NSh 4, 1986, pp. 50-60 & 79.

[173] Ramzaeva, T.G. & L'vov, M.P., Metodika prepodavaniya russkomu yazyku v nachal'nykh kl. M., Pr., 1979.

[174] Razumovsky, V.G. (ed.) et al., Science and Mathematics Education in the General Secondary School in the Soviet Union.

Paris, UNESCO, 1986.

[175] Razumovsky, V.G., "Soderzhanie obucheniya fiziki" in [222], pp. 154-269.

[176] Riordan, J., "Development of Sport in the USSR". Jnl of Russ. Studies, 34, 1977, pp. 19-29.

[177] Riordan, J., "School Physical Education in the Soviet Union". Conference paper, Glasgow, 1986.

[178] Riordan, J., Soviet Sport. Oxford, Blackwell, 1980.

[179] Rogers, E., "The Materialist Conception of History" in A Commentary on Communism. L., Epworth Press, 1952. pp. 94-100.

[180] Rooney, P., Recent Developments in Vocational Guidance in the USSR. Birmingham, Centre for Russian & East European Studies, 1985.

[181] Rotkovich, Ya.A., "The History of Literature Teaching in the Soviet School". Sov. Ed., xxii, 7 & 8, pp. 6-160.

[182] Rutkevich, M., "Is the School Reform Another 'Mistake'?" CDSP, xxxviii, 47, 1986.

[183] Savin, N.V., Pedagogika. M., Pr., 1978.

[184] Shapovalenko, S.G. (ed.), Polytechnical Education in the USSR. Paris, UNESCO, 1963.

[185] Shapovalov, N., & Chernikova, I., "Shkol'nyy kurs informatiki: pervye itogi". NO, 9, 1986, pp. 47-54.

[186] Shenfield, S., "The Reform of Mathematics Teaching in Soviet Schools". Sov. Ed. Study Bulletin, ii, 1, 1984, pp. 22-26.

[187] Shore, M.J., Soviet Education: Its Psychology and Philosophy. New York, Philosophical Library, 1947.

[188] Shtykolo, F.E., "Physical Education". Sov. Ed., xxvi, 4, pp. 71-82.

[189] Smart, K.F., "The Polytechnical Principle" in [114], pp. 153-176.

[190] Smirnov, S.A., "Zamechaniya i predlozheniya po Programme". Shkola i proizvodstvo, 5, 1986, p. 61.

[191] Sorotskaya, O.N., "Soderzhaniye, formy i metody prepodavaniya predmeta 'Oznakomlenie s okruzhayushchim mirom'". NSh, 7, 1986, pp. 52-55.

[192] "Sovershenstvovanie prepodavaniya russkogo yazyka v obshch. shkolakh RFSFR." Russkiy yazyk v shkole, 4, 1984, pp. 3-12.

[193] Starkovsky, A.M., "O propagande russkogo yazyka v shkole". Russkiy yazyk v shkole, 2, 1986, pp. 34-35.

[194] Straut, E.K., "O prepodavanii astronomii po novoy programme". Fizika v shkole, 2, 1986, pp. 61-62.

[195] Szekely, B.B., "The New Soviet Educational Reform". Comparative Ed. Review, xxx, 3, 1986, pp. 321-343.

[196] Tekuchev, A.V. et al., Osnovy metodiki russkogo yazyka v 4-8 kl. M., Pr., 1978.

[197] Tikunova, L.I. et al., "Zadachi dal'neyshego povysheniya kachestva obucheniya i vospitaniya uchashchikhsya v svete trebovaniy XXVII s'ezda KPSS". NSh, 8, 1986, pp. 2-7.

[198] "Tipovaya instruktsiya ob ekzamenakh, perevode i vypuske uchashchikhsya obshch. shkol". NO, 2, 1986, pp. 100-102.

[199] "Tipovye pravila dlya uchashchikhsya". BNAMP, 8, 1985, pp. 32-

34.

[200] Tomiak, J.J., "Education and Vocationalism in Eastern Europe".
Secondary Ed. Jnl, xvi, 2, pp. 7-9.

[201] Tomiak, J.J., Soviet Education in the 1980s. L., Croom Helm,
1983.

[202] Trace, A.S., What Ivan Knows That Johnny Doesn't. New York,
Random House, 1961.

[203] Trethewey, A.R., Introducing Comparative Education. Rush-
cutters Bay, Pergamon, 1976.

[204] Trushin, A., "Novuyu programmu po muzyke - v zhizn'". NO, 10,
1981, pp. 45-46.

[205] Tsvetkov, L.A., "Soderzhanie obucheniya fizike" in
[222], pp. 170-190.

[206] Vince, L., "Physical Education in the Soviet Union." Unpublished M.Ed. dissertation, University of Nottingham, 1980.

[207] "V Ministerstve prosveshcheniya RSFSR". Muzyka v shkole, 4,
1985, pp. 71-73.

[208] Volkov, B., "Protivostoyanie tsenoy v million". Uchitel'skaya
gazeta, 20 Feb. 1986, p. 3.

[209] Volkov, I.P., Priobshchenie shkol'nikov k tvorchestvu. Iz
opyta raboty. M., Pr., 1982.

[210] Volobuev, O.V. et al., Metodika prepodavaniya istorii SSSR
(VIII-IX kl.). Posobie dlya uchitelya. M., Pr., 1979.

[211] Volovnikova, G.M., "Curriculum and Teaching Methods in the
Soviet School". Sov. Ed., xxvi, 4, 1984, pp. 20-39.

[212] Wattez, D. (ed.), "L'Enseignement musical a l'ecole: la meth-
ode Kabalevsky". Aspects de la musique sovietique, 1, 1985.

[213] Wilson, B. (ed.), Mathematics Education. The Report of the
First Anglo-Soviet Seminar Held at St Antony's College, Oxford...1981. L., British Council, 1981.

[214] Wilson, B. (ed.), Mathematics Education. The Report of the
Second Anglo-Soviet Seminar Held in Moscow... 1982 L., British Council, 1983.

[215] Yasmann, V., "Mass Computer Instruction in Soviet Schools".
Radio Liberty Research, RL 479/84, 21 Dec. 1984.

[216] Yurova, V. et al., "Energiya dushy". NO, 10, 1986, pp. 43-46.

[217] Yuzbash'yan, Yu., "Tvorcheskaya realizatsiya printsipov novoy
programmy po muzyke v shkolakh Armyanskoy SSR". Muzyka v
shkole, 1, 1985, pp. 16-18.

[218] Zepalova, T.S. & Meshcheryakova, N.Ya., Metodicheskoe rukovod-
stvo k uchebniku-khrestomatiyu 'Rodnaya literatura' dlya 5 kl.
Posobie dlya uchitelya. M., Pr., 3 edn, 1983.

[219] Zepalova, T.S. & Meshcheryakova, N.Ya., Urok literatury. Posobie dlya uchitelya. M., Pr., 1983.

[220] Zhuravlev, I.K. & Zorina, L. Ya., "Didakticheskaya model'
uchebnogo predmeta", Novye issledovaniya v pedagogicheskikh
naukakh, 1, 1979, pp. 33ff.

[221] Zverev, I.D., "On the Problem of the Sex Education of Schoolchildren". Sov. Ed., x, 8, pp. 47ff.

[222] Zverev, I.D. & Kashin, M.P., Sovershenstvovanie soderzhaniya
obrazovaniya v shkole. M., Pr., 1985.

INDEX

This index includes the principal topics covered in the text. To list here every matter contained or every person mentioned in the school subject syllabuses would obviously have been impossible without making the index as long as the book. Occasionally, when a topic contained a syllabus is held to be of wider significance, it appears in the index.

Novgorod 36
NVP: elementary military training; see Military

Octobrists 27
Ognyov, N. 14
Optional subjects 6, 19f., 173, 174
Orenburg 78
Orlyonok 169
Otlichniki: pupils gaining consistently high marks 176
Overloading of syllabuses and reduction of workloads 18, 99, 121, 140
Owen, R. 35

"Paracurriculum" 175ff.
Parents 28, 108, 128, 178
Parkhurst, H. viii, 13
Patriotism and patriotic education 23, 43, 95, 127, 145, 168–170
Payment to pupils for labour 4
"Pedagogics of cooperation" 183
"Percentomania" 7
Personality development 22f.
Pessimism 107
Pestalozzi, J. 35
Peter I (the Great) vii
Philosophy of education 10–21
Physical culture and education 17, 19f., 24, 159–167
Physics 17, 19f., 60, 80, 88–94, 95
Piaget, J. 15
Pioneers 23, 27–28, 160, 169
Play 49, 60, 178, 180; see also Games
Podolsk 36
Poetry 67
Pogorelov, A. 53, 57
Poland vii
Political education 23, 31–33, 141–143, 176
Polytechnical education 35ff., 94, 124
"Potential" 16
Pragmatic view of curriculum 12
Pre-school education 2, 46, 80, 124
Primary education 46, 47, 49, 80–81, 109–111, 116, 124–125, 126, 177–179
Principles of Soviet government and law 19f., 23, 31–33
Problem-solving 54, 59, 60, 127
Production practice 36
Professional orientation 37, 39, 42, 89
Prokof'ev, M. 172
Proletarian internationalism 24, 95, 145
Proletariat 34, 38
Psychology of education, Soviet 15–16
PTU: vocational-technical college 4; see also SPTU

Quakers vii
Questioning 180–181, 182